PERSONAL
AND
ORIENTAL

AUSTIN COATES

ILLUSTRATED

HARPER & BROTHERS, PUBLISHERS
New York

PERSONAL AND ORIENTAL

Copyright © 1957 by Austin Coates
Printed in the United States of America

Library of Congress catalog card number: 57-6126

CONTENTS

NOTE.—Except where otherwise stated, the illustrations are by the author. For reasons which the reader will appreciate, they do not include pictures of any of the people described in the book.

After bringing me unexpectedly to India, just over twelve years ago, my work led me gradually further eastward, almost country by country. Where work did not take me, holidays did. Mentally I faced eastward, and continued to do so till, three years ago, I reached the ultimate eastern point in this progression—Japan.

There, in the mountains of Koyasan, I mentally turned round, and, by an impulse unexpected but clear, faced the other way—westward. I wanted to look back, to survey. Looking from those heights over the plains of western Japan, I found that the view, spectacular as it was, was not enough. I wanted to climb a mountain so high that from its summit I would be able to see right back into India, where I started years earlier. Cluttered up with impressions, I wanted the simple outlines again, which I was losing sight of, and the long perspective that is often hidden by detail. I had what may be called a desire for panorama.

As there was no mountain high enough for this, the only possibility of obtaining such a view—and even this a remote chance—would be to travel back the same way I had come, passing in fairly quick succession through the countries I had been to before. If I could not see them panoramically, at least I would try to see them processionally.

Due to return to Europe shortly on leave, I planned my journey with this processional idea in mind. I began in the deep snow of a Japanese winter. When I left Japan, the snow was beginning to melt below Mount Iwaté and the first daffodils were in flower. I spent a tropical summer in Hongkong, and in early September started to move again, going first to the Philippines, thence westward through Burma, India, Pakistan, Iraq and Turkey, entering Europe at Istanbul in the second part of November. A month later my journey ended in Christmas snow and foggy gloom in London.

When we think of panoramic or processional views of continents these days, we assume that the panorama will be political or historical, that we shall encounter famous men and hear great events recalled. This was not what I had in mind. The review I wanted was of my own experience as an insignificant traveller, staying in the homes of personal friends, or wandering quietly through cities where I knew no one, a pedestrian's view, a subjective assessment of a mental climate lived in. The basis of such an assessment, and of the book that now follows, is in fact a thin line through an area too vast to be thought of objectively, a glimpse of the people standing beside that line, and the sound of their voices caught in a sequence of time.

I

It was bitterly cold. Though the rush hour was over, the underground train was still full. There was nowhere to sit except on my own suitcase.

Drowsy and hungry, I was dreaming with my eyes open. I had only left Hongkong that morning, but, such are the advances of science, here I was already home in London, stuffed into one of the old-fashioned carriages still operating on the Inner Circle. Strange really, I thought they had all been replaced years ago. What a crowd always seemed to get on at Euston Square! Nothing to do but count the stations; it was impossible to see their names each time the train stopped. There was nothing to be seen, in fact, except the dingy raincoat of the man standing in front of me. Formerly an army officer's coat, now greasy and worn. Yes, those fine officers who used to chase us around: they were looking for jobs now, poor fellows.

And then—how ever many more stations were there? I had lost count—a puddle of melted snow off people's boots dribbled down in my direction and I had to move my feet. How ridiculous my light suède shoes looked in these surroundings—so suitable in Hongkong, but here . . . I had forgotten how many people in London wore wellington boots, ugly ones with no sheen on them any more. The snow must have been very heavy.

At last some people got out, and there was a seat for me. I glanced along the row of tired faces opposite me. Everything looked drab these days, each expression wan in the baleful, unshaded electric light. There was a lean, narrow-faced intellectual reading a book; a rotund petty business man with frayed trousers reading the commercial page of a newspaper; a thin woman worn out from years of city toil sitting with her eyes shut, a spotted kerchief tied about her hair. In imagination one could place them all. Further along was a borough politician, and beyond him a trade union worker, an underpaid teacher, and a student wearing a school uniform that made him look like a German cadet. There were incidents of colour —the heavy features of a labourer suffused dark red from drink, and a baby tied up asleep on its mother's back, its cheeks like two fat bright red apples. Everywhere rubber boots, coarse jumpers and scarves, dingy raincoats too thin for the bitterness of the season. Instead of despatch cases, men seemed to be using large squares of variously coloured cloth, in which to wrap their books and papers. There was no conversation; the train made too much noise. Most people were reading something. Others, indrawn within themselves, stared into the eventless gap between office and home.

The man next to me was reading a book in French. The subject was something scientific. He had earlier indicated the empty seat beside him, helping me move my suitcase when I sat down. From my drowsiness I was now aroused by the feeling that I should say something civil to him, lest he should leave the train before I did. I murmured a few words in French about the coldness of the weather.

He looked quickly across at me through his steel-rimmed spectacles, and, with a just perceptible tremor of social confusion, withdrew again into concentration on his book. With the intuitive speed that often accompanies contact with unknown people, I realized the reason for his confusion. Though he read a French book, he could say nothing in that language, never having heard it spoken.

At that instant my mind was suddenly shaken out of London, and wrenched eastward—ten thousand miles eastward.

What had I been dreaming of? This was not London at all. This was Tokyo. And these men and women around me—they were Japanese.

.   .   .   .   .

I dined with a European friend in a small restaurant with a cellar designed in German style. The food was German, prepared by a Japanese chef; the beer was of German type, made in Japan; and throughout the evening, softly through a concealed transmitter, German music was played—Haydn, Schubert, Brahms' Hungarian Dances. At the bar upstairs were some Europeans and Americans. Below, most of the diners were Japanese.

'How they love music!' my friend commented. 'I should say

that Haydn's music is played more here even than it is in Germany. But they prefer simple music—anything with a good melodic line.'

Every now and then throughout dinner, whenever my mind wandered, the sensation returned of having come back to Europe, to a fully formed society, secure in its traditions and ideas. Glancing mentally backward over the way I had come, it occurred to me, as something hitherto unrealized, how stirred and uncertain were the other parts of Asia in which I had lived, and to whose ways of thinking I had become accustomed. Here in Japan was a quality strange and unexpected—stability. The stability of an island civilization, perhaps, undisturbed by continental pressures; or of a nation which, despite defeat in war, had found its feet in the modern world, taken its decisions, and held to them.

. . . .

We took the district train out to where my friend was staying, a village thirty miles from the capital. It was getting on for midnight. Just before the electrically operated doors slid to a close, a poorly dressed man in a torn greatcoat and muffler lurched into the carriage, swayed about uncertainly in the comparatively bright light within, leaned against a seat, and slowly collapsed into a heap on the floor.

At the first stop, another passenger, who did not know the drunken man, got up and helped the fellow to lean more comfortably against the doors on the non-platform side.

'Which station are you going to?' he shouted at him, shaking him slightly.

The pale, cadaverous face, upturned now to the light, remained unmoved. One by one the commuter recited the names of the stations on the line, and at one of them the drunk gave a slight nod. The passenger resumed his seat and we proceeded in peace.

Chinese hold their liquor admirably. One may see flushed faces and hear loud voices in Hongkong, but one very seldom sees a man drunk. It was strange to come back to a country where people moved about drunk in public. There must have been a Cup Final; I seldom read the sports pages of newspapers. Surely we must be getting near Rickmansworth.

Three stops further on, in the silence that fell when the train stopped, the drunk could be heard singing softly. He had a good voice too. Even in that state, his phrasing was artistic. But something about that plaintive melody, its peculiar minor cadences—it was surely an oriental song . . .

And once again, finding I had mentally drifted off to Europe, I shook myself back into Japan.

At the correct station two passengers got up, lifted the man out of the train, dumped him on the gloomy platform, and resumed their places. He lay there, motionless in the snow, as the doors slid to and the train moved on through the night.

·   ·   ·   ·   ·

My host, Father Johannes, was a young missionary newly arrived in Japan. The mission house he stayed in was a two-storeyed wooden building, very simple within. Like most Japanese houses, it was cold. In whispers, for fear of waking the parish priest, who slept in the next room, Father Johannes continued an account, begun at dinner, of his first reactions to the Japanese, the first oriental people amongst whom he had lived.

I listened, but was at the same time revolving other thoughts in my mind. After living for years in Asia, this entire first evening in Japan was like an electric shock, from which I was still struggling to pull myself loose. In Asia when one lands at an airport there are palm trees round the perimeter, it is warm, one's baggage gets lost, the town is several miles away, and there is—no, sorry, sir—no taxi just now. And maybe there never was a taxi.

What was this place? Was this really Asia? It was awfully cold, and I had not heard those Schubert dances for years. On second thoughts, though, it must be Japan, because the labels on the beer bottles were written in Japanese, and when Japanese beer is exported, the labels are in English.

After drinking a nightcap, we separated to our respective rooms. Mine was of plain wood, with no carpet, the only furniture a wardrobe, a table, and an old iron bedstead with a thick mattress piled high with gaily-coloured Japanese quilts. Something about it all, from the underground train to this frugal house, was trying to remind me of something I could not define. I lay under the quilts, trying to determine what it was, until the weight of them put me to sleep.

(ii) *Japanese bed*

When I awoke it was very early in the morning but already daylight. The moment I moved under the quilts I realized it was almost too cold to get out of bed. But as I was curious to see what lay outside the window, I sat up, quickly pulling on a coat. It was then that my mental searchings of the evening before became clear.

Outside was brilliant morning, a blue sky, and snow covering everything. In the distance I could see a pine forest, and quite near the window were the bare branches of cherry trees. The wooden walls of the room, the double windows to keep out the cold, the old iron bedstead, a crucifix on the wall, and the bright winter view— yes, I knew what it was now. It reminded me of all I had read of Russia.

At this moment the sensation was unexpectedly perfected by the opening of my door and the peeping in of the maid, ostensibly to enquire whether I was ready for tea, but actually wanting to see what the new guest looked like. She was a plump, bonny, middle-aged woman, wearing an apron and with a bright spotted kerchief over her head. I suppose, if I had been landed blindfold in the country without being told where I was, I might have guessed, seeing her, that I was in Japan. But only just. She had laughing brown eyes; her face was as round as an apple, and her cheeks as rosy. In these surroundings, with the cherry trees behind her, she seemed to have stepped straight out of a Tchehov play—the wife of one of Madame Ranevsky's tenants, perhaps.

I saw too that the Tokyo underground reminded me now not so much of London; at its drabbest the Inner Circle is never as drab as that. But the people in the train did strongly remind me of what I had read of Soviet Moscow. Tokyo itself too, with its excellent trains and main roads, but neglected side-streets, suggested the same thing.

In the words of a Japanese friend I met a few days later, in modernizing the country the reformers could not do everything at once.

'They had to choose between immediate necessity and what were desirable as future improvements. So far as transport is concerned, the choice was made in favour of a first-rate railway system and a few major roads. The rest had to take its time. That is why you can travel comfortably by rail anywhere in the country, but in

Tokyo, once you are off a main road, you have to make your way as best you can in mud or snow.'

It accounted for the rubber boots in the train.

It also accounted in part for the similarity I sensed between Japan and what I had read of Russia. Both are countries that have been subjected to rapid alteration and modernization according to a fixed programme designed by a handful of outstanding leaders. Men are not omniscient, the broadest mind cannot think of everything, and in such modernization, directed from above downwards by a few men impelled by strong motives, development is bound to be angular and fractional. Only where it is impelled from within the great mass of the people can it be rounded and complete, embracing every need.

The Japanese since 1868, like the Russians since 1917, have been moulded into a certain manner of living that seemed desirable to their leaders. Comparing our own development with theirs, we of Western Europe and America would call theirs abnormal. We have developed into what we ourselves wanted to be. They have developed into what a Pygmalion wanted them to be. Our shortcomings are of our own construction; we made our bed, we must lie on it, and if it is uncomfortable we must improve it. Their shortcomings are not entirely of their own construction. They may not understand that there is anything better than the bed they are lying on, and when they do understand this, they may have difficulty in improving it. Their bed was made by someone else.

One of the angularities in Japan is the accidental survival of mediaeval conceptions of war.

(iii) *Shadows of war*

At the inn where Father Johannes and I stayed at Nikko, the pug-faced, cheerful servant assigned to look after us was a young former soldier. His elder brother, he told us, was still a prisoner of the Russians, somewhere in Siberia. It was seven years since they had had word of him, yet from the way he spoke he clearly had the dogged expectancy of one day seeing him again.

When the servant discovered that I was English—it is a post-war tendency for Japanese to think every red face is American—and had been in the Japanese theatre of war, he went to fetch the inn-keeper, another former soldier in his mid-thirties. While we took dinner, the innkeeper sat with us on the smooth but chilly *tatami* mats, stoked the little ash fire sunk in the middle of the floor, and talked of war and his experiences overseas.

He was a quiet, square-faced man, spare and strong. A freshly caught hill-stream fish, which he was to have had for his own dinner, was diverted to ours. Conversation, thanks to Father Johannes' rapidly advancing knowledge of Japanese, developed in an atmosphere of friendliness.

It was the first time I had dared mention the war to a Japanese, and had it not been for the inn servant I doubt if the subject would have been touched. Because I had never worked out in my mind what such a conversation would be like, I was surprised by it, although in fact it probably differed hardly at all from any similar conversation after any war in history.

The innkeeper had been a sergeant. Obedient and friendly, but obviously self-disciplined and as tough as nails, he probably had a good record of service. He spoke passionlessly of Japan's defeat, rather as, in his later years, a boxing champion would say, yes, he was the champion for five years, but in the end was defeated in such a year by such a person. In a contest, after all, one side has to lose. Everyone understands that. There is no shame in losing, and all the glory in having been a champion.

A general or student of history might analyze the causes of defeat; our innkeeper did not.

'The Americans and the British were stronger than us,' he said simply.

Noticing that round his wrists were two deep scars, I asked Father Johannes to enquire how he got them.

The innkeeper glanced down at his wrists, turning his hands palms upward as he did so; then, looking at me, he said without affectation or emphasis:

'From the British.'

Father Johannes, who was Swiss, stirred uncomfortably. Having studied at London University, he was more familiar with our side of the story than with the Axis Powers', so far as war morals were concerned.

But, having got so far, I thought we had better go on. Surely one could be confident that there was some reason for it—although, war is a sordid affair; there might not be.

'Where?' I asked.

'In Malaya, at the end of the war.'

'What happened?'

Again without affectation:

'We were roped closely together and marched for several miles in the middle of the day. The rope soon wore through the skin—' he laughed slightly, '—right through to the bone.'

Father Johannes again rearranged himself on the *tatami*, translating in a conflict of embarrassment and neutral Swiss curiosity.

'But there must have been some reason for that,' I said sternly. 'Was there a reason?'

The innkeeper smiled good-naturedly.

'Yes,' he replied. 'Our officer killed some Malays.'

I do not know whether Father Johannes noticed my sigh of relief. When the British landings took place in Malaya, the war had already ended, the Japanese knew it had ended, and for a Japanese officer to have ordered the execution of some Malays could only be interpreted as a final, impotent outburst of savagery, well deserving a few scars for life.

During our conversation the pug-faced servant, attending to our meal, came and went, occasionally contributing a remark. By the way he spoke in front of the innkeeper I judged them to be related. He had been a prisoner of the Russians, of whom he spoke scathingly.

'When we were taken prisoner, you know, sir, not even the Russian sergeants could read and write. They took everything we had of any value—fountain-pens of course, and cameras. But not only things like that—soap and towels, boots, and even our shirts and underpants, because they were of better quality than theirs.'

Japanese are wide readers and set great store by literacy. To this country lad the justice of surrendering his underpants was not in dispute. But to surrender them to a man who could not read and write even his own language—such a simple script compared with Japanese . . . It was this that produced his tone of shocked disapproval.

The sliding door was open, and in the corridor outside an old maidservant stopped to listen to our talk.

'And why. don't they send my son back?' she said in Japanese.

'Where is your son?' asked Father Johannes.

'He's a prisoner in China.'

There was silence. Another seven years—of hope, of waiting, of slow hardening of the heart, as hope becomes a mechanical attitude, gradually drained of its connexion with the person for whose return it was born. Perhaps it were better he did not return. Perhaps, by processes of which it is better not to know, another man would come back.

They were used to the old maidservant. Turning away from her, the pug-faced servant went on with what he was saying.

'America and Britain are up here,' he said, raising his hand above his head. Lowering it to his chest, he added: 'Japan is here.—Russia . . . !' He snorted contemptuously and dropped his hand to below his knees. Then, remembering the old maidservant's son in China, he added forcefully: 'Why should he be kept by the Chinese? Make no mistake, sir. We were defeated by the Americans and the British, not by the Chinese, or the Filipinos. They could never have won a war against us.'

It was a distinction that had not occurred to me.

(iv) *The former champion seen with Madam Butterfly*

At the inn, those confusing moments of thinking one was in Europe no longer occurred. We moved away from sovietic drabness, lost sound of muted Schubert dances, stepped out of the vernal Tchehov setting, into a more familiar Japan, known since childhood, since that first visit to the opera to see *Madama Butterfly*, or since reading *Madame Chrysanthème*, Pierre Loti's elegant story of his temporary Japanese marriage. Here we touched what we had always considered to be the authentic Japan, the land of smiles, of exquisitely-dressed women, flower decorations, and petite houses with sliding paper partitions, the Japan which always sounded so much more pleasing than, and such an· incomprehensible contradiction to, the land of frock-coats and military uniforms, carefully imitated Zeiss cameras and binoculars, battleships and guns.

There being no chairs in a Japanese inn, we sat cross-legged on the spotless *tatami*, our dinner being served on low tables, a cluster being set before each of us. On each basic table was a set of even smaller tables, each holding one dish or a bowl of side ingredients. These very small tables—really trays on legs—could be moved about, and served only an aesthetic purpose, the creation of a co-ordinated artistic design in the initial presentation of the meal. *Saké*, Japanese wine (similar to Chinese *shaoshing* but with less body and colourless), was served hot in small jars which, I noted with some amusement, would in China have been used as flower-pots. The winecups were, if anything, even smaller than those used in China for *shaoshing*.

Each dish was in its way a tiny work of art, served in a bowl or dish of different shape or colour to match its contents. Porcelain, earthenware and lacquer, of vivid and unusual design, were all used, their colours and textures blending harmoniously.

The soup was a miniature representation of the depths of the sea. At the bottom of the bowl was sand, with an open clam-shell from beneath which long swaying plants arose. As one gazed into it and, suddenly, like a primitive tribesman seeing a photograph for the first time, caught its scale and dimensions, it deepened, the clamshell became larger and more mysterious, the sea-plants more hectic and writhing. Disturbing them slightly as I moved the bowl, I was reminded of Shelley's

'. . . sea-blooms, and the oozy woods which wear
The sapless foliage of the ocean . . .'

trembling and despoiling themselves.

As my chopsticks reached down to draw up the shell, however, the sand puffed up everywhere, revealing itself at once for what it really was—beancurd. The sea blooms disappeared in a soup that was now in appearance milky and no longer transparent. The oozy woods dripped over the edge of my delicate lacquer spoon. The fiction was over, the soup light and delectable.

There was, of course, raw fish—*sashémi*. Before going to Japan I had often wondered what on earth I would do if socially obliged to eat raw fish, but, on arrival, *sashémi* can seldom have found a more ready devotee. It is unquestionably delicious, and no visitor who likes smoked salmon need have the slightest hesitation about eating it. The meat of the particular fish used is somewhat similar to salmon, and is cut into small slices, convenient for picking up in chopsticks, but cut thicker than we serve smoked salmon. With it comes a little pulverized radish, which has to be emptied into a small dish of soya sauce, and the fish dipped piece by piece in the tasty concoction thus formed.

It is not etiquette to fill one's own cup with wine. Father Johannes filled my cup; I filled his. When dining alone at an inn a maidservant usually sits with one, making sprightly prattle and performing the important functions of refilling the wine-cup and serving honourable rice—the Japanese outdo even the Germans in honorifics.

To my surprise, the fish which the innkeeper insisted on our taking from what should have been his own dinner was served fried. In South China it is said that a first-rate fish should be steamed, to reveal its merits, while a second-rate fish should be fried, to conceal its defects. Before serving it up, the cook had furthermore removed the head and tail, inexcusable in China, where these parts are considered by many to be the most tasty. Yet, good as Chinese food is, it was a relief to escape temporarily from these over-exploratory tastes.

So we toyed with the little cups and bowls of classic Japan, savouring tiny pieces of dried seaweed, delicate nuts, tasty little roots, finely prepared ginger, and rice—honourable rice—with a raw egg broken over it. While we ate we talked of politics, rearmament, the obsolescence of battleships, and the difficulty of finding jobs in Japan now that the country no longer ruled Korea, Manchuria and Taiwan (Formosa). And as we did so, those two conflicting impressions, the Japan of *Madame Chrysanthème* and the Japan of frock-coats, uniforms and guns, gently fused into one. It had formerly been incredible to me that the grandiose ideas of the Greater East Asia Co-Prosperity Sphere could have been conceived in wood and paper houses, amid the chatter of *mousmés* and the clink of tiny tea-cups. But, as I appreciated that evening, raw fish is Spartan food, wood and paper houses are cold in winter, and the people who live in them must be tough. Just as a small bowl of soup reproduces the vast depths of the ocean, so from the warmth of a little tea-cup, clasped in the fingers in winter, can arise the comfortable dream of an empire embracing the tropics and covering a quarter of the globe.

(v) *Setting out for Koyasan*

For any traveller trying to acquire knowledge of strange lands, there are two primary guiding rules. The first is: keep away from capital cities. Because of their international connexions, capitals often convey false impressions of nations. The second is: never rush about. If possible, go to one place and sit down. A week spent in a single village will give a clearer and truer picture than a year spent visiting fifty cities.

The ideal is, of course, to go and stay with a family of the country. Unfortunately, when I went to Japan I knew no Japanese sufficiently to be invited to stay. I therefore had to make a random choice where I would go and sit down.

On the advice of a wise old friend, the place I selected was the Buddhist settlement of Koyasan, in Wakayama prefecture.

'I have not been there myself,' my friend wrote, 'but, from what I have heard, this is a place you should visit.'

Father Johannes, who had not previously heard of it, could not understand me.

'Why do you want to go there? I asked Father Lancret about it, and he says there are not even any hotels. Where will you stay?' he asked.

'In a monastery,' I answered, without batting an eyelid. 'And I have my talking book.'

Father Johannes, who was about to leave for the far north to assume his duties, would be unable to accompany me. In place of his excellent interpreting, a talking book had to be brought into play.

After living among the Chinese, it was a relief to come to a country where talking books are a practical possibility. In China they are not very practical. The page on 'Arrival' may begin with the phrase 'Please take me to the best hotel', and after it will come the romanized Chinese words, followed by the actual Chinese characters. Try speaking out the romanized version, and see what happens. Expressions of blank astonishment, or else peals of laughter. One has evidently got the words on the wrong tones. On looking at the romanized words more carefully, one notices that they are encumbered with accents and mysterious apostrophes, some curling forwards, some backwards. In order to understand what they mean, one has to refer to the key at the beginning of the book. The key, however, turns out to be a ten-page essay, to master which will take about a week's concentrated study. Hopefully one turns the book towards the person one wishes to address, possibly a pedicab driver, and points to the Chinese characters, only to find that the man cannot read. And so on.

Japanese, in certain respects an even more difficult language to read and write well than Chinese, has nonetheless several distinct advantages for a stranger. It is more or less uniformly spoken throughout the country, the Chinese characters used are simplified and much easier to recognize than the full characters used in China,[1] and, above all, there are no tones to contend with.

Having mastered the stress indications in romanized Japanese, which takes no more than a few minutes, as master of one's talking book one sets forth with a fair confidence.

(vi) *Kyoto after dark*

In any unknown town, the selection of a hotel should be made by daylight. In Kyoto it was my misfortune to arrive after dark.

When speaking of Kyoto, amateurs of Japan use the same ecstatic expressions as sinophils do of Peking—and indeed as impressive people do of almost any place of consequence with which one happens to be unacquainted. Kyoto, capital of Japan from 794 to 1868, is still recognized as the cultural centre of the nation. It is here, they proclaim, that one must go in order to see Japanese life and art at their best.

As a traveller without illusions, I realized that even this aura of enlightenment would not penetrate the darkness of an innless night, and in the last hour before the train drew in, punctual to the minute after a fast all-day journey from Tokyo, I memorized from my talking book the phrases that would be needed.

In Japan there are two completely different types of accommodation for travellers—hotels (*oteru*) and inns (*ryokan*). At the former one stays in the detached grandeur of European hotels as they once were, in the days when royalty led the way to the waters at fashionable spas. The food is approximately European, but sometimes—thrilling novelty—it is possible to have Japanese food, cooked in the

[1] The present Chinese Government is making important modifications.

special style which, by long experience, Japanese have discovered that Europeans like. At an inn, on the other hand, one stays in the conditions which the Japanese, who are great enthusiasts of travel within their islands, provide for themselves, with Japanese food cooked for Japanese palates. Apart from the fact that the latter is more attractive than the former, it is also a great deal less expensive.

At the entrance to Kyoto station, I saw that if I wanted a hotel, there was one right across the square. But to admire the classic city of Japanese culture from such a viewpoint seemed to be excluding half the experience. I therefore selected the most intelligent of the jinricksha drivers politely offering their services—Japan is a country of wonderful politeness, but within a minute of being in Kyoto one is aware of even greater refinement in this respect—and asked him if he could take me to a good inn.

He consulted two of his colleagues, one of whom asked me whether it was really an inn I wanted. I repeated my set phrase, there was general comprehension, and we set off.

The first feeling of spring was in the air. The night was not so cold as it had been when I arrived in Tokyo. With a pleasant sense of anticipation of the morning, I saw we were passing the dark shadows of huge classical buildings, evidently temples. Here indeed was one of the great sights of the East, the city which the Allies, in the interest of world culture, spared from any form of attack.

We crossed a bridge and entered a small dark street lined with trees. Two-storey wooden houses stood back in gardens; the atmosphere was of a secluded but respectable suburbia. The driver stopped in front of a garden gate, and, taking my suitcase, led me inside. At the door of the inn, under a small lantern, he asked whether there was a room. A woman ushered me within, to await the inn-keeper.

Once within, I noticed instantly, compared with the inn I had selected by daylight at Nikko, a slovenliness which, had this been China, would have been perfectly acceptable, but which in Japan, with its higher standards in regard to cleanliness and tidiness, I considered curious.

There were chairs in the hall—that could pass—but the two women and a man who were lounging in them were wearing shoes, and there was no rack near the door for guests' shoes to be deposited, and no pile of slippers for their use when going within. The wooden floor and the stairs were slightly dirty.

The owner, a well-built woman with a pleasing manner, wearing a simple flowered kimono, came down the stairs. Glancing up at her, I was struck by the comparison between her own dignified appearance and that of the cheap coloured porcelain head and shoulders of a western girl, with languorous eyes and a long lock of hair over her shoulder, which hung as a stark decoration on the wall the lady was passing.

Yes, they had an available room. Food?—a slight expression of concern—what sort of food did I want? Ordinary Japanese food. Yes—there was still some doubt—it could be arranged.

For some reason, I was now on my guard.

'I wish to see the room,' I said—blessed talking book—and as she assented I leant down to undo my shoes.

'Please do not trouble to take them off,' she said.

But, with knowledge of China, I insisted. Too often one is told in that country not to obey a convention, only to find afterwards that, by not obeying, one has merely opened the door to discussion about foreign devils being pigs with no manners. I took my shoes off, amid a slight tremor from the onlookers, and followed the lady upstairs.

'This room,' she said.

Unlike the austere but inviting charm of the Nikko inn room, with its *tatami*, its simple flower decoration and scroll of Japanese writing, its tidy ankle-level drawers in the walls, and its central sunken ash fire, with kettle and tripod for preparing tea, this room had bare wooden floors, a calendar of a foreign airline on one wall, a central light with a glass shade ornamented with pink roses, and a small double-bed with black iron bedstead and dingy coverlet. In China, excellent, but here, surely not? . . .

I turned round to look into another room in which two women in European *négligées* were lolling on another similar bed. As they saw me, they began to get up, while from another room came yet a third girl, looking at me expectantly.

Talking books are not made for handling awkward occasions, but at this moment mine did not altogether fail me.

'Thank you,' I said. 'I am hungry. I want something to eat.'

'But we can provide food,' the owner exclaimed, with some

anxiety; 'and you can stay here,' she added, following me rapidly downstairs.

'Thank you,' I said, concealing my embarrassment as I leant down again to put on my shoes.

The people lounging in the hall watched me without emotion.

'My house very good,' the owner said, in English this time.

'I'm sure it is,' I replied similarly. 'But I just want somewhere to sleep.'

'Can sleep here, that room you alone,' she said.

I moved to the door, where the jinricksha driver was waiting to be paid.

'Let's go.—Goodnight,' I said to the lady, and as I did so I caught sight again of the porcelain figure of the western girl on the wall. The first time I had no more than glanced at it. Now I saw that, in effect, it came down below shoulder level, and that the drapery covering one of its breasts fell so as to reveal completely the other.

Can one ever be sufficiently old, seasoned, and perceptive to avoid making mistakes in this complicated world?

.   .   .   .   .

'An inn!' I said hotly to the driver, once we were out again in the street. 'An inn! Do you understand?'

He understood. He looked crestfallen. We started off again.

Within ten minutes or so we stopped. This time the neighbour-hood selected was not so attractive. Instead of trees and garden, the approach was through a yard full of disused pieces of machinery. The driver indicated a door at the end where there were some signs of culture, a door lamp and a dwarf tree in a pot.

But as I made to alight from the ricksha there were sounds of disturbance from within the building, and two American soldiers appeared at the door, arguing with the owner of the house, who was another distinguished-looking but formidable woman of the type I had already met.

I signed to the driver to move on, and, as I saw his expression, understood why he had looked crestfallen. At the railway station he and his friends had estimated that I was a foreigner (an American, naturally) of some means. It had therefore been decided to show me the best first. When he saw that I was unable to agree a price with the owner of the establishment, he realized I was stingy and going to be a bad fare. Having taken me now to a second-rate establishment and found that even that was too good for me, he did not know where to take me next. Did I want the sort of place he himself went to?

As we headed into what was obviously a still more down-at-heel section of the city, I saw crisis approaching if we did not quickly disentangle our cross-purposes. Stopping him, as a last resource I dug out of my case a tattered *Baedeker* of 1933, which a friend in Hongkong had lent me. In Hongkong, and in all parts of China that have been involved in the almost continual disturbances of the last fifty years, one is soon conditioned to a situation in which hotels, restaurants and shops are seldom to be found in the same place for more than a few years at a time. I had brought this conditioning to Japan. Japanese inns were wooden, a sure mark of the transitory.

Nevertheless, being on the edge of resignation, I found the list of Kyoto inns given by *Baedeker* in 1933, and read out the first one.

To my surprise, there was an immediate reaction. Admirably concealing what he now recognized as his mistake, the driver hastily repeated the name of the inn, and within ten minutes we were at the door. It was only then that it began to sink into me that the flimsy wooden houses of the older Japanese cities are sometimes, carefully repaired, several hundred years old, with, in the case of inns and shops, long and honourable traditions. By the strength of their culture the Japanese have given permanence to wood as no other civilization of wooden buildings has so completely succeeded in doing.

The innkeeper, an elderly, benign man speaking some English, informed me with regret that the inn was full, advised me of another, and told the driver where to go.

'It is only a small place,' he said, 'but they will look after you there. The owner is a good woman.'

So, thanks to *Baedeker* and this kindly old man, I at last found what I needed.

(vii) *Winged apples*

In spite of being small—poky is a better word—it was in the very heart of the city. Its owner, used to every kind of visitor, was an experienced hostess who knew what each guest wanted even before he asked for it.

'My hotel makes beefsteak,' she said firmly in English, as, seated before me on the *tatami* in my room, she awaited my dinner order.

With some difficulty I managed to convince her that I wanted Japanese dishes, my knowledge of the names of a few proving of assistance. With a perceptible shrug of the shoulders, she resigned herself to the crankiness of a guest with no proper sense of values, and wrote down the dishes I required; but she was too much a woman of the world to believe I would really enjoy them. As she left the room she turned at the open door.

'Then, breakfast tomorrow—you want bacon?'

'I said Japanese style!'

She gave a nod of comprehension.

'Oh—with liver.'

I let her go, ordering my breakfast later from the less sophisticated maidservant.

My room was small and stuffy, the communal bathroom lugubrious, the food only just adequate; but the ladies' manners were those of a palace—combined with tight-lipped observation lest a yen be wasted. Honourable rice was served with ceremonies greater than any I had yet seen, while in adornment the slender meal of fish, seaweed, caraway seeds and roots was sheer fantasy and inspiration. Even a tangerine was served with a small part of its skin cut and folded in, giving it the appearance of some timid creature from the depths of the sea, while the apples had thin slices of skin cut and bent outwards, one in the shape of gay swallows' wings, the other as rabbits' ears.

For this was the great centre of Japanese culture, where everything is seen at its best. Confronted with the apples, though, I had the disconcerting sense of a swimmer who, having laboured far out from the shore, relaxes to tread water, only to bump his knees on sand, the water being still only a few feet deep.

The hostess had a younger relative, a large-bosomed woman with a white face and soft laugh. Late at night an American came, taking the room next to mine. There were intimate greetings, and by the comings and goings in the passage it could be known that the emperor had come to his small palace. What marvels of invention,

I thought, must his saucers of seaweed and apples be, what ceremonies and manners those of the favoured empress. As I fell asleep I knew through the paper partition that she was seated in the doorway of his room. She was talking softly, talking—and then she laughed. There was a rustle of silk, and silence.

Still, it was more or less an inn.

(viii) *The great conservatory*

As soon as I became aware in my dingy room that it was dawn, I got up and went out in search of the temples whose profiles I had seen in the darkness of yesterday's arrival. It was warmer, a flat, overcast day; and here, slightly ahead of Tokyo, the first cherry trees were blossoming.

As I saw the long silhouette of the first of the great temples, and its austere treatment of the Chinese classical style of architecture, I recognized another of the deceptions of Mesdames Butterfly and Chrysanthème. These ladies had led me to imagine Japanese buildings with gaily curved roofs and upturned eaves, fanciful creations suited to the bizarre lines of women's hair arrangement and dress, another petite art allied to the apples with rabbits' ears. China can show many famous examples of this graceful, light-hearted style. Surely it was these pleasing appearances that the Japanese must have borrowed from China.

The silhouettes in the grey light showed otherwise. The immensely long roofs with no more than the faintest suggestion of curvature, their economy of decoration, their tense control of design, their grave aspect, betokened again the Spartan quality in Japanese life, expressed here in terms of architecture—sternly masculine modes of thought monumentally embodied in wood.

It was a Buddhist day of festival—one of the reasons for the inns being full—and even at this early hour pilgrims, most of them women, were entering the spacious precinct, removing their sandals, and in their white-stockinged feet shuffling up the steps into the gloomy interior.

Within was a single vast hall, its roof and recesses hidden in shadow. At three altars a forest of tapers reflected fire in the golden faces of the gods. Old women crouched before the statues, bowing and reciting over and over again the holy names of Amida Lord Buddha. There was a constant movement of devotees placing new tapers before the altars, in great bronze urns of Chinese design. Elderly men in classic day clothes of dark colours stood patiently with folded hands before the immaculately smiling faces, while their wives bowed, crouched, murmured and sometimes wept as they brought into this solemn sanctuary the troubles of their distant homes. On the soft *tatami* one's socks could slide. The feeling of walking on very thin cushions created for each pilgrim a sense of ease and luxury, of bodily harmony, seldom found in temples in other lands. Gradually, deep colours of wood and faded gold were discernible, the perfect forms of the tree-trunk columns, lacquered an autumnal red.

The statues bore indications of contact with the Buddhist art of India. For a moment, even, one might have mistaken some of them for Hindu gods. The three Buddhas of the past, the present and the future suggested by their gestures and the objects held in their many hands their affinity with Brahma, Vishnu and Siva, the creative, the preserving, the destructive and re-creating. From these Japanese altars it seemed one could traverse China in a single stride, enter the dusty temples of India, and hear again the noble measure of the Vedic hymns.

Such, I suppose, was the Buddhism of China before and during the great T'ang dynasty, before eaves were twisted upward in sprightly curves, before the carving of Buddha statues was reduced to the reproduction of a bland, meaningless smile, before temples had rubbish piled up in their corners, and before monks sat beneath the images splitting melon seeds in their teeth and talking of their adventures.

There had been adaptations in Japan too, of course. The majestic styles of T'ang architecture had to be reproduced in wood, where the Chinese often used stone and brick; and although, through the medium of art, the spirit of Buddhism penetrated the islands, its written philosophy hardly entered at all, being replaced by attractive ritual and the endless repetition of the holy names. Yet so perfect was the artistic reproduction that in this great Kyoto temple there dwelt something that could not be defined otherwise than as a long-sustained rumour of another age, another country. Within this carefully maintained building, in the faces of the gods with their innate concessions to Gupta art, could be identified the fervent acceptance of a new religion, the spirit that must once have pervaded the temples of Loyang in the heyday of the T'ang.

When Japan is called the great conservatory of Chinese culture, it does not mean, as in a museum, that the best Chinese porcelain and paintings are to be seen there. It means this other form of conservation—that of the spirit, which in China has so nearly died. Coupled with intense curiosity and desire for novelty, the Japanese have as a national trait an equally intense conservatism. When something foreign is adopted by them, having adapted it slightly to their needs, they maintain it for hundreds of years without further alteration. As, in a sleepy moment, the Tokyo underground seemed to be in truth London's Inner Circle, on which it was modelled, so perhaps a man of T'ang, set down today in Kyoto and tired of the noisy streets, might turn into a temple precinct and imagine for a perplexing instant, from the appearance of the temple, and from the clothes and manners of the people passing in and out, that he was once again in Loyang, twelve centuries ago.

(ix) *The idyll of Nara*

From Kyoto I moved on to Nara, where, having taken the precaution of arriving by day, I was able to find a first-rate inn. The window of my small but elegant room looked over the ornamental lake Sarusawa, in which a famous beauty of the eighth century committed suicide. The cherry trees were now in full bloom, the green landscape lit with their astonishing whiteness, with here and there a tree of the palest pink blossom. Beside the lake the weeping willows that commemorate the beauty's unhappy fate were in fresh leaf. Old people sunned themselves in the first warm days of the year, watching the deer as they wandered in small concourses under the trees and over a road where all transport respectfully waited for them to cross in safety. Children tried to make friends with them, offering them food, which they nibbled like connoisseurs, until a small hand was put out to stroke them, when they hastily skipped away. Groups of students in dark German uniforms walked past on their way from one historic building to the next, a visit to Nara being part of their education. On the quiet road leading through a park to the Todaiji passed to and fro a constant file of tourists, most of the women wearing their traditional costumes, a line of sober colours, enlivened by the bright silk squares on their backs, and by white socks, padded within against chill and damp. Partially concealed among trees and by another wing of the inn were the eaves of a tall five-tiered pagoda, whose resonant bell, of great antiquity, would strike twice a day, at six o'clock morning and evening. On a gable of the inn sat a white cat, sunning itself.

At Nara one steps further back into Japan's past, for Nara was the capital from 710 to 784, prior to the foundation of Kyoto, which succeeded it. It flourished at an idyllic period of Japanese history, when the genius of this remote island people was first awakened by the impact of Chinese civilization and the Buddhist faith, and in keeping with the conservatism already referred to, not only the historic memory, but the idyll itself, is preserved wonderfully intact.

Staying at the same inn was a young Japanese doctor, travelling alone on holiday. Having set out independently from the inn, we met again by chance in a museum, decided we wanted to see the same things, and from then on did our sightseeing together. We walked together beneath the aged trees of the park; we admired with complementary exclamations the gigantic wooden buildings of the Todaiji; we shouldered our way in through the pilgrims to gaze up at the passionless smile of the Daibutzu, the largest bronze statue in the world (as high as a three-storey house); we examined with pleasure the excellent bookstalls selling illustrated histories of Japanese art for a shilling or so. At the Great Bell, cast in the eighth century and so large that every time it has fallen down has been recorded in history (it being such an event to haul it up again), we watched with equal fascination a young man swing above his head the wooden beam that strikes the bell, swaying it back and forth, gathering momentum, until, flinging himself sideways with the beam, he flew through the air, the weight of his body causing the wood to reach the bronze at last, producing a note of wonderful richness, heard right over the city and into the fields beyond. Finally we mounted to the Temple of the Second Month, and from its terrace looked down on the roofs and trees below.

'I had not expected to find people like yourself so interested in these old places,' I said.

'Why not?' he enquired.

'Because you are what we would call in other Asian countries so westernized. The word has a special meaning. A westernized Asian is usually a person with new roots, new traditions. He feels more at home talking about London or Paris than in discussing the culture of his own country. People with old-fashioned ideas or conservative traditions are like old trees. The westernized Asian may be grafted from an old tree, but he is newly planted. I have always thought of westernized Japan like that too. I could understand these pilgrims coming to the shrines of Buddhism, because they belong to the old Japan. But you, as a western-trained doctor, I had expected to be one of the young trees, with little feeling for the old.'

'I don't think you can make that distinction,' he replied. 'You mustn't be deceived by a change of dress or the adoption of some western ways. I have my roots in this old country, the same as anyone else. The history of France is split in two by a revolution, but culturally there is no split; the story runs on continuously. Our adoption of Chinese culture was a kind of revolution; our westernization during the Meiji period was another. But the way we look at it there was no break. We did not stop and begin again as something new. We became richer, that's all. But we went on as before.'

It had not occurred to me till then that the Japan of frock-coats and battleships was descended from the Buddhist idyll of Nara, that the officers who, by thousands, unmurmuringly surrendered their swords at the end of the war might, on reflexion, have said they were surrendering two thousand years, that this nation aggressively vaunting the costume of a *parvenu* was in fact not a *parvenu* at all.

In all Europe, what building of comparable size is older than the Todaiji, complete and still in use? In Rome, the Pantheon; in Istanbul, the Aya Sofya; little else. What were Florence and Venice when Nara was in its prime? Charlemagne was not born, and Wessex was not yet head of the miserable Anglo-Saxon heptarchy.

(x) *Assimilation*

One of the things that has made possible this sense of continuous tradition is the completeness with which foreign innovations are assimilated.

On our way back to the inn I alluded to the Chinese style of all the architecture. The doctor quickly corrected me.

'These buildings are not in the Chinese style,' he said, and opening one of the books I had bought he indicated a photograph of a more ornate structure, with upturned eaves and a curved roof. 'That is the Chinese style.'

Admittedly the distinction was no more than one of terms, but its suggestion was illuminating. The architecture of Nara is basically that adopted in the seventh and eighth centuries from T'ang dynasty China. But the Chinese styles of later periods, introduced into Japan after the great era of assimilation, had to be somehow distinguished. As they were new and foreign, they were called Chinese, for by this time the styles of the greater T'ang period had established themselves—they were Japanese.

Another illustration of this appeared a day or so later when I was dining with Japanese friends in the town.

'I have prepared a special Japanese dish for you,' my hostess said proudly, adding more slowly, to make sure I caught the name: 'It is called soup.'

She then served a quite ordinary European vegetable soup which I duly praised as a delicious manifestation of Japanese culinary taste. To have done otherwise would have been useless.

At the inn, furthermore, the maidservant had no idea that ham-and-eggs was not a Japanese dish.

In fact, this is no more extraordinary than the failure of most of us to realize that tangerines are Chinese. Tangerines have, in their small way, been integrated into our culture, and are thus regarded—justifiably—as European. A Chinese would look at it in quite another light.—How curious! he would think; they eat Chinese dwarf oranges—and would be upset by the irritated reply that they were not Chinese at all.

The maidservant expressed similar irritation when I told her about ham-and-eggs.

(xi) *Where the whole world must bow*

To see the supreme manifestation of this cultural tradition one has to travel half-an-hour or so out of Nara, and back in time yet another hundred years, to the late sixth and early seventh centuries, to a group of Buddhist monasteries and nunneries surrounded by peaceful gardens. In one of the oldest of these foundations, the Horiuji, is a simple wooden image of a woman, tall, slender, plainly robed, on her head an aged metal crown, and from every inch of the wood a veritable emanation of tenderness and sanctity. This is the Kudara Kwannon, the Korean Goddess of Mercy, unexcelled by any work of sculpture that exists, one of those dateless moments in which, as before the most ancient truth, the eyes and heart of every beholder become those of a child. Designed around the year 610, she stands in a small room on her own, and she is so beautiful that, though the building is a museum, the guardians cannot bear to leave her without each day placing vases of flowers beside her, set assymetrically, in true Japanese style, a tall vase on one side with long-stemmed blooms, on the other side a smaller vase with humbler wild flowers.

A short distance away is an old nunnery, the Chuguji, where amid incense and flowers in a light, harmonious room is a meditating Amida of the same epoch, seated with one leg resting gently over the other, his right hand raised reflectively to his chin and just drawing away at the moment of inspiration—of understanding at last a secret that from others is hidden—and held thus for ever, timelessly. In these works of art, comparable only with the greatest masterpieces of Hellenic and Italian creation, Japan touches universality, reaching the highest pinnacle of human expression.

The sole visitor to the nunnery on a clear, fresh morning, I became aware that an old nun kneeling before the statue had broken off her recitation to watch me with wondering interest. Then she too looked toward the statue, and sighed.

(xii) *A Nara home*

After a few days I was invited by Japanese friends to a tea cere-mony, that quintessential moment in Japanese manners and etiquette which, from the time I first heard it, had always seemed, for so dynamic a people, an incongruous anticlimax in the negative and effete.

My host was a young timber merchant, whose father had recently died, and his house, in the centre of the town, was run by his mother and his elder sister, a teacher of music. The furnishing reflected the father's personality more than that of any of the occupants. Having achieved a fair degree of prosperity, he had clearly determined to fulfil an ambition by building a home which, with Japanese eclecticism, would incorporate what he considered the best of everything.

To begin with, inside the front door was a porch with an English umbrella-stand, coat-hanger and mirror combined. There was a doormat, it being unnecessary in this part of the house to remove one's shoes, unless a feeling for etiquette—instinctive in most Japanese—demanded it. There thus had to be a shoe-tray as well as a doormat.

The doors at this stage—for progress through the house was, as it were, by esoteric stages—were European, of dark stained wood of very high quality, a contrast with the drably provincial umbrella-stand. Through one of them one entered the main living room, furnished in the English style of my grandfather's day, sombre, and encumbered with imposing but valueless things under glass. There was a leather-topped writing desk, some dark book cabinets, Italian pastoral scenes in gilt mounts and frames, a small bust marked 'Athene' (one wouldn't have known), and an old German upright piano with candlesticks. These dignities of the Victorian era were shielded from vulgar view by frosted glass in the windows facing the street. On the desk was a large typewriter, and on top of the piano was my young host's first incursion of personality into the house, an excellent radio. There were leather-bottomed swivel-back chairs, and two old-fashioned armchairs with faded flower-pattern covers. On the floor was a thin dark red carpet, probably made in England, reminiscent of boarding houses at Margate.

Although Nara was once the capital of Japan, within itself, and apart from the drifting tourist world, whose inhabitants it seldom meets except in the street, it is a small provincial town of merchants and shopkeepers. I find it necessary to explain this at this point, lest it be thought that there was anything tawdry about my friend's house. Far from being tawdry, this outer living room was the town's final mark of cultural distinction. It was triumphantly cosmopolitan, demonstrating a knowledge of Europe such as few others possessed. In the town it was an expression of the *avant-garde* of the new Japan, while among the country wood merchants with whom the family had dealings it was the *coup* that bestowed social paramountcy.

It was also a convenient room. On the many occasions when business has to be conducted out of office hours, the Japanese conventions of removing shoes and settling down on the floor are awkward. If it is snowing or raining, the caller's trouser-legs will dampen the *tatami*, and he himself, coming in his rough winter clothes into the serene tidiness of a home, will feel uncomfortable and ill-at-ease. Let us not sully the domain of Butterfly, but sit in its outer confines, on chairs, surrounded by the barbaric but intriguing impedimenta of those big-boned people of the West who cannot sit neatly cross-legged like gentlemen.

In Europe we have our phases when anything barbaric or primitive is the rage; we are in the midst of one at the present time. Japan indulges in the same exotic tastes, but, with conservatism added, the phases do not wax and wane as ours do. There is addition, but no subtraction; glass cases, but no dustbin. The novelties of the barbaric, instead of being removed to an attic (being found inconvenient during a pre-Raphaelite revival), find their immutable position in the national life, and remain in a state of dignified preservation, albeit only near the front door.

It is as if, in England, our houses today had Roman central heating, floor mosaics, mediaeval stained-glass windows, Chippendale furniture and the latest types of refrigerator, all of which we somehow managed to harmonize into a practicable way of living.

.   .   .   .   .   .

I hardly noticed at first sight that the inner wall of the room was a sliding screen, by opening which the size of the living room was rather more than doubled.

Within was a Japanese room—*tatami*, cushions, low lacquered tables, a subtle flower decoration in a low niche in the wall, a scroll painting and two couplets of only moderately good calligraphy—the owner, after all, had no pretensions to being a scholar. Lying across two cushions was a Japanese lute, near it a metal music stand about six inches high. My host's sister, the music teacher, played the piano reasonably well, but was at her best in traditional Japanese forms of music. Later she played the lute for us, a single piece of wood, exceedingly light to hold, lacquered, with thirteen strings of silk lying across delicately carved ivory bridges.

Beyond this room was a small interior courtyard in which there was a dwarf garden of gnarled trees, a lake, bridges and a rustic shrine, all less than two feet high. The secret of these famous gardens is that they must be seen through an aperture that conceals all surrounding life-size objects. Thus excluded, the miniature dimensions assume the reality of a natural landscape seen at a distance through a window. This feature having unfortunately been overlooked, the garden was reduced to an affectation.

Stairs led from the courtyard to the upper rooms of the house where, in the principal bedroom, was the father's large European bed, now occupied by the son. Although in winter a bed of this kind is much warmer than the traditional Japanese bed of quilts spread out on the floor, my host's mother had never cared for it and was glad she no longer had to sleep in it. None of the female members of the family had ever desired such a bed; it was the only one in the house.

At the foot of the stairs was the bathroom, where once or twice a week a big immersion tub of scalding hot water was prepared, each member of the family using it in order of precedence—which means men first.

Beyond the courtyard a small door led into a further, though separate, building at the rear, the *kura*, or earthquake-proof storehouse.

The four fears of Japanese people are humorously expressed as earthquakes, thunder, fire and Father. Earthquakes are justifiably put first. Hardly a day passes without an earth tremor somewhere in the islands; I experienced three in my first week. To those who come from countries where earthquakes are seldom or never experienced, it encloses all one's impressions of the country in a frame of impermanence, misshapen and awry. One links it with the people's love of, and gift for, daring, unusual design in everything from painting and temple decoration to dishes and neckties; one associates it with their fundamental dislike of symmetry—so utterly at variance with the Chinese ideas that have otherwise deeply influenced them—and their unique artistic gift for the grotesque. In the night, at first for no apparent reason, one awakes; and it is not for a second or so that one realizes that the whole sturdy wooden structure one is sleeping in is shaking gently from side to side, as if it were about to loosen itself from its foundations and creep away in the dark to some other place. The gentle rocking continues; stops for a moment; then there is a single and quite sharp shudder, such as we make when, in sleep, some uncomfortable nerve forces us to move with a jerk. It is for an instant as if we were lying asleep on the back of a vast creature with the same nervous reactions as ours. Stillness follows, and silence over the town. Thousands of people have been partially wakened by it, have turned over under the quilt, and, as we did in London in 1940 when we heard the fifth bomb fall to the east and the sixth to the west, said sleepily to themselves, 'It hasn't happened.'

A minor tremor such as this would probably knock the glass out of the windows of Westminster Abbey and damage the intricate roof of Henry VII's Chapel. A slightly stronger tremor might bring down the four pinnacles on the Victoria Tower at the Palace of Westminster and upset the mechanism of Big Ben. Such tremors might be expected to occur every ten days or so. Unless we were exceedingly active and determined, all that in London enshrines our national traditions would quite soon disintegrate. Under such conditions, would we ourselves be the cool, impassive people our friends and critics call us? Would we have the same sense of justice, of helping under-dogs, of resisting aggressions that do not immediately concern us? Might we not, under these conditions, be a very different people from what we are? What traditions would we have? Would they have any depth or strength?

Any family that can afford it will build a *kura*. Most of them are small squat buildings, with one or two very small windows, strong foundations, thick earth walls and double-tiled roof. It is an expensive building to construct. In it will be stored all articles of value that are not in daily use, clothes, fabrics, spare quilts and cushions, jewellery, plate, glass, porcelain, scrolls, books, wine and even stocks of tea and rice. Pictures and other decorations, for example, may be used for a month or so, then returned to the *kura*, from which others will be brought out to replace them. In an earthquake strong enough to bring houses tumbling down, a *kura* may crack or be damaged in some other way; but if one's goods are inside it the chances are that one will be left with enough to furnish a new house. It is not difficult to ascribe the origin of the Japanese manner of decorating rooms with the minimum of furniture or other possessions to the earthquake problem, and see in it a limitation imposed by nature, but converted by man into an art.

(xiii) *Tea ceremony*

With his Italian landscapes, piano, armchairs, double-bed, dwarf garden, scrolls and *kura*, Father had hardly left anything out. Perhaps, though—it would have been interesting to know what the Nara people thought—he went too far when he ordered his contractor to build a tea room.

It lay at the far side of the courtyard, an enclosed square room, of the classic nine foot by nine, bare and clean, approached by an equally bare corridor, passing through which the world is left behind. The tea room may be used for nothing else except the tea ceremony. Mother had always considered it a waste of space, but Father had his way.

Perhaps people might laugh at him. Perhaps an aristocrat would sneer. True, as he prepared tea for his guests with as much as he could manage of the prescribed etiquette, he was unable to discuss the merits of paintings or bowls or verse, as had the originators of the ceremony, and as its principal devotees had subsequently done, with varying degrees of sincerity. But from the price of wood he could turn to the quality of wood, to its intrinsic beauty, to the splendid temples, palaces and tombs built with it, or to the forests themselves, their beauty in snow, or in autumn when the leaves turn gold and red. There were many simple subjects that could be discussed with dignity at the tea ceremony. It was, as its inventor knew, a supreme relaxation. But, while learning its conventions, he would not be its slave, barrenly imitating the groans of aesthetes praising the glaze of a pot. He chose adequately good utensils for the ceremony—relatively the same standard as the calligraphy in the living room. The immense prices paid for really old utensils were beyond his means. There was nothing spectacular about his tea ceremonies, nor yet anything pretentious.

How he still lived in that house, the old gentleman! An independent character, he had insisted on his daughter studying the tea ceremony and perfecting one of its many schools of etiquette. In former times I imagine it would have been unheard of for a woman to have performed the ceremony; yet here she was. Since returning from school she had changed out of tweed skirt and jumper into a superb silk kimono, re-doing her hair in a style to suit the mood of the silk's colours. A vase of cherry buds had been placed in the room—its sole decoration—and before each of us, on a plate of great beauty, reposed a small green cake on a square of plain paper.

With slow, deliberate movements, each conveying an impression of controlled strength, she performed the ritual, cleansing one by one an already spotless set of delicate utensils, warming in boiling water the bowl in which the tea for each guest in order of precedence would be served, a sturdy deep-glazed bowl such as can be clasped warmingly in both hands. First some pale green tea-leaves crushed to powder, a little boiling water added from a slender wooden ladle, one turn of a whisk to make the preparation frothy. She examines it. Satisfied that it is perfect, she offers the bowl with both hands, while we, when our turn comes, with a slight obeisance accept it likewise. We hold it for a moment, savouring its colour, shape and warmth, then, allowing ourselves to hiss as we absorb it, we drain the contents and, with suitable appreciation, return it for more ceremonious cleansing and wiping, in preparation for the next guest.

We now take the small cake. Using the piece of paper on which it lies, we lift it to our mouth, the paper shielding from view the actual transmission of the cake between our lips. Nor must the stained paper be left screwed up, lest its uncontrolled appearance disturb the tranquillity of the mental atmosphere. With deliberation we fold it into a small square and replace it on the plate.

Madame de Sévigné would have been charmed by it, Proust would have described it in eighty or so pages, and if music were ever allowed, it would have been by Mozart.

Although, with a foreigner present, conversation lacked the beauty and dignity prescribed, a sense of ease enveloped each one of us. The grave movements of our hostess, movements elaborated and analyzed through the centuries by scholars and warriors, had the artistic beauty of intimate music—a string quartet played by musicians of great experience and sympathy—and into our drab, ordinary relationships, into this little room excluding all the world, there entered a dreamy hint of perfection.

At the instant of identifying this subtle hint, I thought of Father Johannes.

'Converts to Christianity,' he had told me, 'often explain that they were attracted to the Church from the moment they first realized that Shinto leads to nothing, that it is ritual, with no real philosophy behind it. The ritual can be perfected; but that is all.'

So with the tea ceremony. The performance of certain movements, each completely mastered, and the use of certain utensils of great beauty, induce a sensation of perfection as an absolute and present state—also, to some extent, a withdrawal from the trammels of outer life into an inner state of calmness, symbolized by the passage from the main rooms of the house into the immaculate tea room. This inner state is not an escape, however. It is a concentration upon reality, the concentration being aided by withdrawal, enabling the mind to be focused closely and its sensations heightened, the reality being conveyed by a number of material objects of high quality (the bowl and utensils), and the entire experience rendered keener by being shared with three or four other men, similarly withdrawn and concentrated.

Few people, anywhere in the world, associate perfection with their own lives, or indeed believe that perfection is attainable in this world. The great religions unanimously interpret worldly life as imperfect and impermanent. If they speak of perfection at all, they treat of it as a future state in another, better existence. For those of us with a Christian background, to contemplate perfection as an absolute state is synonymous with lifting our eyes toward God. In all our highest forms of self-expression, in all our strivings for perfection, in music and the arts, there is a pointer to the skies, a suggestion that the highest standard reached on earth is but an imperfect reproduction of something that can achieve perfection only in Heaven. The great choruses of Bach and Handel, the frescoes and statues of Michelangelo, the poetry of Milton, are among the more obvious manifestations of how, in seeking perfection, we seek at the same time to draw back the veil of the sky, and reveal another, greater world. But in fact this same quality permeates the most diverse art. Who would deny its presence in Keats' 'Ode on a Grecian Urn', in the Roman sonnets of Joachim du Bellay, or in

Van Gogh's 'Nevermore', all of them dealing ostensibly with material subjects; while, in the greatest tragic portrayals of earthly life, in the self-portraits of Rembrandt, in *King Lear*, and even in *Macbeth*, are we allowed for a single moment, while watching the gradual destruction of a human life, to forget that that worn frame is but the vehicle of an inextinguishable spirit, which in death is restored to its true nature? In the Shakespeare tragedies, death heals, liberating some from the imperfection of life, restoring others to their sober senses. But always there is the pointer to the skies. Often too, as in the paintings of Botticelli, it is the very quality of imperfection which disturbingly impels our awareness of another state beyond, which the artist knows, but is powerless to express.

In Japan, if we except those supreme moments of universality, the moments of the Meditating Amida and the Kudara Kwannon, it would be true to say that there is traditionally no attempt to glimpse a further shore, to rend the veil of the sky. What is beautiful is not the concealed world hinted at in the tangible object. It is the object itself. Perfection does not lie in the future. If it is to be found at all, it is in the present. Perfection is a state, and a state, in order to exist, must be present. If you run after a state, you will run for ever.

True, the act of running may bring happiness. But that is not perfection. Why search the sky for great, unattainable things? Shade the window, close the door, sit down with friends, and take in your hands the forms and colours that the mind and hand have fashioned.

Profound in sentiment, but not in the emotions that give sentiment its strength; profound in artistry, but not in the searing thought from which great works of art are produced. Such was Father Johannes' verdict on the night of my arrival. Reaching the harmony of the tea ceremony, he would feel himself in shallow water, as I did with the apples. If tangible objects—the kettle, the bowl and the whisk—were to be inducements to reflexion, it could only be, according to his philosophy, because they were symbols of something intangible beyond. As they are not symbolic of any such thing, let them be moved out of the way. Let us look without impediment toward the Trinity.

As in China, however, the elaborations of thought required in projecting beyond what is tangible are considered obscure and dry. What quality have these ethereal avenues that can compare, in China, with the immense, overwhelming certainty of the continuity of human life, expressed in the family? Why should Japan lay aside the gilding of the hour, beautified for its own sake by the limitless contrivances of art, and set out instead on a gloomy route march, the pursuit of happiness, at the end of which, on a date unspecified, she will behold a way of life that is unlikely to be artistically superior to what she has already?

In both countries there is a mental resistance to clearing the tangible out of the way, in order to contemplate the intangible. To do so is what Father Johannes would call going deeper. To a Chinese it is escapist, negative and unrealistic. To a Japanese it is—well, let me not run ahead of my story.

(xv) *The world and the nation*

Yo had come up to Koyasan to buy wood from one of the timber merchants who, apart from Buddhist monks and their novices, are the place's only inhabitants.

'You are English?' he asked in surprise, finding me walking through the forest in search of a monastery in which to stay. 'The last Englishmen I met were prisoners under my charge in Shanghai.'

'Before coming to Japan,' I replied, 'the only Japanese I had met were prisoners under my orders in Singapore.'

With a slight laugh he offered me his hand. Here was a basis for understanding. From his frankness I assumed that in the matter of prisoners he had nothing to hide. Nor had he, evidently. He later showed me a letter—as good as a passport in some countries—written by an ex-sergeant in Yorkshire, thanking him for his good treatment of himself and his fellows.

He was short and thin, with an evenly pale skin, curly hair, and eyes widely spaced, aided by rimless glasses that gave him an appearance of intellectuality. With kindly firmness, he made himself responsible for the rest of my stay at Koyasan.

Yo was a Catholic, and the son of a Catholic. Being a country-man he was not so quick and shrewd as the young doctor at Nara; he expressed himself with less erudition. Yet there was a mellowness about his personality which was absent in the doctor, despite the latter's genuine friendliness and captivatingly good manners. (On the morning of my departure I had been unable to find him, to bid him goodbye. Although he himself was due to leave in an hour or so, he had rushed to the station and searched the train till he found me. We would doubtless never meet again. There was no object in such a gesture other than the observance of politeness as an end in itself, the artist's innate distaste for allowing a work to leave his studio unfinished.)

In Yo one sensed an additional breadth of outlook, the consciousness of belonging to a worldwide community, as well as to a nation. One could well understand how, amid the hatreds of war, he had preserved his cool convictions. His moral outlook had governed his relations with friend and foe alike. His comments on the war were different from those of the innkeeper at Nikko. To the innkeeper, Japan tried, and only failed because her opponents were stronger; she might—it was inexpressed, but there all the same—try again. To Yo the war was a stupid moral mistake; and the magnanimity of the victors, and the friendships he had formed with individual Americans during the post-war occupation of Japan, had given him confirmation of his view.

In the difference between the two views lies the still unresolved conflict between Japanese and western morality. The innkeeper's morality is a code of behaviour applicable in the closely defined relationships of Japanese society, but not necessarily applied to persons outside that society. Again from Father Johannes:

'In a school, which is in a sense outside the frame of defined social contacts, one notices, when teaching, how Japanese boys never complain to the teacher if they are being bullied. The bully is stronger, and the weaker accept that as a verdict on themselves.'

Filipinos, Malays and Burmese, with wider conceptions of morality, were not prepared to accept such treatment as a verdict. To them the bully was cruel and uncivilized. To them, due variously to Christianity, Islam, European influence and a more mature awareness of the outside world, morality—even in its most restricted sense of a code of behaviour—was more clearly recognized as universal. Confined within the framework of a single national society, it was no better than tribal law.

Yo shared this wider view, but although there are many Japanese, Christian and non-Christian, who do likewise, this way of thinking is one of the aspects of modern civilization which Japan has not yet absorbed. It has not, like soup, become Japanese. Yo would like it to, but the innkeeper was unaware that a difference of outlook existed.

.   .   .   .   .

After leaving our luggage in one of the monasteries—Father Johannes was right, there were no inns—Yo conducted me through the town, a single street of timber merchants' houses and small supply shops, into the forest beyond.

Everywhere beneath the aged trees were tombs, some marked with stone or wooden inscriptions, others so old that no name survived, their monuments engaged in slow dispute with the roots of trees. There were tens of thousands of them. For twenty minutes we walked on through the chill shade, past the names of famous families and of almost every region of Japan, past calligraphy in Japanese, Chinese, Pali, Sanskrit and even English.

In the heart of the forest was the tomb of the great ninth-century sage, Kobo Daishi, founder of Koyasan and of the Shingon sect of Buddhism, who visited China and established contact with Indian Buddhism in the last years before its final submergence as a religious force in the country of its origin, To be buried near the sage is for devout Shingon Buddhists a final act of merit.

Near the sage's tomb, pilgrims were pouring water from long wooden ladles over statues of the Buddha, small watercourses providing a never-ending supply for the purpose.

'You must do that too,' said Yo, who had already made me draw lots at a temple, with the object of knowing my fortune.

'Are you going to?' I asked, remembering again that he was a Christian.

'Of course,' he replied with enthusiasm. 'That's what people come here for.'

So we uninhibitedly paid our respects to the Buddha.

On our way back we paused before a Sanskrit inscription.

'Can you read it?' he asked.

'A word here and there. I can't understand what it means.'

Yo looked round the forest.

'This is a world place,' he said simply.

Even though I knew it was true, I was surprised to hear him say it. Kobo Daishi's breadth of mind survives in the spirit of Koyasan, as the idyll of Nara survives; and Koyasan as a result belongs to the world, as Rome and Athens do. To us in Europe there is nothing strange about 'world places'—our capitals and university cities are all more or less so; one might almost call it their *raison d'être*. But in Japan, until a hundred years ago so exceedingly remote, accustomed to remoteness and using it as a conservative measure of self-defence, the very idea of a world place sounds foreign. The innkeeper would have sniffed contemptuously, feeling that Japan, by native cleverness and her ability to study the ways of others, had developed well enough without risking the unknown dangers of internationalism. To take from other nations is sensible enough—as the smug saying goes: the West made the pills, Japan had but to swallow them. Was there more to it than that?

The innkeeper would not think so; and, in accordance with the innkeeper's philosophy, Japan's foreign relations since the dawn of history have been exclusively based on getting something—whether culture, scientific knowledge, or territory.

We retraced our way through the forest, passed through the settlement again, and out to the Taimon, the Great Gate, on the farther side.

The Taimon, a huge wooden edifice like a triumphal arch, with a small tea-stall in its shadow, stood in solitude at the edge of the forest. As befitted a world place, it was an open gate. But, expressive of its limitations in a land with gates traditionally shut, it faced nothing. Beyond it the mountainside dropped abruptly away to an immense view of the plains below. Through it entered only the soft evening sunlight.

'Tea, sir?' the stall-keeper said in English.

I looked at him, a man of rough appearance, unshaven, with some teeth missing. He was dressed in drab white cloth, a sort of tunic many times too big for him.

'Let us take,' said Yo.

We sat on narrow wooden benches, placed clear of the Taimon's long, cold shadows, and talked in the diminishing sunlight. It was one of those still afternoons when one season hesitates on the margin of another: down on the plains, between spring and summer; here in the mountain, between winter and spring.

The stall-keeper was a former soldier who had served in Singapore and could speak some Malay.

Oh yes, he said in reply to my question, he had liked Singapore, a fine city, clean and well built. He would be glad to go there again, except that, well, he'd never have enough money to get there now. And besides, even if he could get a visa—he looked down, and following his eyes I saw he had only one leg, although, placing the stump of his lost leg on a stool, he appeared to be standing naturally.

He came from Osaka, where before the war his father had had a shop. At high school he had been a promising student, he admitted with a deferential smile. He had ended the war at Singapore, one-legged and a prisoner. When he was repatriated, it was to find his home and family shop gone. From neighbours he learned that, in a single American air-raid, he had lost everything, parents and possessions.

The shapeless tunic he wore was the outfit of those wounded soldiers to whom the Government gave concessions such as this, to run a tea stall beneath the Taimon. In fact, he was luckier than some. Many of the wounded could be given no concession other than the right to beg at the gates of temples popular with pilgrims.

'Had you ever been to this place before the war?' I asked.

He grinned.

'Yes, once, when I was a small boy. I came with my mother.'

To pour water over the images at Kobo Daishi's grave doubtless, a small, happy boy, enjoying the varied and exciting journey into the mountains, and the mystery and awesomeness of the forest. How he would have scoffed if, on that far-off excursion, someone had told him he would one day be pinioned to the forest for life. Yet here he was, this maimed bird, caught and dangled tantalizingly above the wide world he would never know again.

So we talked, the three of us; and, glancing up at the heavy beams of the Taimon, I thought how succinctly it represented Yo, and people like him in Japan, this great gate open to the world, enduring unchanged through wars, hatreds and stupidities—there all the time, but unused.

And, at its foot, the once promising student, the trapped—how complete an answer he provided to the Nikko innkeeper, and people like him, who within the framework of social relations courteously give the best fish to a guest, but who, outside those charted relationships, commit murder (no, I am afraid I do not believe it was only the officer) in a last, spiteful demonstration that might is right.

Were not Yo and I too part of the tableau?

War had, like a hurricane, thrust us wide of our courses. Had it not been for the tumult which Japan initially let loose in 1931, Yo would have been a teacher, and I would never have left Europe. Torn away into undreamed-of journeys, fed on a mass of new knowledge and sensations, we were thrown down into peace again, quite abruptly, as the hurricane passed. Like children who have learnt hard lessons, we re-entered the same valleys we left in the morning, but at the end of day, with long shadows stretching before us.

(xvi) *Wood*

Leaving me to make my own way back to the monastery, Yo went off to attend to his affairs. Coming up from Nara to Koyasan was like stepping backwards from April to March. Far below and away into the distance, the plains were still enjoying the warm sunshine of a spring day. Here, on the edge of the great mountain forest, the temperature was already falling, and in the gaps among the vast pines mist was forming, white and clammy, as the forest prepared itself for a night which, despite spring in the lowlands, was here still winter. The cherry trees would not bloom for another three weeks.

Wood, everywhere wood: the solemn Taimon, the monasteries within the forest, the soft road surfaced with brush and needles of pine, and every unseen house on the plains below, from here to beyond the horizon. Even the Emperor's palace at Kyoto was of wood, with roofs of compressed cypress bark secured by wooden nails, the only metal used being the gutters, which were copper. Against earthquakes, fire and the ravages of insects this complex wooden civilization had to be painstakingly preserved. Of every important edifice an exact model was kept which, in case of destruction, would be used, in order that the wrecked building be replaced by another exactly similar.

All the time, in some part of the country, restoration was in process, with wood minutely selected from the most perfect trees of the great forests. The Emperor's palace had to be rebuilt every seventy years, important temples every hundred or so, depending on funds.

This continuous effort needed for the preservation, not only of houses, but of the national culture and artistic tradition, differentiates

Japanese creative art from that of other countries. Our creativity, like our temperament, is different. We are in any case more lackadaisical and pleasure-loving than oriental people. We value leisure far higher than the East does. To us there is something ant-like in the way Japanese artists and craftsmen work away year by year, repairing temple after temple, restoring each decaying fragment, re-tinting each fading fresco. It seems to us to be almost more than art is worth.

But for the Japanese there is no doubt whether it is worth it. It is vital to them. Without it they would have no cultural heritage and few traditions. Without it they might today be no more than a primitive race of fishermen and forest hunters, living in miserable huts liable to be thrown down by even a moderate earth-tremor. Nor, as we saw when inspecting the earthquake-proof *kura*, is the effort for cultural survival limited to public buildings. It is part of the life of every family that can afford it, which feels it has something to lose.

To admire Japan's cultural heritage is not to admire the past. It is to admire the present. The creation of a splendid building is not, as it is in Europe, a superb fling of creative activity, followed by generations of passive admiration. The execution of the original design is only the first day in the long subsequent history of caring for the masterpiece, restoring and protecting it.

Does this not provide a clue to the mysterious temperament of the Japanese as a nation, to the morose side of a nature which, in its dealings with others, wishes only to dominate, or else stay in seclusion?

Sometimes a schoolmaster will give a clever pupil a problem harder than he gives the others to solve. Having solved it, however, and received no extra mark for his cleverness, the pupil feels aggrieved, despising, and feeling superior to, those who received the same marks as he did for solving problems that were easier. It might be said, in the classroom of nations, that Japan, faced with an extraordinary struggle against impermanence, had a harder problem than others to solve.

Here is a people who in their collective soul know they are as capable of creating an enduring civilization as any race on earth, yet who, while they live in their trembling islands, are obliged to work far harder than any other people for each column of tradition they possess. Wood is their achievement—an astonishing achievement—but it is also a sentence, a limitation. It is as if a race of stonemasons and sculptors had been restricted by the austere gods in such a way that, knowing the real extent of its capabilities, it was for ever rendered impotent to fulfil them.

Is there not, behind the artistry of such things as deep-sea soup and the tea ceremony, an element of unrecognized frustration, from which the achievement of perfection, in what is small and attainable, is an escape?

I re-entered the forest. On several sides arose pine-covered hills, on their lower slopes the long sober roofs of the monasteries. Small lanes led to them here and there through the trees. The smoke of cooking fires—pine smoke—rose to mingle with the falling mist. Woodcutters were returning to the village in rough-cut winter coats and cloth shoes. As I reached the canopied gate of the monastery where we were staying, and entered the age-old garden with its dwarf groves, lakes and ornamental bridges, two of the novices were just finishing a game of tennis. They greeted me, and the elder, who spoke some English, asked me to wait while he lit a lamp.

We sat on the steps of the long verandah and took off our shoes before going within. One of the novices brought me a pair of soft noiseless slippers.

(xvii) *A Koyasan monastery*

Eliminating linguistic sounds, it might have been possible to think for a moment that this was some romantically remote part of China—the gentle curve of the eaves, Chinese characters over a doorway, the garden, mist in the pines, the thin supple figures of the tennis-playing novices, one of whom could well have passed for a southern Chinese. But the comparison would not have gone far.

Prior to 1949, the larger Chinese Buddhist monasteries were, like most of what is distinctive of Chinese life, a bursting mass of vitality, conflicting personalities and tensions concealed by diplomacy so natural and deep-rooted that anyone unused to China would be totally unaware of it. The denizens of Chinese monasteries and nunneries often turned out to be—duly shaven-headed and clad in robes—retired wash-amahs and baby-amahs, discarded concubines, political refugees, disgraced officials, unsuccessful bandits, deserters and retired shopkeepers. Occasionally in a monastery one met a true scholar, in nunneries very rarely. Only vegetables were served, of course (with the exception of oysters, because they are bloodless), which was more than could be said for Burmese monasteries, in which, however, the standard of scholarship was higher.

In China a foundation of equal size to this great Koyasan monastery would have lodged about thirty monks, while near and around it there might have been the lonelier cells of contemplatives, come to settle in the shadow of the larger institution. Monastery servants in China were often young boys, orphans or with parents who could not support them, inveigled into living and working in the institution in return for food and a few cast-off clothes. Sometimes they were taught to read and write, but for the most part the monks were too busy with their own souls to find time to teach them. On rare occasions, such boys became novices and monks. The atmosphere of the place would be convivial, slapdash and pleasant, hospitality excellent and free—except that on departure one should make a gift sufficient to cover all costs. The rooms, though swept daily, would somehow never be clean. Rats would trundle around and over the beds at night, and sometimes, as in hotels in various parts of China, hanging from the roof there would be strings on which, before retiring, one dangled one's shoes in mid-air, so that the rats could not gnaw them in the season when they are shortening their teeth. Washing arrangements would be primitive, and lavatories non-existent.

Here at Koyasan everything was different. Despite the size of the monastery, there was only one monk, with four novices, and they occupied no more than two small, unadorned rooms, where they studied, ate and slept. All the rest of the building was designed for the reception of guests coming on pilgrimage at certain seasons. There was a domestic staff, under a manager, to cope with them, and a kitchen like those of our Norman castles, suitable for preparing food for several hundred people on a day trip.

At a sign from the monk, the manager was dismissed and not seen again, our requirements being met entirely by the novices. The novices, again in surprising contrast to China, were all well educated and rather modern in outlook. Two of them held degrees from a provincial university, where the senior had been tennis champion for his year. To find such people devoting their lives to Buddhist study was a pleasant surprise.

After a few minutes the senior novice, returning with a lamp, led the way within. Although in the garden there was still some fading daylight, the interior rooms, due to the shading verandahs and double windows as protection against the cold, were dark. The first room was a fairly long, *tatami*-laid hall, used at popular seasons of pilgrimage. As the light swung into it, the walls were transiently lit up with gold, being panelled throughout with sumptuous paintings on a gold base. I drew in my breath with astonishment and wanted to go no further, but the novice was still walking ahead, his lamp carrying the glimmering mystery forward into the depths of the room, awakening to life its silent glory.

Passing through corridors and up stairs of flawless wood, we reached an upper passage, plain and immaculate as only a Japanese interior can be. He slid open a panel, and we entered the suite chosen for us.

I count the simple act of entering the monastery as one of the great artistic experiences of my life. The last light of day outlined the low windows within, vitalizing from the walls another effulgence of golden panels, that seemed to breathe warmth and life into the room, as if the monastery itself were a sentient being, with pulse and heart. Above the sliding panels—how effortlessly, silently, they could be opened and closed—were two scrolls of calligraphy in contrasting styles, each containing in four or five Chinese characters a subtle Buddhist truth. In the alcove hung a slender scroll depicting a famous mediaeval warrior, beneath which was a Buddha statuette, a museum piece several hundred years old. Beyond lay the garden, perfected through five centuries of devoted attention and artifice, with the forest rising up so high beyond it that until coming near the window one could not see the sky.

The novice watched me curiously as I took in each detail of the scene. For him these were the daily sensations of life. As I gazed out at the garden he took from a small drawer, level with the floor, a silk cushion, which, interpreting my desires, he placed on the low window seat.

'I will bring tea,' he said, and departed.

The window seat would have been entirely comfortable without the cushion, but the Japanese sense of harmony between art and life requires one to sit on a cushion. Dutifully I sat on it, studying the dwarf trees twisted into tortuous shapes, the grotesque rockeries amid which a little stream tumbled, past miniature shrines and grottoes.

Then, drawing back into the room, and, within the frame of the window, excluding all life-size objects, I looked again at its wild mountains, fearsome cliffs and valleys. A great river rolled down, shaded by towering rocks and trees wildly twisted by the winds of a hundred summers. Ancient paths led up into the more remote hilltops, on some of which giant Buddhas, carved out of natural rock, smiled impassively down to where puny men had made their bridges over the water. As in a Chinese painting, I searched the landscape for a ragged wayfarer in a broad-brimmed hat, following a mule and tapping the uncertain path with his long staff.

The light faded. The ferns and bamboo leaves, bent by gentle winds across the golden walls of the room, were losing themselves in unremarkable night. The perfect proportions of the room were being erased by shadow.

In Europe we are accustomed to approach a work of art as an onlooker, as a visitor to a gallery, a spectator at a theatre, a member of a large audience at a concert. One could wrap oneself in the canvas of the Primavera and still not be part of it. Reading books indeed we enter the world created for us by the author, but only by detaching ourselves from our actual surroundings.

Here in the monastery was another kind of art, more vivid, more present, than the forms we are familiar with. Instead of looking at it, one entered within it, became part of it, possessed it. No longer a spectator, one found oneself an actor in the play, a model in the picture, a character in the book—not by escaping from one's surroundings, but by the mere act of being alive, of being united with the present.

(xviii) *A silent climax*

Shortly after Yo's return, a novice announced that the bath water was ready, and, after changing, as custom demands, into Japanese clothes, we descended to the ground floor, into the room of steam with its sunken tank of scalding hot water which is one of the comforts of a harsh winter.

When we returned, warmed and comfortable, to our suite, the double windows had been closed, and the electric current turned on, an unshaded globe drawing from the golden walls, faun-coloured *tatami* and russet wood a warmth of colour compensating for the low temperature—for like many traditional Japanese upper floors there was no form of heating, apart from the scarcely noticeable warmth from the ash-hearth, with its tripod and diminutive kettle. The low dinner tables, of orange-coloured lacquer, with their exquisite superstructure of lesser tables, bowls, leaf-shaped plates and small vegetarian preparations laid on colours that offset the humour and style of each dish, were chosen to harmonize with the room, like well-matched furniture. On separate tables, equally low, stood the covered lacquer bowl of honourable rice, and a pot of hot *saké*.

A silk cushion was placed before each eating table. The cushions were of that exceptionally dark, dolorous colour which maple leaves reach when, in autumn, they fall on damp ground and gradually turn from red to black. As the novice took them from one of the silent-sliding drawers below the window, their wonderful colour, purple and iron, unexpectedly brought to life the white feathered bodies of storks which, on the gold walls, moved in and out among the wind-caressed ferns.

The tables were placed so that when taking dinner we would be face to face. As we knelt formally on our cushions I was thankful for the warmth generated in me by the bath, for a Japanese silken kimono, with its open neck and wide sleeves that do not reach the wrist, is not really suitable for cool mountain nights such as this. Strangely, though, in these surroundings of extraordinary luxury, the ever-present Spartan element of discomfort somehow seemed to matter less and less.

The wine-pot was brought. With ceremony Yo wiped my wine-cup with a small square of paper and filled it for me with hot wine. Leaning over to his table, with equal ceremony I filled his cup. We raised them to drink.

And at that instant there occurred something I have never known before or since, a flash-like sensation of absolute worldly fulfilment and perfection. It was so totally unexpected that I could have cried out in astonishment, had I not been, as it were, paralyzed, dream-ridden by it. And to this day, and perhaps all my life, that moment stands, and will stand, alone—a pinnacle point of earthly existence, a Kanchenjunga on whose summit one cannot stay for more than a moment, yet from which the unique view, though never again actually experienced, can be borne in memory along every ordinary road travelled in later years.

It seemed in that moment as though everything learnt in the past, every enjoyed experience, every friend, every wise counsel, every impression of beauty in life and art, unexpectedly revealed itself in an entirely new form. The past was no longer a road departing straight into distance, but a crooked way, every mile of which was visible from this point, as when, ascending a mountain defile with no views on any side, we emerge on a pass, from which we see, curving down beneath us, every step of the way we have come. Remembering our experiences as we struggled upwards, the sight of the whole route revives the hours that have gone, which, by a trick in the shape of the hills, revisit us like a company of guests entertained long ago. Their return, though, does more than remind. It is as if all we learnt in earlier days partially, and neglected for want of a full understanding, together with all that we knew well but could not place in the scheme of our lives, came back so ordered and clear that we at last recognized them as something more than the miscellaneous remembrances of a diverse life. They were part of us, and we welcomed them, drawing them within our own house. Nor were they any longer separated by years and circumstances. We may have encountered them one by one. In returning, they came together.

This is fulfilment and perfection; and the experience of it is perhaps the only fulfilment completely attainable in this life, when, for one crystalline instant, one is aware that every angle of the past is united to the centre of the present.

Everything contained in that moment could not be written down. The impression gained was too quick—and yet so profound it was as if, in the space of a second, one had read five hundred pages of a book. It was an intensely personal experience—Yo was, and still is, unaware of it—and it might have happened anywhere. Yet to me it was the climax of a train of thought induced by spending several weeks thinking about and savouring Japanese life, and while it showed me something that is certainly universal, it showed me in addition something which I believe to be deeply and distinctively Japanese. As the indescribable excitement of the moment passed, as the cup touched my lips, and the *saké* warmed my throat, as we refilled the cups and broke the wood of our chopsticks into two pieces, preparatory to taking rice, I knew that my answer to Father Johannes' observation about lack of profundity in the Japanese people was that their deepest thoughts are experiences, which either (as in Zen philosophy) cannot be written down at all, or else can only be recorded in the comparative unreality of an account composed after the event, the thought-content of the account containing only a feeble glimmering of the philosophic magnitude of the experience. In the West we too closely associate depth and print. Japanese depth, while revealing itself in art and experience, is resistant to print. It is for this reason that, in the sphere of Japanese Buddhism, there is the somewhat unusual combination of masterpieces of art and a negligible interest in philosophy, and, in the Christian sphere, many devout, sincere and good-living Christians with little or no interest in dogmatic argument. It is for this reason that we concentrate on the objects in the tea room, instead of engaging in speculation on the existence beyond us. What is the use of such thoughts, with their definitions of what is not and what may be? Where thought is experience, you either know or do not know, and no amount of reading, listening, thinking or talking will produce the knowledge sought after.

After one of these profound thought-experiences, a clever man, by taking a book of manuscript and filling it from cover to cover, might succeed in describing a part of what actually took place. Above, in the case of my own unexpected encounter with it, I have set down one exceedingly small fragment. An uneducated person would possibly be reduced to saying 'Something happened to me, and as a result I understand something.' And that is possibly the best of all explanations.

It is not possible to say precisely what happened and what was understood. Because it is not possible, there is not much about it in print. Because it is not in print, it is not included in our general knowledge of Japan.

But, albeit inadequately, I feel I must include it, because I cannot think of Japan without it. It explained something to me which no human association or study could.

What was that something?

I can go no further than to say it was the thing that Father Johannes had not realized.

(xix) *Hope with a limit*

When, after dinner, it came to going out to see some of Yo's friends, Japanese toughness again became apparent. Yo was going out into the clammy mountain night in the clothes provided for us by the monastery, his legs and forearms bare, and part of his chest also. It might be thought that, having coped with raw fish, scalding baths, tea ceremonies and winged apples . . . But no; there is a limit in international relations.

'Very sorry,' I said, and put on a thick shirt and trousers, with the Japanese clothes on top. Even then I was on the point of shivering.

His friends were, of course, wood merchants. One of them spoke French, and another some halting English, so conversation was comparatively easy. During the evening I was conscious, as one is on all occasions in Japanese company, of how vastly the Japanese travelled during the war, and, whatever the ill effects, how much broader their international outlook has become in consequence. As our talk ranged from country to country, it was refreshing to observe their interest in foreign people and their ways. This broader outlook in the ex-soldier generation could, properly handled, become the genesis, in Japan itself, of a new attitude in international relations, putting paid to the age-old policy of only coming out to grab something, then hurrying inside again and locking the door.

By the time we returned to the monastery everything was in darkness. A watchman opened the gate and guided us up to our suite. Here the panels opening into the inner sleeping-room had been drawn back, revealing the classic beds of quilts spread out on the *tatami*. I looked apprehensively to see if I would also have to cope with a classic pillow, one of those small porcelain blocks, sometimes softened—an extreme refinement—by a piece of paper laid over them. Happily, small cloth pillows were provided, stuffed hard like balls with what was presumably rice straw. So with two or three quilts beneath us, and at least four above, we slept in the heavy flat warmth of Japanese beds, with around us the deep silence of the hills, in which even the garden stream had by artifice been made to run smoothly, uttering not the least sound.

.   .   .   .   .

Long before dawn I stirred and lay awake in the darkness, listening.

At first I could not tell why I had woken up so early. With my senses I searched the black room for some sound or movement that might have aroused me. When nothing but silence answered my enquiry, I knew I had woken up expecting to hear, as in Chinese monasteries, the drone of prayers in the last hours of night. For in spite of being the retiring place of deserters, disgraced politicians, and ruffians of all kinds, Chinese monasteries strictly maintain certain traditions, one of which is prayer at about four o'clock in the morning. Being anxious to hear the Japanese version of this, I had evidently determined, without being aware of it, to wake up at the right time.

It was too early, however, so I dozed off again.

The second time I woke it was still dark, and still there was silence. The third time the first light was already clarifying the paper squares of the windows, and still there were no sounds of devotional exercises. I had got up, washed, shaved and dressed before I heard the monk and his disciples pass through into the temple.

After that I went to sit at the back of the small, intimate room, magnificently caparisoned with hanging silks and fine ornaments, while the ritual prayers were said. Three elderly women devotees, who had arrived the evening before, were kneeling behind the monk. At some point in the ceremony each of them went singly to light a taper of incense, placing it in the great bronze incense-burner before the altar.

The prayers were of course more melodiously intoned by the monk than they would have been in China. The musical instruments —small drums, strangely shaped cymbals, silver-toned bells—were sweeter to listen to. And the responses came from the novices in confident unison, quite unlike the muttered uncertainties produced by the disgraced officials and deserters.

Over everything there rested the atmosphere of worldly perfection, a wonderful blending of the things in life that the body needs and the mind desires, art not merely on walls or in theatres, but fused inseparably into every ordinary action, which is Japan's peculiar gift to human existence.

When the service was over and the monk had gone, I went up closer to the altar to look at the musical instruments. Lest there be some religious scruple involved, I touched nothing, but bent down to examine some of them carefully. The Japanese know more about bells, gongs and cymbals than we do.

The senior novice—the tennis champion—was rearranging various objects on the altar. My attention was drawn from the instruments by the sensation that he was watching me.

I glanced up. He was indeed watching me, and though he hastily turned away I was not too late to see a cold look of disdain, a sneer on his lips.

What should I want with these things? his expression seemed to say. They did not belong to my way of life. They belonged to his.

I looked at my watch.

Just about now, beneath the Taimon, the one-legged soldier, in his white sack-like uniform, would be setting up his tea-stall for the day.

II

(i) *Three Chinese sisters*

I returned to Hongkong by a night plane from Tokyo. We sighted the British colony at the first light, when its gaunt, impressive peak was still girdled with chains of little lights, red, green, blue and gold, like the enchanted city of a child's dream, a fairy place, not belonging to this world at all. But by the time we touched down at Kai Tak and stepped out into the humid warmth of an early summer morning, the lights on the peak across the water were beginning to go out, and the scene to assume its daytime appearance—green, treeless hills, choppy blue sea, monotonous grey buildings, and towers not of churches, but of banks.

It was pleasantly homely to be back again in the rude, animated hurly-burly of Cantonese life, back to Chinese politics and pornography, the uncouth voices, oaths and sarcasm, the frankness that somehow compensated for the lack of Japan's engaging politeness and thoughtfulness for others. It was a relief not to have to think first before saying something, lest it be misinterpreted by over-acute sensibility, and not to have to answer the hundred-and-one questions, motivated by personal curiosity, which are a feature of Japanese life. How large and imposing the commercial buildings looked—no earthquakes here. And mentally I reconditioned myself to the Asia with which I was familiar, with its solid outer appearances, hiding the fluttering of an instable heart.

The clothes I was wearing were far too warm, and as soon as I had crossed to the island and reached my flat in the heart of the city, I flung them off and had a bath, while my servant laid out a light tropical suit.

I was still in the bathroom when I heard agitated knocking at the front door, followed by a woman's voice insisting in Cantonese that she see me urgently.

A moment later there was a soft knock on the bathroom door, and Li appeared.

'Mrs. Liu,' he said, making a gloomy grimace.

'All right, sit her down and give her some tea.'

'Oh, I'm so sorry to disturb you so early,' I heard Geneviève say outside, between what were evidently sobs. 'But something terrible's happened.'

'Please wait just a moment,' I said, completing a shave. In Hongkong something terrible is always happening; it is part of one's conditioning to be accustomed to it. After a volatile youth, I have acquired in Hongkong the calm of a volcano believed to be extinct. 'Now, what's the matter?' I asked, entering the living-room.

Poor Geneviève, she looked terrible. Middle-aged and inclined to plumpness, her hair was not done properly, and one small clip of her dress was untied. Her eyes were red with crying, and her rather heavy Cantonese lips looked swollen as she blubbered out:

'It's John! He's been arrested!'

John was her husband, whom I had not met and knew little about. They were refugees from Shanghai and moved in a different circle from mine. I knew Geneviève only through her own family, who were Hongkong people.

'Drink your tea,' I said sternly. A cup of green tea—how wonderfully fine and astringent Chinese tea was after the Japanese varieties—rested untouched on the arm of her chair.

Like a child she did as she was told, a tear falling on her sleeve. Then she began again.

'He's in Victoria Prison. You must help me to get him out. What can I do?'

'What's he been arrested for?'

'For nothing!' she moaned. 'Nothing at all. He would never do anything wrong!'

I waited while she had another good sob.

'I appreciate that, but what did they say they were arresting him for? Geneviève, pull yourself together. Surely you must know what it is.'

In effect, now I came to think of it, it was strange how, on all my many visits to the home of Wu Hon-leung, Geneviève's brother-in-law, I had never seen her husband. Could it be that he was keeping away from the family, or that she was keeping him away?

'He was just about to fix a very big deal,' she sobbed. 'We were going to Europe to see our eldest son, Lucas. It was all arranged!' She sipped more tea. 'And now—everything's ruined!'

She leant back in the chair and covered her eyes with a soiled handkerchief.

'I'm sorry, I don't understand why it should be. Can't the deal still go through?'

'No! They've arrested him! They think he's a criminal!'

'Why? What sort of deal was it?'

She moaned under the handkerchief.

'In guns and ammunition!'

'For Heaven's sake!'

'No!' she wailed, throwing herself forward towards me. 'It's not what you think. He was buying for the —— Government. But the Hongkong police won't believe him!'

Well, whether he was or was not buying for a foreign government, his absence from the Wu family gatherings began to look more suspicious.

'You'd better go and see the —— Consul-General, then,' I said, after a moment's thought. 'If it's a bona-fide transaction, he should be able to get him out.'

Her sobbing stopped, and in a suddenly normal, practical voice, she said:

'That's what I thought. I know you're friendly with the Consul-General. Could you please telephone him, and ask him to have John released?'

Dear Geneviève. In spite of the tears, she had worked it all out well beforehand. Still, it was evidently serious.

'No one can give orders to a foreign consul-general,' I said, 'but I'll find out what the position is, and let you know tomorrow. Now, please excuse me; I have to go out.'

.   .   .   .   .

On reflexion, I decided to phone the police first. It was lucky I did.

'Straight case of gun-running, sir, sorry. Nothing anyone can do.'

'I see. Would it be any use my speaking to the Consul-General?'

'It's up to you, sir. But I think you'll find he doesn't know anything about it.'

'What will happen to him?' I asked.

'Not sure yet. We're recommending banishment.'

There were emergency regulations covering cases of this kind. It looked as though Liu had had it.

It was awkward. I did not want another unhappy interview with Geneviève, yet I had to let her know.

It then occurred to me that the best person to handle the matter would be Geneviève's sister, Winkle, who happened to be in Hongkong on a shopping spree from Manila. Geneviève was one of three sisters. They were Cantonese, of Chungshan district, but only Dora, the wife of Wu Hon-leung, had remained in Hongkong. Winkle and Geneviève had both married into other provinces, and gone to live in Shanghai.

Winkle Miao, who was older than Geneviève, was a widow. Her husband had been a prosperous building contractor, and she had grown-up children in America. Yet, when the Nationalist *débâcle* of 1949 took place, Winkle could not bear the thought of going to America and isolating herself from the stimulating environment of Chinese politics to which her husband's financial standing had procured for her the *entrée*. Instead, she enterprisingly took a job with a large Sino-American trading corporation, with branches in Bangkok, Singapore, Manila and Hongkong, and lived in what seemed to her many friends to be a state of perpetual motion between these places. As a widow it would have been contrary to Chinese custom for her to entertain on her own, though she would have liked to, but her wit and liveliness ensured that she was entertained by others. She was a pillar of the Chinese (Nationalist) Embassies at Bangkok and Manila. When Winkle Miao was in town, no ambassadorial party was complete without her dry remarks, calculated indiscretions, superb dresses and slightly greying hair ('Someone once said I ought to dye it, dear, but lord knows we need a bit of distinction in these trying times'), and if an ambassador was unwise enough to think he'd had about enough of Winkle Miao, she soon resorted to means whereby he would hear about it. She was a determined supporter of the Taiwan régime, talking about it as if she were herself one of its ambassadresses—as indeed, in a way, she was.

She answered the phone immediately—she usually sat near it, so as to grab it first—and, as soon as she heard my voice, began without giving me a chance to say a word.

'I can't stand it, dear,' she said. 'I can't stand it a day longer. I'm going back to Manila.'

'What's wrong?' I asked apprehensively.

'This house, of course! Everything's so gloomy, and no one seems to go out any more. I don't know what's happened to Hongkong. It's not the same place it used to be.'

She said this accusingly, as though I were personally responsible.

'What should we do to it?' I asked.

'Put a bit of life into it again! I want a bit of fun. Don't you go dancing any more?'

'Well, yes—sometimes.' Winkle, I should add, was quite old enough to be my mother, and was herself a grandmother.

'Well then, honey, let's go,' said the dry voice.

'Steady,' I said, 'first things first. What about that sister of yours?'

'Oh—that!' said Winkle vexedly.

'She's wept so many tears on my carpet this morning the colours have run. Don't you think you'd better come down and dine quietly with me this evening?'

'No, not in your dingy little apartment. Let's go to the Ritz.'

'Winkle, it looks as though she may try to involve me with one of the consuls. You'll have to talk to her, and you and I must have a talk first.'

'M'm,' said the voice. One could imagine her pouting. 'Spoil-sport!' Then reason dawned. There was a pause. 'You'd better come and have dinner in the bosom of the family.'

And with the chuckle of indescribable naughtiness which was part of Winkle's passport, the conversation ended.

(ii) *Tradition and superstition*

The bosom referred to was that of Wu Hon-leung, or, more properly perhaps, of Mrs. Wu, Winkle's and Geneviève's sister Dora; and it was to be found in an old house near the University, with a porch of Doric columns, and decaying pediments over the ground-floor windows. It had such an appearance of neglect, not having been painted for years, that when going there by taxi it was unnecessary to remember the house number: one could simply say the name of the street, and ask the driver to stop at the dirtiest house in it.

'Don't talk to me about whitewash,' Winkle had once said, when I first knew them. 'If he paints the house, people will stop eating rice.'

For Wu Hon-leung was a rice merchant, among his other commercial interests, which were numerous; and, like many who have made their way by luck, he was superstitious. The front door opened into a narrow hall, with stairs leading straight up to the first floor, a passage leading through to the kitchen and basement, and a door into the drawing room on the left.

'Don't walk up the stairs,' Winkle had warned me on the same occasion as we entered from the street. 'Well, you can maybe, but we' (meaning her brother-in-law) 'never do if we want to avoid ruin. No,' she continued, opening the drawing-room door, 'when *we* want to go upstairs, we go this way, through this room, out through that far door, into the passage, back into the hall again, and *then* up the stairs.'

'What on earth for?'

'Oh, *fêng shui*,'[1] she said with some contempt. 'There's a box of rubbish up there given him by some monk or other, and he must walk under it every time he enters the house and goes upstairs.'

I looked at the inner door of the drawing room. Over it a shelf had been fixed, on which lay a small camphor casket with a brass lock.

'Doesn't your sister find this rather a strain?' I asked.

'She doesn't care. She never did. Besides, she's never been out of Hongkong, except during the Japanese occupation. Until then, she thought the whole of China was like Hongkong.'

Winkle had once been an exceedingly attractive woman. Her skin was slightly darker than that of other members of the family, and testified—though this would not have interested her—to the diverse racial origins of the Cantonese. Her eyes were larger and more expressive than those which in the West we regard as typically Chinese. The habit of pouting, of expressing her feelings by grimace (a rare habit in China, against the canons of conservative behaviour),

[1] Geomancy, used here in a looser sense, meaning superstition.

had brought two drooping lines from the sides of her mouth, making her chin into a square of shadows. Her children might have described her face, when in repose, as severe; and in a way there was a severity about Winkle which had only recently begun to show itself in her features.

All her life she had been ambitious. The family had risen in the world. Their father had come as a simple young countryman to Hongkong, where he started as a salt-fish hawker. He prospered. After a few years, his mother and his illiterate country wife joined him. He established a rice shop, invested in house property, and operated two cargo junks. Two daughters were born, Dora and Winkle, but no son.

Meanwhile the grandmother's ambitions were being aroused by her son's commercial success. One of these ambitions was that he should marry the daughter of an official. In normal times such an alliance would have been unlikely, but in the last days of the Manchu dynasty there were many officials down on their beam ends and willing, for financial reasons, to eat pride and marry their daughters to petty merchants. Thus, on his mother's advice, the father took as his second wife the well-educated daughter of an officer. The first wife, who had been sickly since Winkle's birth, died soon after. The family said she died of a broken heart. But the second wife, the mother of Geneviève, became a true mother to them all. On her insistence, all the girls were educated in English and Chinese at the best Hongkong schools—her own daughter, Geneviève, going to a Catholic school, where she was converted to Christianity.

As there was still no son by the second marriage, the grandmother, who had a *mui-tsai* (a servant girl maintained as a family dependant in what amounts to a form of slavery), made her son take the girl as a concubine. A son was born, but died when only a day old, and after a few years, when no more children were born, the third wife was installed in a room of her own in another part of the town. There she lived, neglected, except for occasional visits from the children, whom she had looked after since they were born. She had an amah under whose influence she became interested in Buddhism, the two of them finally retiring to a nunnery.

Not until the grandmother's death was the second wife secure in her own house. When she was, she found an outlet for the social humiliation of her marriage by instilling into the three daughters her own negative impulse of ambition, which was that no one should ever say of the children she had brought up that their father was once a salt-fish hawker. In this she completely succeeded. In a single generation the family moved from one social class into another. But, from what I know of the family, it is my impression that she instilled more into Winkle than into the other two. It was this influence, I think, that in later years made Winkle cultivate the high society of Nationalist China, the foreign embassies and American business magnates. It was this that still kept her going now.

Dora's marriage to Wu Hon-leung, the son of a prosperous Saigon merchant, was the mother's first essay in that difficult art which in China's modern commercial cities can almost be called that of dynastic alliance. Possibly in her later years (she died during the war) she may secretly have regarded the marriage as an indication of her own inexperience. Certainly she did better when Winkle married Jenkin Miao, an America-returned student of engineering, who was sensible enough to see that there was more money to be made as a contractor than by working where the Government would have said his services were really needed.

Geneviève's Catholicism had made her marriage more of a problem. Her mother was determined she should not marry into a Hongkong commercial family, but at the same time the girl was being influenced by European priests not to consent to any marriage other than to a Catholic. Finally, as a measure of emergency, Geneviève being already twenty-three, agreement was reached on John Liu. He came of a good Shanghai family, was a Catholic, and although he subsequently showed himself incapable of remaining for long in any occupation, the Church—perhaps feeling it had a stake in the matter—had time and again helped him at crucial moments to scrape more or less unscathed through the rapids of a disjointed life.

Not even the upheavals brought upon the family by the Japanese invasion of China had seriously marred the serenity of its success. Only in the new conditions produced by the triumph of Chinese communism did it look for the first time as though the tide had ceased to flow.

I shall never forget my first visit with Winkle to Wu Hon-leung's house. It was winter. There were no curtains over the windows and no shades on the lights. On various parts of the walls strips of old plaster were hanging down dejectedly. The blackwood chairs with their marble seats were too cold to sit on, and in any case the arms and backs were loose, coming away in pieces in one's hand, while the entire room suggested that the house, once occupied, had for some reason been deserted. The sofa and armchairs were set, in old-fashioned Chinese style, with their backs to the walls, leaving the centre of the room empty except for a table, on which were some torn American magazines several months old.

In the midst of this sat Winkle, the last word in chic, in a modern Chinese winter suit of quilted silk, with a short surcoat lined with white lamb's wool, sticking a cigarette into a long holder and automatically looking round for the table lighter which was not there and obviously never had been.

'Isn't this just the grimmest house you've ever seen!' she said, with her fruity laugh, while I found a box of matches on the top of the old marble fireplace.

It was at the moment of final political collapse, the week the National Government leaders established themselves in Taiwan. Yet the Nationalist sympathizers who flocked to Hongkong during that fateful year brought with them far more of an atmosphere of gaiety than of defeat, and Winkle Miao reflected this. There was hope. There would be changes yet. One day they would all go back to China.

.   .   .   .   .   .

As I entered the house on the evening after John Liu's arrest, three years later, I recalled that first evening. Things had not turned out as expected. Instead of remaining fluid, the pudding had set in two hard lumps. Return to Shanghai was now remote.

Still, Winkle had carried on wonderfully. Wherever she went, the days of her arrival were like a festival. Even into hot, drab South-East Asia she seemed to be able to bring the cool crisp smartness of Shanghai. Though in a restricted sphere, her ambitious character exerted itself.

On Dora's house, for example. The drawing room had been redecorated, and some of the chairs pulled from their stiff square positions round the walls. The blackwood had been repaired. There were flowers, curtains and new chair-covers.

The end of the sofa which was nearest to the telephone still had broken springs, but by putting an extra cushion under the top one, Winkle had brought it up to the same level as the other end. The fortune-teller who had advised Wu not to paint his house had also warned him against buying new furniture, and not even Winkle had been influential enough to have the sofa replaced, or even repaired. Still, there was an improvement in almost everything. A worn carpet had been replaced by a new one, although, as Winkle later showed me, the old one was still there, underneath the new, Wu having forbidden its removal.

Receiving me in these improved surroundings, Winkle looked far more in her own setting.

'Remember that first evening?' I said, looking round at everything, and added, to tease her: 'Really, Dora's done wonders.'

'Nonsense,' she retorted. 'I did it. Dora wouldn't mind living in an igloo.'

A servant brought tea, followed by iced water. Winkle and I sat where we could enjoy the cool breeze which passed through the room from the front window looking on the street to the back window with its view over the harbour.

I explained in detail the position regarding Liu. Winkle was not surprised.

'It nearly happened several times in Shanghai,' she said.

She became pensive, and in that moment I could see how she had aged in the past few years. In repose her face was indeed severe, and with a hint of resignation I had never noticed before. After all, what had her ambitions led to?

Her political *milieu* had evaporated. Her sons, to whom she had determined to give the best American education, did not care if they never left America. To every point of the compass the circle of her life had been scattered, leaving her alone, unchanged, a comparative stranger in every city she went to, a woman of whom other refugees in Hongkong said: 'I think I saw Winkle Miao the other day in the street, looking much older. She used to be somebody.' Surely, even with her intense vitality, she could not much longer revolve at the pace of the whirlwind, now that the whirlwind had died.

(iv) *The family at dinner*

Dinner, served upstairs at the traditional round table, was inharmonious, everyone wishing to discuss the arrest, but considering it improper to do so during the meal.

I sat between Wu Hon-leung and Hayley Chen. Wu, a quiet, inoffensive person of middle age, with close-cropped grey hair, thick lips and heavy features, said little. Though he spoke English fairly well, I noticed that, whenever in the presence of Europeans or Americans, he liked to have Hayley with him to bear the brunt of conversation.

Hayley Chen was his secretary and interpreter, a Hongkong man with an excellent command of English and good Chinese calligraphy, who managed all Wu's foreign correspondence. He had held the position for twenty-five years and, still a bachelor, was almost a member of the family. He was noisily cheerful, enjoyed food and wine, and, with occasional references to dancing girls and actresses, and *risqué* remarks in English, gave Wu the comforting sensation that he was still in touch with the wicked outside world, had not become solidly respectable, and was not growing old.

Hayley, while loyal to the Wu family, was an artist at preserving his association with them. The artistry was probably needed too, for, in spite of being the life and soul of the party, Hayley Chen was by no means young. Humorous wrinkles round his eyes and mouth sank deep into his well-fed but restless features, and when reading he used magnifying spectacles. He had good features, with a jaw and chin larger and better formed than is usual among Cantonese; but in his jollity one detected here and there something forced, a concealed sadness. He sometimes came unshaven to his office, and when he laughed he showed one or two teeth that were beyond repair. He would laugh off the fact that he had no clean shirt or needed a shave by saying he had long ago found that Bohemian life was the best, to be free as an artist, to get drunk, write poetry, or paraphrase some difficult Chinese composition into flowing English—all of which was indeed part of his life out of office hours. Yet for a

Bohemian existence, who would choose Hongkong, a city of counting machines, with humanity on contract from nine to five each day?

This question had clearly never occurred to Wu Hon-leung. He believed that Hayley could and did live a Bohemian existence in Hongkong. Hayley's remarks about it were in fact one of Wu's flattering excitements. Then, with Hayley out of earshot, he would look serious for a moment, and say 'Poor Hayley! But he's a very good fellow'—which confirmed my own view that Hayley Chen was a lonely, uncared-for man.

It was only necessary to look at Wu's son, Ho-man, seated beyond Hayley, to appreciate how slim were Hayley's chances of staying with the firm should anything happen to the father.

Ho-man was the youngest of Dora's three children, but if the communist régime in China continued, he was evidently going to be the head of the firm at some future date. His only elder brother, Wai-man, was my first contact with the family. We met shortly after the war when we were both travelling to England in the same ship. Wai-man had a British Council scholarship to study engineering in Britain for three years. In Glasgow, where he spent most of his time, he became deeply interested in industrial relations, made friends with all classes of people, became acquainted at close quarters with industrial poverty and its causes, studied trade unions and socialism, his reading and personal contacts steadily veering to the extreme left. At the end of the three years, the British Council would probably have been disconcerted to know that its scholarship had produced a convinced communist. Wai-man returned to Hongkong, announcing to his mortified parents that he would only remain there for three days, arrangements having already been made for him to travel on directly to Peking, where, in view of his engineering knowledge, there was a job waiting for him.

Three days of family crisis followed, in construction like a typhoon, hectic on the outside, calm at the storm centre. Aunts and uncles advised and chattered, the telephone hardly stopped ringing, but Dora and her husband said little. Dora told me afterwards she cursed the British, but her husband was less pessimistic. In Chinese wars and conflicts the family tradition is to try to ensure that there are members of the family in every camp, so that, whichever side is strongest, the family will not unduly suffer. In keeping with this tradition it might be advantageous to have a son in a good position with the communists—engineers were badly needed, they said. True, it was a pity the boy was a real convert; for the purposes of the family, crypto-communists were better. Nevertheless, Wai-man in Peking or Manchuria might some day be useful.

Within the calm of the storm centre, none was more vehement against Wai-man's departure for Peking that his younger brother, Ho-man. Each time they were alone together he tried by every means to dissuade him from going, and on the last night the two brothers lay side by side on one bed throughout the stifling summer darkness, arguing without pause till dawn. But Wai-man went.

That also was three years ago. At the time, Ho-man had been a junior assistant in one of the communist banks in Hongkong. Two years later, his father by then considering him sufficiently experienced and ready for more responsibility, he left the bank and went to Singapore to manage his father's branch firm there. From time to time he visited Hongkong.

He was a pale good-looking lad with soft hair already, in his early twenties, receding at the temples. His eyes were bright and humorous, but his manner of speaking was short and quick, suggesting underlying anxiety or dissatisfaction. An experienced business man would have said he did not inspire confidence. When spoken to at dinner, his replies, though good-natured, were rapid almost to the point of rudeness, and in his remarks to me, each one with a slight twist or challenge in it, I sensed a mental antagonism to me as a foreigner which was disturbing if he was ever to prosper in the Eurasian commercial world on which the family's fortune depended.

He was seldom at home during his visits to Hongkong, his evenings being taken up with parties and dances, among people the family did not know. After taking two bowls of rice and a few mouthfuls of *sung*,[1] he excused himself and left, before the rest of us were half-way through our meal.

In the place next to him was his sister Jenny, her mother's chief pride and anxiety. Poised and intelligent, Jenny was exceptionally attractive and able. Of all the younger members of the family she would have been the most fitted to manage her father's affairs, but to the chagrin of both her parents she had no inclination toward commerce, her interests being centred on literature and teaching.

[1] The courses in a meal, as opposed to rice.

In Jenny the family's development in the direction of westernization reached that extreme point where, as is the case with certain rare orchids, the attainment of perfection of form brings with it a suicidal sterility. The first language that Jenny learnt to read and write was English. She later studied in England and France, speaking both languages perfectly. She was one of the very few young Chinese I have ever met to whom one could speak with the same complete sense of ease as to an educated Englishwoman. She was well read, with a keen interest in social problems, on the subject of which she could hold her own anywhere in English or French society. Had she been born European, there is little doubt that with her sweet disposition and penetrating intelligence she would have been married within a few months of her début. But in Hongkong society it was different. In the words of a Chinese mutual friend:

'Jenny will never get married. She's far too clever. She'd scare any Hongkong Chinese boy out of his wits. To begin with, she would fundamentally upset him by not minding whether he had a large or a small car, or even no car at all. She has no interest in swimming at Repulse Bay, dancing at the Ritz, playing mahjong, or going to American musicals. In short, the chap wouldn't know where to begin.'

Dora knew it. That Jenny was still unmarried at the age of twenty-eight was her greatest worry, about which, before her husband, she blamed only herself. The ambition of her old foster-mother, the officer's daughter, had worked too hard and too far, and on Jenny's return from Europe Dora recognized with something almost like fright that here she had produced something she herself could not understand.

Jenny was utterly different from her. Indeed, looking at them side by side at the table, it was impossible to tell they were mother and daughter.

Dora was fat. Dora was more than fat; she was blousy. In summer she found the Chinese *cheungsam* so suffocatingly hot round the neck that she wore European dresses with open necks. For this reason many people who saw her in Hongkong thought she was Eurasian, for, feeling that Chinese hairstyle was too severe with European clothes, she additionally had her hair permanently waved in western style. She looked faintly like a Chinese version of a retired actress who has ended up as landlady of an actors' lodging-house, one of those sensible motherly people to whom all secrets can be safely confided. I have seldom met anyone so thoroughly kind in all she did.

When she became aware of her daughter's interest in social welfare, Dora thought she saw the providential opening by which she could penetrate what she knew to be Jenny's speechless unhappiness at returning to Hongkong. Dora's social ambitions had brought her into the forefront of social welfare work in the colony. Through this she had maintained cordial personal relations with a succession of governors and their ladies. She served on numerous committees, organizing charity entertainments and flower days. Jenny wanted to work, to do something for the betterment of the people. Here was an obvious opportunity for her.

Slowly, perplexedly, Dora came to understand that what Jenny called social work had little or nothing to do with committees or flower days. In fact, mystifying as it was to Dora, she realized that in her daughter's eyes she herself was not doing any social work at all, whatever the Hongkong newspapers might say. Instead of helping her with her committee work, Jenny took a dry-as-dust job at the University, spending most of her spare time learning to read and write Chinese—and not Cantonese either, but Mandarin, useless in Hongkong. What future was there for her in this? Dora asked herself. What else could a decently brought-up girl do other than what she had suggested? Did she want to become a communist worker, and live in China on a pittance, without any comforts at all?

What did Jenny want to do?

'I don't know how anyone with any imagination can enjoy living here,' she once said to me. 'Everyone's so smug and pretentious. Oh, yes, you too. You may not be pretentious, but you're as smug as any of them.'

Sometimes we would go out with other friends, all of them former students in Europe, to obscure Chinese restaurants where we could risk talking politics without being mistaken for a new party under formation. At such discussions, usually ruthlessly frank, Jenny invariably defended the communists—really, I think, because she would have preferred anything to what she considered the nihilistic political atmosphere of Hongkong. She produced arguments none of us could refute to her satisfaction. In addition there was the personal pull that Wai-man, her favourite brother, was in

Manchuria, married with children, and writing strongly advising her to come.

Only the Church stood in the way. At an early age Jenny had become a Catholic. She was very devout, and had, what is rare among Chinese, an interest in the doctrinal differences between the various Christian Churches. She would not even go inside a Protestant church. When taking her around in London, I had to pretend that Westminster Abbey was still under Rome, otherwise, regardless of its architectural beauty, she would not have gone inside. Once within, of course, she soon discovered my trick, and did her best that we both get out as soon as possible without attracting attention. Never mind; she saw it. I dawdled behind her, while she whispered to me anxiously to hurry up. Whenever she turned round I used it as an opportunity to point out this and that. She appreciated it angrily, being a person of discrimination.

In her aunt, Winkle Miao, there was a sense of waste in the latter part of an eventful life. In Jenny it was something infinitely more pathetic; a life that was wasted before it had even fully begun. Behind her pale features and almond-shaped eyes, behind her modest manners and faultless Oxford English, lay a burning enthusiasm, a zeal for service, a clean bright truthfulness of character, that could not, whatever Dora's hopes, breathe in the suffocating airlessness of her home. Of the world-wide conflict between Catholicism and communism there was little Jenny did not instinctively know, for all of it was happening within her. Sooner or later she would have to declare herself for one side or the other. The smell of sun-tan lotion on the plage at Repulse Bay, the chromium-plated laughter, the calculations of the prices of other people's cars, jewellery, houses and furniture, only served to intensify the conflict, which no one in her family circle seemed to understand—except Wai-man, who was too far away.

The other three members of the family present were Geneviève, her elder son, Lewis, and his wife, Vivienne. They had all arrived together, just before the dinner hour. Vivienne, with whom Winkle could quickly become exasperated, was a taciturn, obstinate young woman of great physical beauty, superior to her husband in will and intellect. She was of Chekiang province, and spoke to the family—when she spoke at all—in English, her Cantonese being only just adequate to deal with her baby-amah. Her skin was exceptionally pale and flawless, her black hair fine and glossy, and her features had the regularity praised in the Chinese classics. To untrained European eyes her face would have seemed expressionless. Actually —though it was not till I saw her with her baby that I identified it— her eyes expressed an inordinate possessiveness, and sometimes, when for a second she glanced at Lewis, contempt for the husband she had dominated.

For the first eighteen months of the communist régime, throughout the first horrifying period of mass trials and executions, Vivienne had been employed in a confidential capacity by one of the principal state banks in Shanghai. But during the period of attrition that followed, when 'bourgeois reactionaries'—most of them people of the same social background as themselves—were committing suicide at a rate of thirty or forty a day by throwing themselves off the tops of the city's higher buildings, Vivienne decided she had had enough, and persuaded Lewis—not a difficult matter—to take her to join his father and mother in Hongkong. Like Lewis, she was born a Catholic, and might have had much to say that would have interested Jenny, had not the physical luxuriousness of Vivienne affronted the more intellectual Cantonese girl.

Lewis was an unhappy product of Geneviève's over-emotional mothering, and her determination that he would be, of all things, a great musician. He played the piano moderately well, but only studied Beethoven and the classics when his mother was at home. When she was out, he played dance music, for which, in his quiet way, he had a flair. Having been brought up on the principle that by Mother's will another Paderewski can arise, his education had been unorthodox, and he now found himself without any practical means of earning his living. Since coming to Hongkong he had had no employment, and Vivienne, unaccustomed to being at home all day (with a baby and no job), was evidently finding his constant presence infuriating. They all lived together in a small modern apartment in the eastern part of Victoria, which, because of its high refugee population, had become known as Little Shanghai. John Liu had illegally smuggled gold bars into Hongkong, but these had long since been used up on one after another of his crackpot commercial ventures, and for several months they had all been dependent on Geneviève, who had a reliable job with an American firm.

After some time Lewis, unable to put up with the neutral subjects of conversation at dinner, asked me directly about his father's arrest. His long serious face, with his steel-rimmed spectacles and weakly voluptuous lips, was paler than usual, a sign that he had been drinking before coming to dinner. Drink was one of his recent discoveries. If this had been a European family they would have been asking themselves why Lewis was taking to drink, but somehow in this family, though everyone knew about it, it did not seem to have occurred to anyone that there might be a reason.

As delicately as possible, and directing myself entirely to Lewis, without looking at the emotional Geneviève, I explained that if the man with whom his father had been negotiating, and who was supposed to be an official of a foreign government, would come and see me, with Lewis if necessary, and satisfy me that he was indeed what he purported to be, I would pass on the information at once to the police, who would certainly act upon it if they too were satisfied. (I should perhaps explain that the reason for all this indirect procedure lay in the deep-rooted Chinese dislike of conducting their affairs other than through the medium of personal connexions, however indirect.) Even while I was speaking, however, I felt sure there would be no further developments in this direction. John Liu was the victim of one of the confidence tricksters with whom Hongkong at that time unfortunately abounded, and this time not even the Church could save him.

When Lewis tried to ask some more questions, Hayley Chen interrupted.

'You're spoiling our dinner, young man. Your father's problem is serious, but our present problem is to fill our stomachs with this excellent food. I propose we talk about something else.'

'Carried unanimously,' said the deep voice of Dora, for whom family dinners were like committee meetings.

'Let's drink,' said Hayley generally. 'Eat, drink and be merry!'

Geneviève, concealing her dislike of the upstart Hayley—how could her brother-in-law tolerate such a man!—smiled sadly and drank from a glass of red tea. Lewis drank whisky, Vivienne soda water, Hayley a strong Chinese wine, Wu Hon-leung and myself beer, Winkle and Dora a sweet sherry, Jenny and Ho-man iced water.

.   .   .   .   .

After dinner we descended to the drawing room, where green tea or coffee was served with a wide choice of liqueurs which, because they were sweet, most people enjoyed. Hayley was now on whisky and showing the first signs of being tight—an increased jollity and a louder tone of voice.

If John Liu was to be banished, he would probably have to be out of Hongkong forty-eight hours after the order was given, and some swift thinking was needed to decide where he should go. Obviously he could not return to China. The Philippines and Singapore were out, because of visa difficulties for Chinese. It would take too long to obtain a visa for Saigon. Japan was too far to go, and the family had no connexions there. Thailand would be possible, but Winkle, with visions of John Liu being a nuisance at one of her firm's offices, hastily said what a ghastly place Bangkok was and that John would have the greatest difficulty earning a living there. Argument narrowed to a choice between Taiwan and Hongkong's Portuguese neighbour, Macao.

Winkle, of course, was all for the beloved Taiwan, which she had never seen. Jenny thought both were dead ends, but that Macao was nearer and the fare would cost less. Dora sighed heavily and (so in character) drank *crème de menthe*. Geneviève began to be tearful again. Vivienne read a magazine, and later went to talk to some of the lesser Wu relatives who kept on coming and going in the background (Chinese families defy counting). Lewis suddenly said, almost vindictively, that he couldn't see any point in his father going to Taiwan, which was a doggone hole anyway, then equally suddenly shut up.

There was silence.

'He'd better go to Macao,' said Wu Hon-leung, adding to me, 'I have a clansman there they can stay with.'

There was again silence.

'Macao,' said Hayley Chen with a broad smile, 'is a very jolly place, excellent for crabs.'

Winkle looked gloomily at Geneviève.

'That won't be much consolation to you, dear, will it? You're allergic to seafood.'

Geneviève sobbed and nodded, and suddenly Winkle, followed by everyone else, burst out laughing. Even Geneviève laughed as she dried her eyes.

'There you are, you see,' said Hayley triumphantly. 'These things have to be approached with a philosophical attitude.'

The release of tension was broken by Lewis saying aggressively to his mother:

'We can't all go there. You have your job, and there's the baby. People say there are no doctors in Macao.'

'Of course there are doctors,' said Jenny, with a slight expression of irritation.

'That's not what I've heard,' said Lewis sullenly. 'Vivienne can't possibly go there. Can she, Mother?'

'No, dear, I suppose not,' replied Geneviève weakly, while I think all of us wondered just what Lewis would do if his mother lost her job.

It was at last decided that John Liu would go to Macao alone, that Geneviève and the rest of the family would stay in Hongkong, but that Winkle would, at her own insistence, take the opportunity of her present vacation to go to Taiwan and explore the possibilities of Liu moving there and setting himself up in some kind of business.

Dora stifled a yawn when it was all over.

'Let's play cards,' she said.

'Cards' being a Hongkong expression for mahjong, some of the lesser relatives, two of them boys in their late teens, brought out a mahjong table. I took this opportunity to leave.

(v) *An outsider*

In the hall, as I went out with Hayley, who was going to accompany me, Vivienne was talking in Mandarin to a young solemn-looking fellow, a friend of the Wu cousins and, like Vivienne, a refugee. It appeared that the lad came from the same district of Chekiang province as her own family.

As, after bidding everyone goodnight, we opened the front door, the boy came with us, saying in stiltedly stiff English:

'I must go too.'

'Come along, then,' said Hayley cheerfully.

'Aren't you going to stay and play mahjong?' I asked.

The boy drew himself up like a Puritan.

'I do not understand to play that game,' he said severely.

I raised my eyebrows, never having heard of a Chinese who did not know how to play mahjong.

It was getting late, and the three of us were able to walk in the middle of the empty street, Hayley's loud voice ringing out among the sleeping houses as he described John Liu's as a hopeless case.

'A hopeless case!' he repeated, still more loudly, as if not everyone had heard.

After a few paces of silence, the stern young refugee continued where he left off.

'Generalissimo Chiang Kai-shek,' he said, 'does not play mahjong.'

I looked startled; Hayley Chen gave an irreverent guffaw.

'Splendid, young man! Splendid!' he said with mock encouragement. 'How can there be any progress without high principles? We must all have them. One of my principles is never to drink more than two catties of *sheung ching*[1] with one meal. It's the application of high principles such as that to one's own life that makes it worth living.'

But the lad was not amused.

'This is the way to my house,' he said. 'Goodnight.'

'*Wai!* young man!' Hayley shouted at him, as without further ceremony he walked off up a steep side lane. 'Why don't you join us for supper?'

He turned beneath a lamp at the corner of the lane, saying slowly and clearly across the street, 'Thank you. I do not take supper'—and with a nearly military about-turn he strode away into the gloom.

(vi) *Supper with a Chinese Bohemian*

Shrugging our shoulders, we walked on together, and after a short time took one of the stairway streets leading sharply down into the most densely peopled and oldest quarter of the city. It was pleasant going out with Hayley. Like Wu Hon-leung, he belonged to that world of Chinese commerce which is outside, and only indirectly influenced by, China. The conflicts that Jenny and other members of the family were going through were foreign to them

[1] Equivalent to two bottles of vodka.

both. They regarded them dispassionately, as problems that did not concern them. Wu Hon-leung, because he had them all round him, due to his family's connexions, had at least tried to appreciate what all the tensions and emotions were about. Hayley had never bothered. To him Jenny was an overstrung girl who should teach in a school or get married.

'But she's desperately unhappy,' I said.

'We all have our little unhappinesses, my dear Austin. But what happens? Tomorrow you make some money. Or, if you don't, you can cheer yourself up with friends and wine.'

'Wine for Jenny?'

'Well, friends at least. Why doesn't she come out with us swimming at the weekend, or hiking in the country during the winter? She will be unhappy—naturally—until she learns to enjoy herself.'

But at the back of my mind I heard Jenny's voice:

'What pleasure can you find in going out with people like that, only talking about eating and drinking, and making coy remarks about rumoured engagements? It's all so shallow.'

To me, Hayley's company was a restful escape from the cloak of disillusion which enfolded so many of my friends from China. Equanimity with regard to the great Chinese political issue was easier for him than for Wu Hon-leung. Hayley's family was, by Hongkong standards, long established in the colony, with few remaining links with China. They belonged to the Hakka, a race distinct in language and certain customs from the Cantonese, and subject to persecution by the latter at various times in the past. During one such wave of persecution, when many Hakka sought shelter in Hongkong or migrated overseas, Hayley's grandfather came to the colony, without a cent to his name, and, having first learnt to cobble western shoes, carefully built himself up until he became the compradore of a large German firm. During the First World War the firm closed down in Hongkong, and the two sons who were then connected with it fell on hard times. The third son, Hayley's father, was fortunately not affected. He had joined the service of the Hongkong government shortly after leaving school, and on a steady income raised a family of nine sons and three daughters. For the last ten years of his career he was a Supreme Court interpreter, a position of trust and respect in the community.

True, there were divisions in the family. But they were Hong-kong divisions, caused by Chinese impact with the West, granted, but with the political element absent. Hayley's younger brother, for example, was a devout Buddhist, the only member of the family to be so. Another brother, who worked in a British firm, had become more than usually westernized and no longer lived in the family house. The eldest daughter of the Buddhist had become, while still at school, a Baptist, much to her father's regret. Another brother had married a Peking girl, far more modern in outlook than the rest of the family, and who found it insupportable living with them. She had persuaded her husband to live separately, in an old-fashioned apartment which she had modernized tastefully with western furniture, from which her husband periodically sloped away to a camp bed in the family house.

When Hayley invited me to take supper with him I thought he intended to go to a restaurant. Later in our walk, when I asked which one we were going to, he answered:

'Let's go to my place. Our cook will be preparing something.'

This still left me in doubt. I knew the family house quite well. It was in the western part of the city, in an old-fashioned street mounting the hillside convincingly for a certain distance, then, giving up the struggle abruptly, diminishing into a narrow twisting flight of steps. Their house was built in one of the styles appreciated in Hongkong by Chinese families fifty years ago. Though it had only a narrow street frontage, it stretched far back from the street, a long narrow interior, each floor consisting of one long room, sub-divided at the rear into cubicles with plywood partitions six feet high, cheap curtains shielding view through the doorless entrances. On each floor the ceilings were fairly high, but the highest, as well as the most pleasing in appearance, was the top floor, of which the only ceiling was the roof itself—long rafters supporting tiles and painted white on the interior. The house was so long that the angle of the roof was very gradual, rising to its highest point far back in the room, falling thereafter in such a fashion that it covered the kitchen, washing rooms and other lesser places into which the house tapered off at the back. This slow rise and fall of the roofline enhanced the upper room's length and depth.

Each floor had kitchens and other offices, and on each level lived various members of the family eating communally. There were too many of them living on each floor for everyone to sit down comfortably to eat at the same time, even per floor. Two brothers, with their wives and children, might eat at a certain time each evening, after which the same kitchen would be used to cook for two sisters, their husbands and children, and possibly some other younger family members. After the first dinner was cleared away, a clean cloth would be laid over the same table, and the next meal session would start.

Only on the top floor, where Hayley's mother lived, a widow for many years, was it arranged that there was only one eating session, the only other occupants of the floor being the Buddhist brother with his wife and three children. The wasted space was sorely needed by those below, for the house now sheltered several relatives from Canton. Nevertheless, the overriding consideration was to prevent the old lady of the house from being worried by having too many of her grandchildren around her.

So while comparative calm reigned on the top floor, the rest of the house seethed with children of all ages, all in different types of schools and different degrees of modernity—like their parents, in fact, except that, while the modern type of parent could be fairly sure of modernity in the children, old-fashioned parents could not guarantee orthodoxy in theirs. The family leaned gently westwards.

But, walking with Hayley down into the heart of old Victoria, I was puzzled by his invitation to supper. We were not going in the direction of the family house, while, as for his remark about his cook preparing the food, I knew the family had no cook, the wives and sisters doing all cooking and housework.

Could it be that there was, after all, some substance in his remarks about living as a Bohemian? I had always regarded these hints as part of Hayley's artistry in his dealings with Wu Hon-leung, but as we walked on—Hayley talking loudly about what people missed in a life without wine—my doubts grew. Recollecting my visits to the family house, I could not recall anywhere having seen Hayley's cubicle, although his books and other possessions were there, in his Buddhist brother's cubicle which was much larger than the rest. Had he perhaps some small room in the centre of town where he could live independently, only returning home for family gatherings? If this was so, why did he keep his books and suits in the family house?

To have found out why Hayley was still a bachelor would have meant delving back twenty-five or thirty years. His attitude towards young women was, in my opinion, unusually idealistic—that is, by comparison with other Cantonese of my acquaintance. His contacts with women were undoubtedly numerous. From what I could gather, the story began when he declined to accept a bride chosen by his parents. Later, or about the same time, he fell in love with a girl from a Chinese Protestant family, the father of whom refused to permit the match unless Hayley became a Christian. This he would not do. A long crisis in both families ended in certain permanent embitterments. The girl was eventually married to someone else, but was at first miserable, while Hayley's relations with his own father were all but severed—an event of great misfortune and ill luck—by the old interpreter's refusal to reconcile himself to Hayley's wish to choose his own wife or to make any approach for an understanding with the parents of the girl Hayley was in love with. The father's objection arose from a promise made to one of his oldest friends that his eldest son would marry his friend's eldest daughter. Hayley, in fact, had been betrothed from birth.

Although that is all I ever discovered about it, I felt certain that it had provided Hayley with the greatest conflict of his life. It occurred moreover at a time when in Canton, only ninety miles away, China's new nationalism was emerging in its most intense form, when filial obedience, arranged marriages, continuity of the family, the entire fabric of ancient Chinese civilization, was in a melting pot. Filled with the passions that motivated many young educated Chinese at that time, Hayley was adamant in defiance of his father's wishes, while with another side of his character he considered that to become a Christian, and obtain the girl of his desire, was weak and unworthy. He despised Christians as people who had turned their back on all that was best in Chinese culture.

Though he never told me in so many words, I gathered that, when his friend married, Hayley, hitherto a celibate, took to another kind of life. And my impression was that, even now, there was a woman concealed somewhere in his present life. I wondered whether she was the reason he stayed away from the family. Was he perhaps keeping her at his apartment?

·   ·   ·   ·   ·

In the densest part of the city, not far from the waterfront, we turned into a small black doorless entrance, a narrow anonymity concealed by the glaring lights of shops on either side, and mounted dingy wooden stairs within. The staircases of old Hongkong houses such as this do not have landings, nor do they change direction at each floor. They mount straight on upwards, so that the door on the first floor is near the front of the building, the door on the top floor right at the back. We mounted to the top.

The door was not locked; it did not even have a handle. As Hayley pulled a string, which swung it open, and some light shone from within down the staircase, I saw an aged plaque of Chinese characters fixed to the wall saying something I could not understand about clubs or associations.

We walked into a large dingy room directly under the roof. The windows were arched and pilastered, a breathless remnant of the last century, when this was a middle-class residential neighbourhood, now taken over by shops with upper floors let out per cubicle, as many as ten families living on each floor.

The room occupied a little less than the ground-floor space of the house, a few steps leading down at the rear to a kitchen and latrine. Around the walls were benches, stacked chairs, stools, and, in one corner, a large stack of square tables with the round tops of various sizes which are laid over them when they are used for meals.

The meaning of the Chinese characters outside now became clear. It was a room that could be hired for club meetings, wedding parties, and private dinners. On one wall, in large gold characters on a red background, was the sign of double happiness customarily hung up at weddings.

Two men, working at accounts on a desk with a telephone, greeted Hayley familiarly as we entered. For economy, some of the fluorescent strip lights in the roof had been turned off. The middle of the room was thus gloomy. At the far end, however, near the arched windows that looked bleakly upon other similar rooms packed with cubicled humanity on the other side of the street, were two men of Hayley's age and education. One was talking with the civilized solemnity of Chinese drunkenness, while the other, only half listening to him, was practising large calligraphy, with scroll paper, brush and Chinese ink (looking like soft black paste) laid on a table in front of him. As we drew near, the talker greeted Hayley, while the writer looked at me gloomily over the top of his spectacles. We were introduced. The talker was a former education officer under the National Government, the writer a refugee professor.

With a yell, Hayley called down to the kitchen for supper. A fat sleepy cook brought Chinese wine, beer, bowls and porcelain spoons. Soon, in the gaunt emptiness of the room, we were making ourselves perspire with wine and bowls of hot congee.

The two exiles relaxed. Patting my knee, the education officer explained that bad economic conditions had sent prostitution rates down to a lower level than he had ever known, with serious effects on the morals of young men. The professor said marriage was all right in theory but he was glad he had left his wife behind. Hayley said they were too pessimistic and should look on the bright side.

Putting down a half-finished bowl of congee, the professor got up, returned to his writing table, looked contemptuously at his own calligraphy, screwed up the thin soft paper he had been writing on, threw it on the floor, and resumed his seat with us.

'How many times is that?' asked Hayley.

'Fourteen,' he said, then smiled with unexpected cheerfulness. 'Anyway, let's drink.'

As we drank, and the conversation grew maudlin and repetitive, I had a sense of inconclusiveness. I had expected to find Hayley's lair, an intimate home concealed from the family, inhabited by a voluptuous slut who would pawn his clothes if he left them with her. Yet, as so often with Chinese, here we were still talking in a comparatively public place, while the inner part of his life, which this time he had almost promised to reveal, still remained a secret.

Then, leaning back slightly as I drained my cup, I caught sight of a narrow ledge on the wooden wall opposite, and on it some discreetly arranged objects: a piece of soap, an old towel, a razor, a toothbrush and a hand mirror. During a wedding party or a committee meeting one would not have noticed them. In the empty room they became conspicuous. More than that. As I stared at them, they loomed large with significance.

'Are those yours, Hayley?' I asked jokingly, not at first daring to believe they could be.

'Yes,' he replied gaily. 'Bathroom, bedroom and living room combined.'

Without knowing it, I had already found Hayley's lair. There was no apartment, no avaricious concubine. This bleak unhomely room, hired out for parties, was where Hayley lived. On camp beds, or on benches laid side by side to make a bed, these three men, for various reasons homeless, spread out their quilts. If there was an evening function, it was late before they could come in to take nocturnal possession. But provided they did not mind that, the owner, who was Hayley's friend, let them keep a few things there during the day. People at wedding feasts were too busy to notice a piece of soap on a ledge, and too happy to bother if they did. Hayley laid out his bed just below the ledge, beneath that symbol hung up for other people, the glittering golden symbol of double happiness.

To my European way of thinking it seemed ridiculous that Hayley did not live at home. That he liked independence was clear; but Hongkong being what it was at that time, with bachelor flats unobtainable, to live as he did indicated an inordinate craving for independence. It was irrational. I knew for certain that there were no differences between himself and his family. He had made his peace with his parents many years ago, long before his father's death. In the circumstances, it was ridiculous that he should not stay in the family house—he, the eldest son.

While Hayley was out of the room for a moment, I expressed this to the professor. He looked at me with surprise.

'But Hayley is a bachelor,' he said.

'Yes, I know. But why doesn't he live with the rest of the family?'

The professor smiled at my stupidity, and, as if explaining kindly to a student thick in the head, asked:

'Who would cook for him? Who would wash his clothes and mend them? His mother is too old. And why should any of his brothers' wives do it? They have their own families to look after. You understand?'

I understood. It was simple enough. I might have known better than to think that in Hayley Chen I had found at last a Chinese who acted irrationally, who lived a Bohemian life because he liked it, who turned up at his office in dirty or torn shirts because he did not care. That was the carefree veneer with which he covered the truth, a veneer which I now saw Wu Hon-leung had picked off, but which in an oblique way amused and flattered him.

The truth was in the last degree rational, in terms of the Chinese family system. Only inexperience had hindered my perception of it. Hayley was an unproductive member of the family, and the family has no place for unproductive members. They must go away to monasteries or scrape along somehow in wretched independence. They have a place in the family, but a place of little honour, in that they have not given the family what it insatiably demands—descendants.

In fact, Hayley could have lived at home, had he insisted or determined on it. It would have meant not much more than engaging an amah and adding an extra place at his brother's table. But, as I later discovered, there had been complaints among the wives when it was once suggested. Hayley heard of these complaints, and as a matter of pride withdrew his suggestion.

There is room for individuality in Chinese society—plenty of it—but only after tribute has been paid to the essential gods. Hayley refused that tribute, and would rue it, perhaps till death.

(vii) *Society facing a blank wall*

Winkle Miao, on the other hand, paid. Her merest whim of individuality received the family's serious attention—she was a grandmother. She had even made Wu Hon-leung redecorate his drawing room, though he knew it was certain to bring bad luck. And, though to some it might be fortuitous and sound absurd, the bad luck came.

The order of banishment against John Liu came through as expected.

'It was appalling,' said Winkle, eating crabs for lunch at my flat after Liu's boat left. 'Everyone was in tears. Anyone would think he was going to the other side of the world, instead of to that stuffy old dump only forty miles away.' (For Winkle the picturesque Portuguese colony had no charms.)

'D'you mean even Lewis cried?' I asked.

'Not him,' said Winkle with a leer. 'He was drunk again.'

Lewis' drinking was becoming serious. He could hold a good deal and never changed colour or became excited. Only by an occasionally disconnected remark, sometimes rude, could one tell when he had been drinking too much. He at all times gave an impression of being cold and calm.

'These crabs,' I said, 'come from Macao.'

'What d'you expect me to do about that?' asked Winkle. 'Burst into tears too?'

Two days later, she sailed for Taiwan on what her friends and relations were certain would be an epic visit to her spiritual home.

.   .   .   .   .

Geneviève had mixed more with Americans than with Europeans in Shanghai. Sympathetic, attractive and a good sport, she had many American friends and was always a popular figure at their parties. Behind her back, these friends often said what a misfortune it was that she should have such an unsatisfactory husband and such spineless sons. In other words, Geneviève had always been placed by those who knew her in a category apart from her husband, and in Hongkong, when Liu was banished, Geneviève did not suffer socially. At her office the Americans openly sympathized with her to the point of tactlessness, and a few days after the event the director informed her that he had recommended to the New York head office that the scope of her work be enlarged and her salary considerably increased. It looked as if the family's financial problem, rendered more precarious by Liu's departure to Macao, where he would certainly be unable to make money, was going to be miraculously solved.

I had this news from Jenny and her brother, Ho-man, with whom I dined a few nights later at a Cantonese restaurant. Since it seemed to me that the director must have made his recommendation with an understanding of Geneviève's financial difficulties, I praised the thoughtfulness of the man concerned.

Ho-man disagreed.

'I don't think it's got anything to do with it,' he said. 'Americans are only out for what they can get.'

'Cool down,' Jenny said to him. 'My brother doesn't like Americans; it's no use saying anything good about them,' she added to me in explanation.

For an instant Ho-man looked embarrassed. Ever since the communist Resist America Aid Korea propaganda campaign at the beginning of the Korean War, America had come to represent a principle almost as much as a nation. To be anti-American was to risk being mistaken for a communist. He looked down at his teacup.

'My sister idealizes things, that's all,' he replied. 'I don't. I believe in facing the facts.'

But beneath the controlled words and expressionless face there were tensions of the type one senses quickly after living amongst Chinese for any length of time. This was the lad who had desperately tried to talk his elder brother out of going to Peking, and yet . . .

'That's why you left your job in the communist bank and went to Singapore,' I said, taking a bow at a venture.

Clearing his throat, he spat heavily into a spittoon beside our table.

'Of course not. I left because my father wouldn't let me attend the lectures the bank staff had to go to in the evenings.'

'Did you enjoy the lectures?'

'I only went to two before I resigned.'

My estimate of Wu Hon-leung expanded. One son in Communist China might one day be convenient; two would be a disaster.

'Oh, he's a real little theoretical communist,' Jenny said, teasing him.

He flushed slightly.

'You don't understand anything,' he said to her. 'You only believe what the European priests tell you.'

I changed the subject. It was three years since the elder brother left for Peking, and in that time one's ideas can change. Perhaps I understood now why Ho-man left so abruptly at the family dinner. Although the family said he went out to parties and dances, somehow I began to wonder. The clipped, restless way of speaking, the undercurrent of challenge to me as a foreigner, started to make a new sense. Did his father also know? It was something father and son were unlikely to have discussed openly, but was that not why he was sent to Singapore? He could have escaped the communist lectures just as well, after all, by remaining in Hongkong in his father's office.

.   .   .   .   .

This particular dinner had been fixed up within the hearing of Lewis, who, with an irritating habit he had, moved towards us at the mere sound of an invitation, so that Jenny was more or less obliged to include him. It was arranged that Lewis would come to my flat first, from where we would proceed together to join Jenny and her brother at the restaurant.

Lewis arrived at the appointed time and was pleasant. The coldness which he invariably showed in the presence of his mother and wife was not there any more. Dominated all his life by their more powerful personalities (in Vivienne he chose his own wife, possibly with the subconscious hope that she would rescue him from his mother), when he was free of them both, on occasions like this, he became a responsible, independent human being.

He moved nostalgically over to the piano, awaiting an invitation to play, then crossed to one of the bookcases and pretended to examine the titles. I had observed on his former visits with his mother that the atmosphere of my flat disturbed him, and I now saw why.

'I think I have spoilt my life,' he said quietly, his eyes still mechanically directed toward the books.

I laughed.

'Aren't you a bit young to say that?' I asked.

'No,' he replied, turning to me. 'My mother understood me when she wanted me to study music seriously. But I didn't know it. I thought it was easy to study; I could leave it till the next day. Now it's too late. I shall never be a really good pianist.' He moved slowly across the room, savouring its colours. 'And I shall never be satisfied either. Yours is the sort of life I would like to have. Pictures, books, grand piano—my mother calls this your studio.'

Geneviève again. Geneviève's idea of an artist's life, derived from novels and the cinema. Geneviève's idea for Lewis. And so, Lewis' idea—until disturbed by contradictory ideas from Vivienne. All that Vivienne was conscious of in my 'studio' was that one had to eat off the arms of chairs, on cigarette tables, or even sometimes on the floor, while cooking was done partly in a windowsill and partly on the edge of the bath. Geneviève's Bohemia included details such as these, which she thought rather fun. Vivienne, who, prior to her marriage, had only read of Bohemia as a country in European history books, thought my way of living was poor and shoddy.

Lewis' visits to me, ever since his one and only visit accompanied by Vivienne, were actually small rebellions against his wife, momentary escapes into his mother-world; and it was as the ally of Geneviève that I was detested by Vivienne.

'Won't you play the piano?' I said.

With the two deferential refusals which Chinese etiquette prescribes, Lewis responded to my third invitation and sat down at the piano. He played some old Gershwin and Jerome Kern songs, improvising on them with the correct degree of restraint, without any strummers' clichés.

When he stopped he did not rise from the piano stool, but sat still with his hands clasped, pale and depressed.

'I shall never get the life I want,' he said slowly. 'There's no room in the world for Chinese musicians anyway.'

The telephone rang. I recognized Vivienne's voice; she recognized mine.

'Is Mr. Lewis Liu there?' she asked, as if speaking to a servant.

Lewis went to the phone. There was a short conversation in Shanghai dialect. He sounded anxious and confused.

'It's time we went to the restaurant,' I said, when he put the phone down.

We went down together into the street. I hailed a taxi, and had opened its door, when Lewis hesitated.

'I have something to do,' he said nervously. 'You take this cab. I'll follow you. I'll be about ten minutes late. You please excuse me.'

Thinking no more of it, I went on alone, arriving on time for the appointment with Jenny and Ho-man. I explained that Lewis would be following.

When half-an-hour passed without his arrival, we ordered food and began without him. Neither of them cared much for Lewis, and conversation went smoother by his absence. When we had been at the restaurant for over an hour and were well into our meal, we were agreed that he was unlikely to turn up at all.

We had reached, with easy consciences, the soup and rice at the end of dinner when to our astonishment Lewis pushed open the glass door of the restaurant and stepped in, bringing a warm blast of street air into our air-conditioned comfort. He no longer wore a tie, as he had earlier on at my flat. His face was ashen and severe, his movements unduly slow. He was more than usually drunk.

'Sorry I'm late,' he said, as the *foki* brought another stool for him.

He made no reference to our having met earlier. He did not seem to remember it. He scarcely seemed to be the same person at all.

With some embarrassment we watched him sit down. But the

fokis in Chinese restaurants are adept in dealing with such situations. In a flash, tea was poured for him, and a new set of bowls and chopsticks arrived. Ho-man quickly ordered another dish, which we all pretended to eat. After some generalities, we resumed our conversation, allowing Lewis to put in remarks where he could. The crisis passed.

We were on the old subject: the mental sterility of Hongkong. Jenny was speaking scathingly of the way in which modern Chinese history was avoided as a subject in Hongkong schools. The three of us went on for some time till Lewis abruptly cut in.

'I hate this place,' he said. 'I wish I'd never come here. I have no life of my own—only my mother's life. No friends—only my mother's friends. You are my mother's friend,' he went on, addressing me, 'not mine. I want to say it bluntly. You are only my friend because my mother told me I should be friendly with you, because you could help me. I speak very bluntly,' he repeated, his eyes fixed stupidly on my chin. 'But I don't believe anyone can help me in this place. And I don't want help. You must understand this. I don't want anyone to say I took help from foreigners. I am a Chinese. I want to explain to you bluntly.'

Ho-man, who a moment before had been running down Americans, with a quick glance begged me to take no notice.

'Did you know there's a tie hanging out of your pocket?' Jenny asked Lewis.

The drunken man's attention was diverted to stuffing his tie further into his pocket. Somehow we reached the moment of departure without a scene.

In a friendly undertone as he swung open the door into the warm street, Ho-man said to me:

'He has no right to talk like that. Mentally we're all half-foreign. That's our difficulty.'

For a young man of his age, it was a colossal admission.

With unusual, and obviously sincere, demonstrations of friendship, both he and Jenny bid me goodnight, stressing their meaning by making another date. Knowing that Lewis, in order to get home, would have to travel the same way as me, Jenny firmly detained him at the kerb while I boarded a tram.

Seated in the cool breeze of the tram's upper deck, I pondered on Lewis' words. In recollection they had the manner of a set piece, something learnt by rote, someone else's words, drummed into him to oppose or strengthen the weak, friendly, disillusioned young man who had sat at the piano playing Gershwin.

But one does not get far by pondering the mysteries of Chinese thought. It is simpler to relax and wait. In time the answers to the problems appear of their own accord. My mind drifted off to other things.

Two stops or so later, my attention was drawn from the tram window by a familiar voice saying in slow, mannered English:

'Good evening. May I take this seat?'

Looking up, I found at my side the anti-gambling refugee from Chekiang whom I had met at Wu's house.

He took the empty seat beside mine. In better light than that in which we first met, I took more note of him. He was tall and well-built, with hard eyes and an obstinate mouth which, when it spread into a smile, showed friendliness but no spark of humour. He had splendidly white teeth and well-kept finger-nails. He probably did physical exercises and took his health seriously.

We talked conventionally of the Wu family. I asked if he had seen them again. He replied that he went there nearly every day to see his friend, one of the cousins. I told him Mrs. Miao had gone to Taiwan.

'It is good,' he said solemnly.

'You really believe the Kuomintang can make a come-back?' I asked.

He looked at me like a lecturer.

'It is the duty of every Chinese to support them,' he said. 'If you cannot agree to communism, you must agree with Generalissimo Chiang Kai-shek.'

'You're the first Chinese I've ever heard say that.'

He smiled disdainfully at me.

'Because you live in Hongkong, and the people you know are Hongkong Chinese. They have no patriotism. They are only interested in money. Every patriotic Chinese must be against communism. You cannot be against communism if you are not for the

Kuomintang. There are only two ways. If you do not take one, you must take the other.'

A man in front, who evidently understood some English, looked round, and the lad became silent.

'Where did you learn to speak English?' I asked the refugee.

He smiled with a hint of pride.

'When I came to Hongkong I could not speak either English or Cantonese. I learn English by reading, and listening to the radio.'

We got down at the same stop, and he walked with me part of the way to my home.

'I go to see Mrs. Liu sometimes because he is my countryman. We speak my village language.' Then he looked down prudishly. 'But he is a communist.'

'Who?' I asked with surprise. 'Vivienne Liu?'

He nodded and corrected his English.

'She is a communist.'

'Of course she isn't,' I replied. 'She came here to get away from communism. They're Shanghai refugees.'

'Maybe his husband does not agree, but Mrs. Liu is communist. She goes to meetings. He—she—invited me to go too.'

We stopped at the corner of my street.

'Are you sure?' I asked.

'Certainly,' he replied, with evident pleasure at knowing better. 'That is what we were talking in the house when you came that evening.'

'Does anyone else know?'

'Of course not. She make me promise not to tell. My friend does not know. But I can tell you.'

Promises of this kind somehow do not apply to foreigners.

Somewhat disturbed, I reached my home. If it was true that no one in the family knew, should I intervene? Could anything be gained by intervention? Lewis certainly knew. His entire behaviour was explicable in terms of this unexpected information: his drunkenness and changeableness, his sober moods of depression; above all, his words to me at dinner, learned beforehand—learned from Vivienne. Torn between his wife and his mother, unable to stand without the support of either one or the other, he was eking out hell, unable to express himself fully to anyone without humiliating himself.

I concluded that intervention was pointless. Geveniève must certainly know. She was intuitively close to both her sons, Lewis and Lucas, the one in Europe. They could not conceal much from her. No doubt the knowledge that Vivienne was attending communist lectures in Hongkong, despite her former views and the influence of the Church, contributed to Geneviève's despair when her husband was arrested. And if Geneviève knew, perhaps they all did, whatever the Chekiang lad might say. Possibly that was why they never attributed reasons to Lewis' drinking. The causes were too obvious for discussion.

The restraint of a Chinese family, the hesitancy to attempt to influence any member within it, except in what, from a family angle, could be called an extreme emergency (an undesirable marriage, for example), is an object lesson in the art of civilization.

(ix) *The family receives a blow*

That same night, Ho-man later told me, Lewis accompanied them to their house, and, having vomited his meal in the lavatory and washed his face in cold water, went in a state of comparative sobriety to announce to Wu Hon-leung that he had decided to return to Shanghai, taking Vivienne and the baby with him. Vivienne would rejoin the bank. The communist representatives in Hongkong—doubtless as jubilant as priests at the rescue of a wayward Christian—had assured him they would be well looked after.

The luxurious, obstinate beauty had triumphed. There is no calculating the types of personality that communism can attract. Selfish and possessive, a lover of creature comfort, with a rich family background, until recently a practising Catholic, Vivienne was one of the last Chinese on earth that one could imagine being attracted. Yet there it was.

I passed Lewis in the street a few days later, but pretending not to have seen me, he hurried by. Sober, perhaps he was still unsure of himself. Within a week they left by train for Canton and Shanghai.

At the end of the month Geneviève received from her American employers a double month's salary and a curt typewritten note informing her that with effect from receipt of the letter her service with the company should be considered terminated. She telephoned, called on American friends, asked for reasons, made explanations, implored people to help her by making the director appreciate she had nothing to do with her son's return to China. Chinese style, she approached everyone except the director himself.

It was useless. Something inside the American machine had clicked, and the holiday was over. With a Republican board of directors in New York, and traditions of respectability that were almost English, the firm could tolerate, even sympathize over, the husband's gun-running. But the son's political frailties provoked only alarm. The Chinese, in the final estimate, were tricky people. One never knew quite what was going on behind their smiling, impassive faces. A competent Portuguese was engaged to take her place.

When Geneviève asked Wu Hon-leung for a loan, he must have inwardly cursed the day he redecorated the drawing-room.

(x) *The shrewdest of the sisters*

Some days later the telephone rang. Winkle was back from Taiwan.

For the first few days she was heavily dated, and I could not see her. Everyone wanted to hear the ambassadress' views and experiences, which important officials she met, what they said to her, and whether the political barometer in Taipei was rising or falling.

Finally she came to lunch. In the windowsill and on the edge of the bath, so despised by the communist Vivienne, succulent and intriguing dishes were prepared. No pains were spared to render honour and distinction to the occasion. Like cardinals who have come straight from the Vatican, like governors who have kissed hands on appointment, or like Chinese household idols that have recently returned from sojourn beside a 'strong' idol in a famous temple, Winkle returned from Taipei with added occult virtue.

She looked wonderful and was dressed, if anything, even better than usual. She was marvellously unchanged by her experience. It was as if she had never been away.

'Don't ask me whether I had a wonderful time, darling. Everyone else has. I did,' she said as she settled in a chair near the fan. 'That's official.'

We both laughed heartily, but I was not sure why.

'Unofficially,' I asked, 'are you going back there?'

'Not at the moment,' she said, looking for something in her bag.

'What did they say?'

'They said "Carry on with the good work where you are," ' she said, making it sound as significant as possible.

'What about John Liu? Will he be able to go?'

'Not much point just now,' she said evasively. 'Ah, here it is. A small present for you, dear.'

She took from her bag a pink paper package.

I accepted it with sincere protestations. Presents from Winkle were always calculated to be just what one wanted—that too was part of her passport—and I undid the package with interest.

Inside, to my surprise, was a pair of beautifully hand-knitted bright yellow woollen socks. Useful, of course, but—well, extraordinary. Winkle had never before given me anything so domestic.

'Don't look alarmed, dear,' she said as I took them out of the paper. 'I knitted them myself.'

This was truly astonishing.

'You *what*, Winkle?'

'Didn't you know I could knit?' she said nonchalantly.

I was still overcome.

'Winkle, d'you mean to say you knitted these for me on your holiday?' I said in amazement.

'Yes, dear. Don't you like them?'

'Of course I like them. They're fine. But I still don't understand. This is a thunder-striking event. You knitted them in—in Taipei?'

'Of course, dear,' she said, with a blank expression, taking a cigarette. 'In Taipei everybody knits—nothing else to do.'

That evening I fixed a party for her at the Ritz. It remains to be seen whether her words were an epitaph.

(xi) *The family struggling in political waters*

In due course Winkle returned to Manila, and Ho-man to Singapore. News from Shanghai was bad. The bank refused to take

Vivienne back on the staff, and due to some legal technicality about having previously surrendered her union ticket she was unable to find any other employment. She and Lewis lived on money sent from Hongkong by Geneviève, until Wu Hon-leung found out and refused to give her any more unless she stopped. Even then, whenever Lewis sent a particularly piteous letter, she sent a little, keeping it a secret from her brother-in-law.

A European friend of mine, who corresponded with an old Chinese friend in Shanghai, told me that his friend's letters contained remarks about Lewis constantly borrowing money from himself and others who could ill afford to give him any. Vivienne, doubtless with luxuriant tears of contrition, had been received back into the bosom of the Church and attended Mass in Shanghai regularly.

In Hongkong the family discussed these and other details sadly. They were of course unaware that justice had given a sly wink.

Wu Hon-leung, who now found himself financially responsible for Geneviève in Hongkong, John Liu in Macao, Lewis and Vivienne in Shanghai, and Lucas in Europe, was far from pleased. In addition to trying to prevent Geneviève sending money to Shanghai (an attitude in which he showed surprising modernity), he made it another condition of his assistance that Lucas must come back to the East at once and stop wasting family money in Europe.

Geneviève meanwhile got a badly paid job with one of her husband's less reputable American acquaintances who, using a watch-shop as a cover of respectability, was actually engaged in a variety of dubious activities. She went daily to services at the Catholic Cathedral.

To the grief of Dora and Wu Hon-leung, Jenny declined every inducement to make her stay in Hongkong. I think that by now she too knew she could never marry a Hongkong man. The curious episode of Vivienne's return to the Church in Shanghai counteracted the letters which continued to come from Wai-man, advising her to come into China. Finally, she took a job in Japan as an English teacher in a Catholic convent school for girls.

I met her one day in the street, a lonely, sad little figure, quite different from the gaily dressed, well-made-up Cantonese girls passing by as we talked.

She told me of her decision.

'I've got to do something useful with my life,' she said.

"If anyone is too old or too sophisticated for this, he has forgotten how to live."

Early morning at Nara, ancient capital of Japan, looking over the ornamental lake Sarusawa, in which a famous beauty of the eighth century committed suicide

When visiting a temple, traditional Japanese costumes may still be appropriate.

but when going out with a boy friend . . .

Farmer's wife   Housewife

JAPAN

Sculptor   University lecturer

KOYASAN, JAPAN

Everywhere tombs, tens of thousands of them, their monuments engaged in
slow dispute with the roots of trees

Sunday in Hongkong: *above*, in the Botanic Gardens; *below*, waiting for a tram at the end of a day in the country

Chow Kwong-Ming

Chow Kwong-Ming

HONGKONG

Old-fashioned streets mount the hillside convincingly for a certain distance,
before diminishing into flights of steps

HONGKONG

A city of elaborate façades and many ups and down, where behind nearly
every house is a ship

In the last Spanish church to survive the destruction of Intramuros, the old walled city of Manila, in 1945

A modern American-style Filipino home on the outskirts of Manila

In the market at Maymyo, Burma, where after haggling over their goods, market women and their customers can relax side by side over a bowl of noodles

Pilgrim at a mountain shrine

Young monk

BURMA

Lady buying fish

Buddhist intellectual

A remnant of Mughal architecture in a congested part of Old Delhi
Brahmins taking their morning bath in the Ganges at Benares

MADHYA PRADESH
CENTRAL INDIA

An old man, seated on a
table in the street, selling
betel-leaves

A brassware merchant
with a customer

DELHI

An open-air barber estab-
lished on the pavement of
one of the main streets in
the old city

LAHORE, PAKISTAN

An area devastated in the rioting and massacre that accompanied the partition
of India into two nations. Several years after partition, people were still cooking
and sleeping on sites such as this.

ISTANBUL

The mosque and
tomb of
Suleiman the
Lawgiver

The
coming
of winter,
a hillside
view
looking
towards
the Sultan
Selim
Mosque

'Yes,' I replied. 'That's your daemon.'

She laughed.

'There you go again, complacently summing people up. I don't think people are much use unless they've got daemons.'

'I didn't mean to dispute that,' I replied. 'And so yours is pushing you out of here.'

'Yes,' she said thoughtfully. 'I don't think I shall ever do anything but blame myself if I stay. Even this convent work may not be what I'm really after. But I must try it and see. It may be.'

'Have you written to tell your brother?'

'Yes. He'll be angry. But it can't be helped.'

Something about this short encounter saddened me. I had always thought that Jenny should reach an absolute decision, one way or the other, or she could never be happy. Her decision to go to Japan was, from her own admission, indefinite. The conflict within her was still unresolved.

As a possible resource, I arranged a dinner for her and some of her closest friends, most of them young people engaged in fruitful social work in Hongkong. I thought they might possibly dissuade her from going, by showing her that there was in fact plenty of useful service she could render in the colony. But she saw through my device, and at the last moment telephoned to say she was ill and could not come. Later the same week she left.

. . . . . .

That her younger brother, Ho-man, also had an unresolved problem and a decision to make was something I had only faintly perceived when meeting him in Hongkong. Not long after Jenny's departure, I had to make a flying visit to Singapore. I wired Ho-man to say I was coming. Not having had time to buy him a present, I thought at the last moment, at the airport, of taking down to him, as a possible breath of his home town, a copy of all the principal Chinese morning newspapers.

He met me at the airport at Singapore that evening, and at my hotel I unpacked the newspapers, to find that I could hardly have brought a more welcome gift. To my consternation he went straight for the two communist ones, the *Ta Kung Pao* and the *Wen Wei Pao*. Picking them quickly out of the bundle, he looked at me with admiration and astonishment.

'You managed to bring these?' he said.

'Why not?'

'Don't you know? They're banned in Malaya. We never see them.'

Until then, I had been unaware of this, and told him so. But he was no longer listening. Avidly he ran through the principal headlines, then, as if I were going to take them back, said:

'May I really take them away with me?'

I laughed.

'That's your risk. If you leave them with me I'll only burn them.'

Spreading them out to half-size, he opened his shirt and carefully packed the newspapers round him, between his shirt and vest. After fixing his shirt again, he made to go, unable to bear another minute's delay talking to me, so anxious was he to get home and read in privacy.

'Thank you. Thank you very much,' he said, nearly overcome with gratitude at this puny gift. He shook me warmly by the hand, and went to the door.

'Don't you want these others?' I asked, pointing to the bundle of more restrained literature still lying unglanced at on the table.

He looked back, grinned, and shook his head.

'Not much in them,' he said. 'Thanks all the same. Good-night.'

(xii) *A refugee from communism*

Sometimes, thinking over the indecisiveness of the family's position, its attainment of a point of retreat from which it was unwilling to go either forwards or further backwards, it seemed to me that the only person in their circle who really saw the situation clearly was the Chekiang lad, with his puritan self-discipline and rationalized loyalty to the fallen National Government.

When he had first made his confession of faith to me, in the tram, he had infectiously passed on a sudden spasm of confidence. The National Government had at one time come to represent in western eyes what Europe had been trying to achieve in China for four hundred years, a stable, secure and independent government, a democracy adapted to China, voluntarily leading the country out of its remote exclusiveness into the age where nations meet as equals, with agreed principles of law and morality. Could it be that, whatever Hongkong people might say, there was still hope for this idealistic aim?

It had been a shattering experience to see that Government driven out and supplanted by another which, though it might greatly modernize China, was based on one of the narrowest schools of European political philosophy, the theoretical merits of which were far from proven in practice. Yet at the time of the downfall of China's democratic experiment, so overwhelming was the swing of Chinese public opinion against it that it was more or less impossible for European observers to feel there was any more hope for it. Had there been two rival points of view, one democratic, the other communist, there would have been more hope. But there was only one view. As it became more and more certain that the communists would overthrow the Government, criticism of the Kuomintang became less and less restrained, until, in the hour of communist triumph, it culminated in a vindictive torrent of condemnation.

In China he who wins is good, until he loses; he who loses is bad, until he wins again. In the dramatic days when Chiang Kai-shek left the mainland for Taiwan, one could search the papers in vain for any reference to his tremendous achievements during his twenty years of rulership. His own propaganda organs prattled on glibly about ultimate victory. The rest spat. An uninspiring demonstration, it appeared to represent the facts as the Chinese saw them. Nowhere could it be seen better than from the neutral vantage point of Hongkong, with its freedom of speech and of the Press.

Later on, when the real nature of the application of communism to China came to be understood, the attitude towards the fallen Government changed to one of negative hope—the hope which expresses itself in sentences beginning 'If only . . .', petering out before reaching a full stop. Among the younger refugees in Hongkong one occasionally met men whose ambition was to go to Taiwan and join its armed forces. But it took months, sometimes years, of waiting to gain admission to the island, and many were refused for one reason or another. The light of even the negative hope seemed to be fading.

In this situation the Chekiang lad appeared like a phenomenon, and later, after thinking it over, a possible portent. The quality of steady optimism which had maintained his morale throughout three tedious years of exile from home, and specially the fact that he was young, boded well for a happier outcome in the future, in tune with the hopes of every westerner who had sincerely devoted his or her life to work in and for China. For he could not be the only one; there must be others like him.

Persuaded at last that I did not play mahjong and would not force him to drink anything alcoholic, he accepted an invitation to dinner. What I primarily wanted to find out from him was what kind of government he hoped to see established, should the improbable happen and a democratic party regain the mastery of China. It would not be sufficient, I stressed to him, to say that such a party would re-establish a government similar to that which the communists destroyed, because such a government would be associated from the outset, in the minds of Chinese people, with corruption and incompetence. Something was required giving a sure promise that these earlier weaknesses would not be repeated.

My question surprised him.

'This is not so important,' he said. 'The important thing is that our people must learn to obey, or we shall never be strong. In all the strongest countries the people are very obedient. Japan is very strong for this reason. But the other countries in Asia never agree. There is nothing but argument. We Chinese must learn not to argue. We must all do our best to build up our country.'

'In fact, the communists would agree with all that, wouldn't they?' I commented, trying not to make it sound offensive.

He smiled faintly.

'The communists are very clever,' he replied. 'But all they tell is lies. You cannot believe anything they say. I know because I was choose for their special school where young men and woman train in communism. I understand everything about communism. I never can agree this thing.'

'But once you were in the school, how did you get out?' I asked. 'I thought they never allowed people to leave.'

'Of course they watch every student all the time. But one other student—but he was a communist, but he was also my very good friend—he tell me, warning me that I must take care because they understand I do not agree and are going to move me to some other place, to another school. I know then I must go quickly, because perhaps that other place is very far from Taiwan or Hongkong, so I cannot escape.'

'So?'

'There was an American missioner in the town near the school. Sometimes before I talk to him in Chinese. When my friend tell me, I went to the American and he gave me money for the train as far as Canton.'

He was of course speaking of 1950, in the months immediately following the establishment of the new government, when many American and other missionaries still carried on their work, in spite of severe restrictions.

'How old were you then?' I asked.

'Eighteen.'

'Did you see your family before you left?'

'Yes. I went straight home. I got there at night and leave before daylight. But I only dare tell my mother and father I go—no one else.'

'Were you ever interested in communism?'

'Never. When the communists entered our town for the first time I lie on my bed for two days—how d'you say?—weeping. I do not want to see the sun again.'

'Then why did you go to their school?'

He shrugged his shoulders.

'There was no other school. And after some time I think I must not struggle against this. I must go like the others. At first it seems a good school. I think I make a mistake. But after some months at the school everyone must write a letter to his father and mother saying "You were no good as parents. You were old-fashioned and your thought all wrong. You should be shame for not telling your children the truth." It sounds stupid when you talk this thing outside Communist China, but it was very important. Every student must write this letter and send it to his father. The instructors prepare everyone for this. They know that for we Chinese it is very disgraceful thing and very difficult.'

'It would be in any country. Did you write your letter?'

'Yes. But for three days I could not. And after I write it and send it I feel terrible ashame. And I understand all this is stupid. And every day after, I listen in the class and pay attention, but all the time inside I say "No, no! You are talking lies. I don't believe that. That is not true." And I wait till I can have a chance to escape.'

'But you think that, in spite of pretending, you were spotted by the communist instructors?'

'Yes. They are very clever.'

'Did anyone not send a letter?'

'Everyone must send.'

'But don't you think they all felt the same shame as you did?'

'I think so. But none of us can speak this. We cannot trust any other student. They must report everything to the instructor.' Reflectively, he hissed through his teeth. There was silence.

'So you came to Canton.'

He cheered up again.

'Yes. And I had not enough money to come by train to Hong-kong, so I walked from Canton to Shumchun.[1] I found out there that the Hongkong police would not let me come in because I could not speak Cantonese. There is one British inspector there who speaks to each person coming in in Cantonese. If he can answer, he can go through; if he cannot, he must go back. So I walk out into the country to find a place to cross the river.'

He went on to explain how he swam the river and got across into the New Territories, dodging the Yellow Ox bandits who were at that time preying on people trying to cross the frontier illegally, demanding a fee to 'assist' them to pass in safety.

Once in Sheung Shui, the first small town in the New Terri-tories, he was safe. With his last remaining dollars he bought some food and a rail ticket to Kowloon, where he arrived with only eighty cents in his pocket.

On his first night in Kowloon he managed to find some of his countrymen, who put him up and fed him. But, as he saw at once, they were only slightly less poor than he, and he could not possibly remain with them. Finally, searching for a missionary lady whose address he had been given by the American priest who helped him escape, he was befriended by two Europeans, also temporarily refugees from China and understanding Mandarin. With their help he weathered his worst months of exile, got a job as an office messenger, and later, when his English improved, a better post as a youth welfare worker.

[1] About 60 miles.

'You presumably teach the youths to be very obedient,' I said.

For once he laughed.

'Of course! This is the most important thing we Chinese must learn.' His face became serious again. 'When I say goodbye to my mother it was the beginning of the light, and you know sometimes there is one big star left in the sky then, the only one. After going some way down the street I look back. I can see the shadow of our house and my mother still standing there, watching me. And just above the roof, that star. When I see this, I know that one day I shall come back.'

(xiii) *Interstices*

A difficulty one encounters when discussing political subjects with any Chinese other than the widely travelled and highly educated is that their knowledge of the world outside China in some ways resembles Europe's knowledge of China in the age of Voltaire. Certain aspects of Chinese life were at that epoch fairly well understood by intelligent people, who had read accounts of the 1635 Dutch Embassy to China or the published letters of the French Jesuits from Peking. But between each item of knowledge were interstices of ignorance hiding the context in which the items subsisted and had meaning. By filling the interstices with conclusions based on western reasoning, the harmony and balance of the truth were upset. Minor details were magnified, vital elements overlooked or misinterpreted. The China fashioned by the savants of the *chinoiserie* was, though fascinating, a place which no Chinese would have recognized.

To some extent the reverse now applies. In spite of much outward westernization, the Chekiang lad had an idea of the West in which, between large chunks of correct information, were gaps filled with impressions drawn from Chinese experience—generals whose loyalty to the leader could not be relied on, palace intrigues, the possibility of poisoning the leader of the opposition, and suchlike—an exhilaratingly colourful frame which, however, altered the tone and significance of the portrait within it, detracting from the salient, heightening the unimportant.

Sometimes the results were quaint, sometimes humorous, sometimes suddenly grotesque.

'When I read books about Europe,' he said, 'I think the country I most like to see is Germany. This people is very strong. You British do not like them, I know. You are always fighting them. But I think the Germans must be a good people.' He paused a moment, and said tentatively, 'Do you know the word Nazi—N-A-Z-I?'

'I'll say we do!'

'This is a very interesting party,' he went on unconcerned. 'I have read a book called *My Struggle*. It is a very good book—by Hitler.'

'Yes, in Europe we know all about that book.'

The expression of faint contempt appeared again.

'You do not agree with it. Because you are British you do not understand it.'

'Have you ever heard of a place called Belsen?'

This time the contempt was more pronounced.

'I have heard all about that,' he said, as if to dismiss the matter.

'Have you ever seen pictures of it? I can show you some.'

'That is exaggerated,' he said, with the authority of a pontiff.

'You read Hitler's book in Chinese?' I asked.

'Yes, of course. I have many books about Hitler.'

And he proceeded to say in what ways he thought Hitler was a greater and cleverer leader than Mussolini. He had books on Mussolini too, and on various other modern dictators.

For one disquieting moment it was as if history were going backwards. The European dictators and all they stood for have been so utterly discredited that it is difficult for us to imagine intelligent people paying any more attention to them, other than as a historical curiosity. We forget that books like *Mein Kampf* have been translated into many languages, and are still circulating in many parts of the world, amongst people who have not had our experience of what they lead to. The political fabric of the East is a crossweave of many threads obtained from many sources. None can say which of them will prove to be significant and which insignificant. For every one the world hears about there are dozens that are never heard of. Probably Nazism will be one of the latter. What mainly impressed me about this conversation were the basic conceptions that lay behind it.

Though the Chekiang lad was undeniably well-read, and although his reading was in many ways up to date (he had Chinese translations of some of the best short histories of the Second World War, for example), the political climate in which his reading thrived bore an unexpected resemblance to the way the world used to think thirty years ago.

Not knowing enough about his home, I could not determine why this should be. Possibly it was due to his father, who was a man of some importance at that time. Or possibly this period was a particularly productive one in Chinese political literature, setting its stamp on the tone of subsequent writing. Anyhow, he spoke of national prestige as people used to between Versailles and Locarno. China had still to be vindicated from the humiliation wrought upon her by the Western Powers. That vindication would be achieved when China stood as the unique oriental equal of the West, as Japan once stood in the League of Nations. Events since that day— the rise and fall of Hitler, the failure of the Versailles experiment, the independence of India and other Asian countries—were not fully appreciated, subsisting as they did in this obsolete setting.

He will mature, widen his knowledge, and alter his ideas. But I am glad that I met him soon enough after his escape from China to see something of the mental framework he came out with.

(xiv) *A day in the country*

At the end of August Winkle paid another visit to Hongkong, and my ties with the family, which relaxed somewhat when she was away, closened again. Though the heavy rain-bearing clouds of summer were already beginning to give way to the thinner, higher, softer cloud of autumn, the weather was still swelteringly hot, stifling in town on a holiday.

On the Sunday after she arrived I was invited to join the family on an excursion into the country. We set off in three cars laden with every imaginable kind of food and drink, and headed in the direction of the high, sparsely inhabited hills west of Taimo-shan, the New Territories' principal mountain. The cars climbed up beyond the last shack-like vestiges of the city. Soon we were high up among the bare green backs of grass-covered hills, with here and there a forlorn fir tree, looking like a lost soldier. About 2,000 feet up, leaving the road, we bumped for some time along a tufted track on the top of a lower ridge with superb views on either side, on our left Hongkong, green island girdled in stone, and on our right the brown waters of the Pearl River, with the Bocca Tigris just discernible on the horizon. After this the cars could take us no farther. With drivers, amahs, and older children carrying part of the enormous quantity of provisions, we started along a small track round the side of the hills.

We went very slowly, taking twenty minutes to accomplish what in the winter could have been done in five. Dora, Winkle and Geneviève fanned themselves and carried sunshades. Wu Hon-leung took off his coat and gave it to the driver, who with a per-spiring grin added it to the already unwieldy collection of things he was carrying. There were no more sunshades, so Wu covered his head with a handkerchief. The cousins ran up and down the grassy slopes, sometimes in front of us, sometimes behind. The Chekiang lad and his particular friend, talking earnestly, went ahead and were soon lost sight of.

Winkle's outfit, which had looked rustic enough in Hongkong, was here seen to be most unsuitably urban. The collar of her dress was too high and stuffy; her fashionable white shoes continually let her down on the stony track. Dora, whose hair had recently been dyed unrealistically black, was looking picturesquely relapsed in a shapeless fawn European dress with a sedate fringe of lace round the open neck. On her expansive feet were espadrilles of indeterminable age. But she was comfortable.

'If you will wear all those Shanghai clothes . . .' she said to Winkle.

Wu Hon-leung next undid his braces, tying them like a belt round his trousers, then rolled up his sleeves, revealing pale fat hairless arms and a heavy gold watch.

Foreseeing something like this, I had come in a sweat-shirt and was comfortably cool.

'For goodness' sake, share my sunshade,' said Dora. 'You'll get sunstroke, and we shall have to carry you home.'

'Isn't this angelic, dear,' came Winkle's dry voice behind me.

'I don't know how long this place has been in existence, but of course no one ever thought of improving the path.'

We rounded another corner of the hill. The view expanded over descending hills and the sea scattered with its innumerable mountainous islands. The south wind caught the sunshades and Wu Hon-leung's handkerchief, which was rescued by the unshakeably cheerful driver.

Situated in a rounded depression between two breasts of the mountain was a grove of dense bamboo, banyan and camphor, at the entrance to it a small iron gate with a Buddhist inscription. Dogs barked. Everyone talked louder to let the inmates know who was coming. Two thin shaven-headed nuns hastened in cloth slippers to the gate and ushered us within. There was animated conversation in Cantonese.

The interior of the grove was delightfully unexpected. Its outer appearance of being no more than a dense clump of trees and bushes was a disguise and protection in a part of the land that has only known real peace and security in the fifty-five years since it has been under British administration—and even that period was sharply broken by several years of banditry and lawlessness during the Japanese occupation. Walls would have been less protection than trees. Walls suggest wealth and invite the stray bandit. The grove was a more subtle and sure device. Only the ramshackle little gate gave any sign that it was a place of human habitation. Although the mere presence of bamboos and such valuable trees as camphor indicated some form of human dwelling, from outside one would have assessed the dwelling as being poor.

In fact, passing through the gate and under an untidily kept tunnel of the thickest trees, we found ourselves on a terrace overlooking a beautiful sheltered garden. It was paved as in the West, with a balustrade and steps leading down to the lawn. Only in decoration did it differ from a European classical terrace. Instead of lions, it had friendly Chinese dragons; instead of Ionic pilasters, green tiled imitations of bamboo stems. In the centre of the terrace, facing the garden, was the high main door of a nunnery, a plain grey building of symmetrical design, with small barred windows and its name written in large strong characters in a recess over the door. In small characters at the side was recorded the date when the name tablet was presented.

Within, on stone tablets set into the walls, were records of each occasion the nunnery had been repaired, the date, the reasons, and the names of those who gave money for the work to be done. The most recent tablet was dated the 17th year of the Emperor Kuang Hsü, about 1890; the earliest was of the 5th year of Ch'ien Lung, about 1740, alluding to the original foundation, and chronicling a restoration of the building. The foundation tablet was for some reason—no doubt some very good reason, at the time—missing. Various other objects were dated, a big bronze bell, an incense urn, and another tablet hanging from the ceiling with a finely written Buddhist saying carved on it. From the wall tablets and these objects much of the history of the place could be gauged.

The sense of historicity which permeates China is a factor of great importance in the maintenance of tradition and the altering of it. What an extraordinary sense of shock one gets, on the first occasion when one asks the semi-literate head of a remote village how long his family has lived there, and he replies without hesitating, 'I am the twenty-fifth generation,' and, taking a little boy on his knee, adds, 'This is my grandson, the twenty-seventh.' We are back in the Yuan dynasty, the age of Jenghiz Khan. But let us still be unsatisfied and ask, 'Where did the family come from?' There is another unhesitating reply. 'From such-and-such a district; the ancestor who came to this village was the fourteenth at our earlier home.' And we are back to the early days of the Sung dynasty and beyond, or, in other civilizations, to Alfred the Great and Harun al-Rashid.

In Europe a few royal or aristocratic families can trace their history in this way. In China nearly every family can. Most of them have a clan record, which in the case of large and important families will be printed, and from time to time brought up to date and reprinted. In it, as well as brief history of the generations and branches, there is usually important information about the ancestral tombs, where they are sited, and for what geomantic reasons. The clan record of an important family is quite often like a history of the district.

Sometimes great historical figures appear, either as members of the family or as persons acquainted with the family. One of the oldest families living in the neighbourhood of the old walled city of Kowloon, for example, has a record containing personal details about the last of the Sung emperors, Ti Ping, who rested at Kowloon in 1278 in the last phase of his overthrow by the Mongols—details unknown to history, but recorded here with the vividness and veracity of a good eye-witness. Further on we see the downfall of the Mongols, the savage sixteenth-century attacks on the coast by Japanese pirates (the epoch in which Portuguese Macao was founded), the coming of other Europeans, the foundation of Hong-kong as a British trading depôt, all this and much more, mixed with family happenings, quaint legends and prophecies.

Even in the humblest countryside, everything has its date, a decaying temple, a well, an ancestral hall, the walls of a village, even woods, paths and bridges. Where a streamcourse has been altered, it will be no difficulty to find out which family altered it, in what year of what reign, although it may be as long ago as the fourteenth century; and old men who occupy their time with these things will be able to point out where the stream ran prior to that date, though no trace of it remains among the rice fields.

It is the people's sense of having each his or her place in an immensely old and minutely recorded civilization that stands basically opposed to the sudden introduction of new systems and ideas. Under compulsion the people of the countryside may bend before the wind, but only with the conviction that in the long run little can be changed. Reformers may push with all their might to veer the course by ninety degrees. As a result it may move five. Let them gather strength and push to a hundred and eighty degrees. It may still only move five. And in the moment when they relax to draw breath it will probably revert to where it was originally.

(xv) *Escaping from both the choice and the family*

In a small cool stone room in the nunnery, tea was served, people mopped up their perspiration, and Dora, with evident signs of contentment, fanned her behind—a great relief in hot weather. Here we found Hayley Chen, who had come separately with Geneviève's other son, Lucas, recently returned from Europe.

Lucas was taller than Lewis, but with the same pale narrow features. He smoked continually and his front teeth were brown. Hayley, who had carried camera and binoculars over a rather longer route than we had come by, had taken off his shirt and was clad in only a vest and shorts. He was as usual talking loudly, making jokes with the nuns, and sampling their home-distilled wine, which was the subject of a good deal of uproarious comment, the timid shaven-headed ladies protesting that they only distilled it for sale and to offer to guests.

Alone among the men, Lucas had removed neither coat nor tie. He appeared to be cool, and though he sat at the same table with Hayley he took no part in the hilarity and looked as if he had no interest in anything that was going on. Knowing well the unsettled emotions of oriental students returning home after their first long visit to the West, I was not surprised when, having been introduced to me, Lucas hung on to me as if he found me more familiar than the members of his own family.

'D'you like coming out to places like this?' he asked curiously, as we went to admire the garden.

'Don't you?'

'Dirty, old-fashioned place,' he said. 'I can't think why they all bother to come.'

'Don't be too hard on it,' I replied. 'We're probably going to get a delicious vegetarian lunch.'

'You can eat food like that?' he asked with mild astonishment.

'Well, if you don't like the vegetables, you can eat the soup and the rice.'

He looked away with a hint of contempt.

'I don't like rice,' he said.

He was an extreme case. I turned back into the nunnery.

It was the abbess' birthday, it now turned out. This was why the family had come, and in honour of the event a particularly large variety of vegetables was being prepared for consumption, with the usual mysterious pieces of beancurd disguised to look like fish, sliced chicken and other dishes forbidden to Buddhists.

The abbess, a bent old lady of over seventy, whose bare scalp was the only unwrinkled part of her head, was watching in her dark grey gown while the nuns in the open kitchen behind the building sliced and prepared vegetables and ground soya-bean flour on an ancient stone wheel. She was much smaller than Winkle and Geneviève, but as they talked her eyes were fixed intently on them, slanting upward from her downbent head and hunched shoulders. I could not catch everything they said—they spoke in Cantonese—

but the sisters were evidently speaking of people or things the abbess knew. There was not the least sense of embarrassment as these well-dressed, sophisticated women talked to the frail old nun in her garb of poverty and simplicity. Only Lucas, with distinctions unhappily imported from the West, was out of place in these remote and frugal surroundings.

'We needn't have brought all that food with us,' I said to Winkle, while the abbess took Dora to see some alterations she had made to the building. 'But I suppose some of it will do for Lucas.'

'Why? Can't he eat with us?' asked Winkle.

'He says he doesn't like rice.'

A sudden wave of irritation swept over Winkle, obliterating every affectation by its intensity. At the same moment Lucas came in from the garden, lighting another cigarette.

'Why don't you go to a dentist, Lucas, and have your teeth cleaned?' Winkle broke out sharply, loud enough so that everyone could hear.

'Don't worry him, dear; please don't,' said Geneviève to her softly.

Lucas showed no sign of emotion.

'I think the dentists are better in London, Auntie,' he said suavely, and smiled slightly, showing again the unfortunate teeth.

Winkle turned to me.

'Have you seen the rock garden, dear?' she asked brightly, as if nothing had happened.

We went outside together.

'That boy makes me furious,' she said, when we were out of earshot. 'Since he came back he's done nothing but complain. As if his mother hadn't enough troubles already, he insists on going back to London to marry some typist!'

'European?'

'Yes. Ridiculous! Quite unsuitable—he should never have been sent to London in the first place.'

'Won't the family stop him going?' I asked.

'I almost wish they would. But it would be far worse if he brought her back here. Mixed marriages are difficult enough any-where, but in Hongkong they're impossible.'

Winkle was socially nothing if not realist.

'Must it be one or the other?' I asked.

She pursed her lips and nodded.

'They've already been living together for several months.'

I looked back at the nunnery. In the doorway Lucas could be seen talking to someone within. He looked thin, relaxed, spiritless. What kind of European woman was it, I wondered, who had laid her hands on those padded shoulders and drawn this man backwards to herself, gently inducing him to a fearful renunciation of everything to which he was born? A woman older than himself, possibly? Really a typist? In any case—the only certainty—someone who did not like the taste of rice.

(xvi) *The unexpected without end*

Two hours of the afternoon were spent eating a splendid meal, supervised by the abbess and her nuns. An hour of somnolence followed, by which time it was five o'clock and time to be thinking about going home. The provisions we had brought with us—and which, I now observed, contained nothing with meat in it—were taken to the kitchen, where the abbess, happily holding a tin of Huntley and Palmer's biscuits, directed the emptying of the baskets and occasionally asked Dora what this or that tin contained (she recognized the biscuits by the pattern on the tin).

I took a final look round the nunnery. At the central altar were three gilded statues of the Buddhas of the past, present and future, with a smaller effigy of Kwan Yin, Goddess of Mercy, in front of them. There was a way round the back of the altar where, in the place approximating to the room of the mother of the family in an old-fashioned house, was yet another and more sacred image of Kwan Yin, the female spirit which is ever behind the male faces of the gods, a faint Chinese remembrance of the Hindu spirit, Shakti.

Beneath was a wooden tablet, carefully gilded and painted dark red and green. Its top was ornamented with imperial dragons and the sun, and in gold characters were written the words that were once kept in every Buddhist monastery from one end of the land to the other: 'Long, long live the Emperor!'

I suppose it must be the last of its kind still maintained in its traditional place.

.   .   .   .   .

Beyond the door of the nunnery the garden was now in shade. In the black frame of the door Hayley was standing outside on the terrace, leaning with one leg on a step talking to Winkle, who was seated on the balustrade between two potted flowers. Hayley's binoculars and camera were hung crosswise from each shoulder; Winkle's elegant white shoes caught the light against the grey flagstones of the terrace. Were they talking of old times, of the days when they were the first Chinese to learn ballroom dancing, drive cars, play tennis—when they were impossibly bright young things? If they were, they did not seem out of place in this quiet haven of tradition. They melted into it. One wrinkled face answered another.

Drawing nearer the door, I could see down the steps into the garden, where Wu Hon-leung, talking to two of the children, was adjusting his braces—methodically, without either a false or an unnecessary movement, rather in the same way as he adjusted his family, one son in China, one in Singapore, his brother in Saigon, himself in Hongkong, and only Jenny—well, perhaps one day Jenny would find happiness. Let the wind blow north or south, cold or hot, dry or humid, Wu Hon-leung would make adjustments and survive unharmed, not entirely by foresight, but far from accidentally.

And looking into a lilypond at the end of the garden, with thick bamboos rising behind them, the Chekiang lad was talking to his friend, seriously as always, his rare moments of laughter invariably derisive—the courageous, proud, unpredictable future. How he could talk! Throughout the entire excursion so far he had spoken to no one but his friend, and to him ceaselessly—dreams of grandeur and conquest, of China invincibly dictating to all who once humiliated her—while gazing at the lotuses, the silent and exquisite emblems of the pacific Buddha,—dreams of the West amazed and dazzled, humbly confessing to shallow-minded misunderstanding, begging only to learn from the fount of civilization—near those slim feet on the terrace that had once danced the black bottom and might even now be learning the cha-cha,—dreams of national power with no national difficulties, of factories with no capitalists, cruisers in which the men lovingly obey the captain because they admire him, incorruptible officials happy to work all their lives with no prospect of a pension, locomotives that run without American oil, heroism and noble sacrifice, with no ambition, jealousy, greed or self-indulgence—while Dora was wondering whether the rumour was true that her husband wished to take a concubine, and whether, quite apart from anything else, it would not ruin their chances at Government House if he did.

As I reached the door, Geneviève came from the interior of the nunnery with the abbess beside her, followed by Lucas. Geneviève was the first to reach the main door. As she joined us on the terrace, the old abbess said something to Lucas. I did not understand what his reply was. All I heard was the name of respect he gave her—Small Grandmother.

I looked quickly round at everyone. It was as if I were seeing them, and the abbess and her nunnery, for the first time. The two syllables of Cantonese I heard Lucas utter established the old lady as almost certainly a relative. And suddenly, in the expressions of Winkle, Geneviève and the others as the abbess came out, I identified the mixture of respect and familiarity I had earlier appreciated, but without comprehension. The old abbess was the *mui-tsai*, or slave, their grandmother had brought into the family as a young girl, who, after helping to bring up Winkle and her sisters, had eventually married their father and retired childless to a nunnery. She had been kind to them as children, and today was her birthday.

With something approaching fascination I listened to the adieux that followed, picking out triumphantly the confirmation unknowingly given to my supposition by Winkle, in whose last words to the old lady I heard the address Small Mother.

We passed under the tunnel of trees and through the gate, amid dogs whining and wagging their tails, the gentle chattering of the nuns, and the rustle of bamboo in the south wind. In another moment we were once again in single file on the bare rough track winding round the edge of the hills.

The children were less excited than in the morning. All of us were quieter. Winkle and I were last in the file, and because of her unpractical shoes we gradually fell behind. The rest of them passed out of sight round a shoulder of the hills, leaving us to the click of our shoes on stone and the silence of our thoughts.

'What's the matter with you, gloomy?' Winkle asked after a time, still walking on and looking ahead.

'I was just thinking,' I replied, also walking on. 'There's no end to China, is there.'

Winkle chuckled effervescently—

'Of course not, dear. Whyever should there be?'

—and her chuckle rose on the wind over the wild coarse grass.

.   .   .   .   .

On the last stage of our drive home, while we were crossing in the vehicle ferry over to Hongkong Island, Wu Hon-leung invited me to change cars.

'I know you admire Chinese calligraphy,' he said. 'I want you to come and meet a friend of mine. The others will go home.'

As we drove off the ferry the cars separated, and we headed eastward, through the central district and Wantsai, toward Little Shanghai.

Our destination turned out to be a block of new apartments. Wu Hon-leung pressed the bell at a ground-floor front door, and after an eye had peered at us through a small glass hole in the middle of the door we were admitted by a middle-aged smiling Chinese lady, a northerner unable to speak more than a few words of broken Cantonese.

The apartment was very small, furnished in simple western style of good taste. We were led at once into the principal room, where the lady's husband, a grey-haired man of quiet temperament, greeted Wu in English and made us both welcome.

We sat down, and after a few moments an amah, closely supervised by her mistress, brought lidded cups of green tea such as would seldom be served in a Cantonese home. After discussing our outing to the nunnery, Wu and our host exchanged views on a business deal concerning some house property in which they were jointly interested, while in silent admiration I looked round at the scrolls of modern calligraphy which were the principal wall decorations. Each was by a different writer, and all were in entirely different styles miraculously embodying the writer's personality, even to a person like myself, unable to understand a word of what was written.

Lost to the rest of the world, I was only recalled to my surroundings by the realization that the business conversation had ceased and that Wu and our host and hostess were all laughing at me. Our host then explained who the writers were. One scroll was by a former minister, another by a general, another by a provincial governor, all of them prominent men of this century.

'And your own writing, sir?' I asked.

He led me over to a table on which was an incomplete scroll in cursive style. Wu looked at it for some time in silence.

'Very hard,' he said slowly at last and with deep respect. 'When I was a boy there were five or six men in Kwangtung who could write like this. Now I'm afraid there are none.'

'Is it very difficult to read?' I asked Wu.

'Very. To tell you frankly, I cannot understand more than a few words.' He turned to our host. 'But this is in an old style. What is it?'

The grey-haired man smiled at us both.

'This is the writing which was used during the Western Ch'in dynasty.'

'Do you often write in this way?' I asked.

'Every day,' he replied. 'In order to keep the facility it is necessary to write every day for about three-quarters of an hour.'

There was silence for a moment, while Wu continued to scan the characters.

'Western Ch'in,' he repeated quietly, as if to himself.

'Just when was that?' I asked. 'About fourth century A.D.?'

Our host, thinking for a moment, nodded with a look of appreciation.

'Yes,' he said. 'About that time.'

III

(i) *Entering Manila at pistol-point*

September is not a sensible time at which to leave Hongkong. The heavy heat and humidity of summer are about to be followed by the year's compensation, a superb autumn of blue, windless days, warm in the sun, becoming each day steadily cooler in the shade, until the tenth moon of the Chinese lunar year (usually about November or December) brings winter clothes and winter fare, including the best dishes of the Cantonese cuisine—snake, civet, quail, raw fish, and the delicious self-cooked meals with the fire in the centre of the table, with hot yellow wine from the north.

The ultimate destination of the plane taking me from Hongkong to Manila was Labuan, in North Borneo, and the passengers were thus varied. Most of the better-dressed ones were bound for Manila. But besides them there were a number of Chinese of the type from which the great overseas Chinese communities in South-East Asia have grown—poorly-clad people, speaking only Cantonese or their district dialect, calmly making their first journey by air as if it were the most ordinary experience for them, their fares doubtless paid for by relatives already in Borneo, and their possessions tied up in a fascinating assortment of parcels and bundles. Near me was a middle-aged countrywoman dressed in traditional Chinese jacket and trousers of black Shuntak silk. Her belongings were contained in two kerosene tins, tied up with wire, and a stiff paper carton, from the top of which emerged a kettle. From the luggage compartment in the stern came the anxious quacking of ducks and—no, surely the aircraft could not be carrying a pig.

In the seat next to me was a young Japanese business man with a movie camera. Although the Chinese air hostess, who was old enough to remember the war, carefully arranged that this gentleman did not get a window seat, she did not succeed in restricting him. As we rose into the great bowl of Hongkong harbour and cruised past the magnificent panorama of the city climbing up the sides of its fantastic peak, the Japanese hissed at me apologetically, leant over and took pictures of the full length of the city.

Ever since the war, which established beyond doubt that a high percentage of all Japanese living overseas were spies of one kind or another, the sight of a Japanese abroad with a camera is disquieting. Photography is a major national hobby in Japan, but abroad it is such a useful hobby. . . . Having photographed everything down to the last departing island of the Ladrone group, my neighbour relaxed with another hiss and said nothing to anyone for the rest of the flight.

It was dusk by the time we sighted the coast of Luzon, the largest and most important of the seven thousand Philippine Islands. About half-an-hour later, in darkness, we caught sight of Manila, a glittering crescent curved round the black water of a bay, with long avenues of lights stretching out on the landward side like the sparkling rays of a star. As the plane touched down, the cabin temperature rose, and though the airport lamps were reflected in puddles of recently fallen rain, we found on stepping on to the gangway that the rain had not had much effect on the heat.

Of all the big cities of modern Asia, surely Manila is the hottest. Singapore is cooled down by rain, and sometimes at night it can be almost cold. The same is true of Jakarta. Calcutta, in spite of appalling heat and humidity in summer, has several months of delightful cloudless winter. Rangoon's winter is shorter but no less pleasant, while winter in Delhi and Hongkong is positively invigorating. Bangkok and Saigon are possible rivals to Manila, a city whose apologetic excuse for a winter consists of a few cool evenings in January; but in these other cities life moves at a gentle tropical pace, whereas in Manila—well, the United States did not rule the Philippines for forty years without effect.

But here is the authentic Asia. Even arriving after dark one is aware that there are palm trees round the perimeter, it is hot, and one's baggage—now, just where is the baggage? no, as you were—has not got lost, but has passed into the custody of an official of some kind, a tough little guy with a murderous-looking face, an American-style khaki uniform, two pistols, a belt gleaming with bullets, and a cap that knocks General MacArthur's into insignificance. He has a hand on each holster and is chewing gum.

'Fill in one of those,' he says, nodding at a sheaf of forms on the counter in front of him, while his expression shows that he has already marked us down as an American or a Britisher, one of those so-and-sos who think they run the world, but this is an independent country, see?

Abased and humbled, we make to do as we are told, but of course—this is one of the tricks we sons of etc. use to show our superiority over coloured people—we have nothing to write with. With maddening civility we ask:

'Could I please borrow a pencil?'

Had we asked for a bullet we would have had more likelihood of delivery. As it is, the official says nothing, but with a nod indicates something the other side of the room. Turning round, we see another official writing at a desk, on which is a pencil. We go over to the desk and ask to use the pencil, but the official does not say yes or no. He continues writing, without looking at us.

Should we shout? Better not, because to force us to shout is one of the tricks these coloured people use to get the better of us sons of etc. Gingerly, we remove the pencil and turn back to MacArthur, who has not yet fired his pistols but now looks as though he may at any minute.

After writing down the answers to a devastating series of questions which seem to be no one's business but our own, and signing a solemn declaration that we have not brought with us any roots, seeds, plants or wild animals, we sign the forms and hand them over.

He taps our suitcase.

But by this time we are slightly nettled and wondering how long it will be before we ask for the telephone number of our Embassy.

'Yes?' we say innocently, pretending not to understand.

'Open up,' he says, shifting the chewing-gum from right to left.

He makes a silent but thorough search through shirts and underwear, while the Philippine pesos which we are illegally importing (due, as usual, to the impossibility of remembering details of the cobweb of currency restrictions in which international relations lie choked) repose peacefully between the pages of a Life of Rizal, the Philippine national hero, which we carry in one hand and which naturally no one would dream of inspecting.

Having tidied up the contents of the suitcase, we pass on to another jaunty military cap, the passport officer. Here there is a sudden change.

After scanning the pages of our passport, the officer looks up at us with a beaming smile.

'Say! You remember me?' he asks. Frankly, we don't. 'I signed you in on your last visit.'

We hastily rectify our memory. The officer rises. We shake hands. Other military caps look up. The scene melts. MacArthur's jaws are motionless with astonishment.

'Hey! Boy! Fetch this gentleman's bags.'

Other passengers are left suspended in mounting fury while we are escorted by the officer himself to the airport entrance. For this is the authentic Asia, where nations get blocked but individuals sail through.

'Wait here, sir. I'll have them get you a cab.'

'Thank you very much, but I think there are friends meeting me. Yes, there they are!'

The officer lays a brotherly hand on my arm—

'You're all right, then, sir? Enjoy your stay!'

—and he returns to the other perspiring passengers.

The comedy of national prestige is over.

(ii) *Into a land of music*

Doming (Domenico) and his wife, Trining (Trinidad), came quietly over to greet me, in the way members of the same family greet each other, without excitement, part of a long continuity. It was as if we had met last week, instead of a year ago. A moment later we were in their large American car being driven at hair-raising speed, in and out of the most dangerous drivers in Asia, to their home in the heart of Manila.

'We thought you might be late, so we're not having dinner at home,' Doming explained, as we off-loaded my luggage at home and set off again.

We dined at a small Spanish restaurant down town. The principal dish, at my request, was *bacalao*, cod cooked in a style which must originally, I think, have been Portuguese. Although it is nearly sixty years since Spain was forced by the United States to release her hold on the Philippines, Spanish cultural influence is still strong. The priests in many of the churches are Spanish, the leading colleges in Manila are run by the Church and many of the teachers are Spaniards. Spanish is spoken widely, particularly among the well-to-do, the children of the rich are often sent to Spain to complete their education—and there is always room in Manila for an enterprising Spanish restaurateur.

In the one-room air-conditioned restaurant—there was only enough space for ten tables—Manila's three principal languages, Spanish, English and the native Tagalog, were being spoken. At one table a Philippine Chinese family was entertaining cousins on a visit from Hongkong. Like many of their kind in the Philippines, they were from the Chiuchow district of Kwangtung, speaking their distinctive dialect, somewhat resembling Fukienese. At another table a lively young Filipino was giving a flawless impersonation, greeted with much laughter from his friends, of a big-shot British business man giving his opinion of 'the natives'—out of date, perhaps, but less so in Manila than it would be in London.

During dinner three guitarists played Spanish and Philippine melodies, the principal player singing in Spanish and Tagalog. They performed with the innate musicianship which is a principal feature of the Islands' culture. In every eastern country except China there are well-developed musical arts. The classical music of India can, intellectually speaking, only be compared with musical development in Europe; in Asia it is in a class apart. Its appeal is limited, however, and if, in speaking of music in Asia, one confines oneself to music's fundamental aim of making melody, the Philippines become unquestionably the greatest centre of this art in the East. Their northern and southern neighbours, Japan and Indonesia, have prolific and flourishing musical traditions, but the Philippines' long connexion with Spain has given their music a quality unique in the continent. Spanish music, singularly suited to the temperament and climate of the Philippines, has acted like a touchstone in the life of a people with profound natural musical gifts.

The guitarists moved from table to table, a custom which in Europe invariably fills me with embarrassment. It is almost impossible to play well when moving about, and though serenading of this kind may be socially amusing, musically it is often no more than a good tune spoilt. The Filipino players only moved between the numbers they performed. While playing, they remained still, rather serious, entirely absorbed in following the singer, and what they presented was art of a much higher order than anything one might expect to hear in similar circumstances in the West. Like all really good musicians, they did not play around with the music. Every tempo was exactly maintained, every harmony as the composer would have wished it, every note in a melody given its true value, every phrase its mood. I temporarily forgot all about the *bacalao*.

(iii) *Where East is West and West is East*

'Now, Doming, we're going to have a quiet time,' said Trining firmly, after we had momentarily exhausted our personal news. 'You haven't come over here to go dancing every night, have you?' she went on, giving me a look to indicate that I had better be firm now, otherwise we might none of us have any sleep for a week.

But Doming reassured her.

'Sure, we're going to give him a quiet time—I imagine,' he ended in a different tone as the street door admitted another highly attractive Filipina whose face broke into a broad smile as she saw us.

'Trining darling, I knew you'd be here. Hi, Doming,' she said, sweeping past the Chinese, who all stopped talking. 'You're their British friend.' She looked me up and down as if I were a horse. 'I just couldn't wait. I had to have a look at you.'

Asia, famed as the continent of downtrodden womanhood, in fact rejoices in having more outspoken women than any other continent. Every country in Asia produces them. I cannot imagine what life would be like without them, and there is one rule in dealing with them: give as good as you get.

I turned icily to the beautiful newcomer, and having noted that she wore a wedding ring, said:

'I take it you are not contemplating divorce.' (I had no idea who she was.)

She gave a rich laugh.

'We're going to have a wonderful time,' she said. 'My! you people are eating *bacalao*. That looks good.'

And so we were four.

Trining looked wistfully at our rapidly-departing quiet evening. Doming, satisfied with the situation, smiled and said nothing.

'This is my great friend Nati,' said Trining, introducing the newcomer, who was already helping herself from the casserole.

'Stands for Natividad, my dear,' said the boisterous one, nibbling at a small piece of cod to see how hot it was, 'but you don't have to say all that every time.' Finding it not too hot, she ate a whole mouthful. 'Say, can you dance the cha-cha?'

'Now, don't you start that,' I said. 'Last time I came here they said could I dance the guaracha, and maybe next time it'll be the meringuo. But the answer is always No.'

'Ever seen a penguin?'

'Yes. We have them in the London Zoo.'

'You have? Well, when you dance the cha-cha, you look like one.'

Doming, observing that we were now heading hard for the Skyroom, encouraged me.

'Nati's the right person. She'll teach you all the steps. Let's go round afterwards.'

Trining appealed:

'No, Doming! Not tonight! He's only just arrived.'

Nati looked at me in amazement.

'You're not tired, are you?'

'Well, not exactly.'

She caught me out that time. I reverted to type.

Once again the street door opened. This time Senen and his wife, Carmencita, came in and it was I who first rose at a sign of recognition. Senen, in his thirties, tall, heavily built and rather Chinese in appearance, with a pale beardless face and large expressive eyes, was a prominent lawyer. Carmencita, one of the most attractive women in a city which boasts a higher percentage than most, was a socialite in her own right, a well-known amateur actress and musician. Her eyes laughed permanently, and the edges of her lips curved very slightly upwards, provocatively.

Doming and Senen were close friends, Carmencita and Nati went to the same parties. There were greetings all round. And so we were six.

Senen and Carmen had just come in for a snack after a cinema show.

'We're going to take him on to learn the cha-cha,' said Nati. 'You'd better join us. The cha-cha is good for the soul, and it'll bring your weight down, Senen dear; you're too fat.'

While more food was ordered, and another bottle of Spanish wine opened, Nati and Carmen chattered, Senen reminded me that his wife exaggerated, and Trining, with a look of resignation, allowed herself to be buffeted, and amused, by the high spirits of the others. With bewildering cross-patterns, the conversation wandered in and out of English and Spanish, with an occasional domestic bustle of Tagalog, a language that sounds extraordinarily like Malay yet is in fact mysteriously different from it, identical words bearing entirely different meanings.

Being momentarily forgotten amid a discussion of the latest political scandal—Nati's husband, I now gathered, was a politician on the verge of cabinet rank—I found myself once more going through the same sentiments of wonder and strangeness as always assail me soon after arrival in the Philippines: that here, so far from Europe, among an Asian people, one can feel so absolutely at home.

Yes, an Asian people—though there are often times when one finds it hard to believe. In spite of centuries of colonization by Spain, it is said that the European ethnic strain in the islanders amounts to less than three per cent. Yet, arriving from Hongkong or Japan or any other nearby country, it is like coming home.

Doming, in addition to having the quiet manners usually associated with Englishmen, had a European cast of features. Of medium height, with a high forehead and receding hair, his eyes, with their slight tints of dark hazel, were entirely European; so too his lips, which were thinner than normal in South-East Asia. One gauged his reactions in the same way as one does with Europeans, without resort to the searching intuitions that are needed among Asians with less expressive features. With his fluent command of English and Spanish it was impossible to feel the least remoteness from him. Only his slightly flat nose and wide nostrils, and his golden-brown Malay skin, reminded me, at rare occasions, that we came from opposite sides of the earth.

Trining, somewhere in her ancestry, must have had some Chinese blood. Her skin was less warm than her husband's, but her soft narrow features, dark eyes, restful and reflective, gave her too a European appearance, added to which of course was a European hairstyle and tropical European dress.

Nati, wearing a tropical version of an up-to-date New York model, was nevertheless more Asian in looks, with wide-set eyes, two dark pools to study in a face that, apart from them, concealed with regularity of features more than it revealed. Her lips were heavy, ruminating, assessing, and her fingers, enhanced by two large diamond rings, were podgy from over-eating. Senen and Carmen both looked slightly Chinese by comparison with Doming and Trining, and in fact they each had one Chinese grandparent, though possibly even he or she, being of the Philippines, may not have been pure-blooded Chinese.

It sounds needlessly analytical to describe one's friends in terms of race. But the Philippines have throughout history been a meeting-place of races, and to anyone who has travelled in Asia and seen the various races in their own surroundings it is intriguing to distinguish them here and there in the Manila crowd, people with Spanish names and a Catholic upbringing, yet wearing the features of other races of whom perhaps they have no personal knowledge. Sit beside the pedestrian walks on Dewey Boulevard, the Manila seafront, for twenty minutes, and you will see the characteristic types of every nation in Asia go by: dreamy handsome Malays, pale expressionless Chinese, pensive heavy-featured Cambodians, sun-tanned Malayan Chinese, dark thin South Indians, and even, now and then, a pale Spaniard with light brown hair—all Filipinos. And about them all, something distinctive—a swing, a swagger in the men, in the women self-assurance and poise—life with a dash of something in it.

'I've finished. Let's go,' announced Nati, taking a rouge-stick out of her compact.

'Hey! Go easy there!' said Senen. 'We've hardly begun.'

Once more the restaurant door opened, and with visions of fearful complications I saw, of all people, Winkle Miao enter with two pale fat Chinese big-shots and a skinny, humourless Chinese woman, presumably the wife of one of them.

But I need not have worried. Winkle would never put a social foot wrong. With a quick glance at my Filipino friends, she waited till her host had chosen his table, and only when they were all seated did she give me a wave of recognition, accompanied by a smile which ended in a comic grimace as the musicians started again near her.

'You know that Chinese lady?' asked Doming quietly.

'Yes, but not the others,' I added hastily, as I saw the two Amoy merchants, socially out of their depth with Winkle, discussing furtively in Chinese what they should order from the patient but faintly supercilious Spanish *maître*.

'Why, what's wrong with them?' Doming enquired with a curious smile.

'Oh, nothing special.'

He laughed quietly.

'I see what you mean. You've got a quicker eye for them than we have over here.'

'Your friend looks kind of nice,' said Nati. 'Why don't you go over and speak to her?'

But there Doming's English nature obtruded gently.

'Give him time,' he said to Nati.

'Some friends of yours?' asked Senen, who had his back to Winkle's table.

'One very good Chinese friend,' I answered.

And, just as if we were in Europe, all of them knew, but none of them looked round.

·   ·   ·   ·   ·

As we left the restaurant I stopped for a moment beside Winkle's table. We had parted company only a few days earlier in Hongkong, so no elaborate greetings were required. The Amoy merchants, looking acutely embarrassed, talked hard among themselves in their own dialect, leaving Winkle and me to exchange a few words in English. Like many merchants of their kind, although they had probably lived outside China for the greater part of their lives, their knowledge of non-Chinese customs and etiquette was slight. It is not customary in China to stop at someone else's table on the way out of a restaurant, and the merchants did thus not know what to do.

'I didn't know you liked Spanish food, Winkle,' I said, as the others all turned their heads away.

'One has to keep alive somehow in this joint,' she replied. 'Most of the Chinese food's uneatable.'

'I know. It's a tough life'—this with a glance at the merchants' backs.

Winkle suppressed an enormous giggle.

'Get away with you!' she said, slapping my sleeve.

With a wink that was promptly reciprocated, I rejoined my friends, leaving her to battle on, trying—if I may misuse a Cantonese expression—to cover a chicken basket with a flowered quilt. Such deceptions are consoling in exile.

(iv) *And the twain meet in a paso doble*

Outside in the warm street it was raining again. While we were waiting for the cars to be driven up, another group of young people, sheltered in twos under umbrellas, came along from another restaurant. They were looking for their cars.

'Felipe!'

'Doming! Hi, Senen!'

There were greetings all round. I had met some of the newcomers on former visits; to others I was now introduced.

'We're going to teach him to dance the cha-cha. Why don't you join us?'

Trining looked at me and silently raised her eyebrows.

And so we were—fourteen?—no, sixteen.

The cars drove up, and because of the haste required to avoid the rain, we piled in without worrying who was with whom. I found myself with Felipe and his lynx-eyed wife, who spent the time talking to another woman in rapid Spanish about the price of cosmetics and how much it was going to cost to have some of her diamonds reset.

Felipe and I conducted an exchange of platitudes. He was a narrow-faced man of thirty-five, with pale skin, small restless eyes and lips twisted with self-indulgence. We viewed each other with mutual disinterest. I had always met him on occasions such as this, and had no idea whether he had an occupation or any interests other than being seen at parties with his over-dressed wife. The only clue I had about him dated from some years earlier when he had driven me, with some other friends, to Baguio, the former summer capital during the American period and a famous mountain beauty spot. Passing through the province of Pampanga he casually mentioned that we were passing through his family lands. In answer to a query from me, he pointed out his home, not far from the main road, explaining that all the land in every direction belonged to his father.

'I suppose you come here for holidays?' I said.

His expression darkened.

'No. There's nothing doing here.'

'Doesn't anyone live there, then?'

'My father used to, but I prefer Manila.'

'What is that crop, anyway?' I asked, pointing to some fields.

'I've no idea,' he replied, carefully lighting a cigarette at the wheel, ending the discussion by addressing someone in the rear seat in Tagalog.

I waited till this exchange finished.

'But I think I would much prefer to live here than in Manila,' I said.

Felipe drew at his cigarette.

'If you could avoid being kidnapped it'd be all right. This isn't England, you know.'

As we drove through the Manila night rain, this conversation came back into my thoughts. The car swung out of the main highway, there was a glare of lights, uniformed men ran down steps to open the car doors. We passed into another air-conditioned coolness where, in the foyer, we reassembled before entering a large ballroom.

It lacked intimacy. On a smaller scale it had the same empty feeling of a drill room that one finds in the popular ballrooms of Blackpool and Hammersmith, and for the same reason—that people came here to dance. A few seconds after the band started playing, the large floor filled up with couples, leaving most of the tables around deserted—white cloths and empty chairs.

The dancers were uniformly smart, most of the men in tropical lounge suits, the women in American cocktail-length dresses of light tropical materials. Here and there were couples in evening dress, some of the women wearing the charming *mestiza* costume of pineapple fibre that is distinctive of the Philippines, with its high butterfly-wing shoulders, stiff and transparent, a colourful mist of pale pinks, yellows and blues. Some of the men were in dinner jackets, others wearing the *barong tagalog*, the pineapple fibre shirt with embroidered front, which, worn outside dress trousers and with only a sleeved vest underneath, is by far the most sensible evening gear for men in any tropical country.

The dancing—spirited, carefree, with easy grace—was of a standard that put most American or European ballrooms to shame, while as for the band—well, the best bands throughout Asia depend on Filipino musicians, this was Manila, and it was consequently a dance band of dance bands, such as can sometimes be found in America, but never in Europe. Every rhythm it played—

'You can dance this,' said Nati.

'No, I can't.'

'I don't believe it. Let's try.'

—turned out to be one which, given the indispensable adjunct of a talented Filipina partner, one found oneself dancing, almost without learning the steps.

(v) *Insecure dance-floor*

Thoughts while dancing are disconnected, yet sometimes, like dreams, at the time they seem to make sense. But they are mixed up with moments of concentration on a tricky step, a sudden swing to avoid another couple, a yes or a no to a chattering partner. They hold together somehow, although no more than stray thoughts, lost when the music stops. But they have an unreliable tendency to become dramatic, picturesque, flamboyant. They are not so much thoughts as indications.

Dancing with Nati it occurred to me that Manila is like the bridge at Avignon: '*l'on y danse, l'on y danse*'! It is part of the national self-expression of the Filipinos to dance. Doming's six-year-old son gave me a masterly display of the rumba, with one of his girl cousins of the same age. Their grandfather, who was looking on, scornfully dismissed my expression of amazement.

'When I was their age I could do much better than that,' he said, and he was not given to exaggeration.

But if you dance on the bridge at Avignon, you dance on a useless structure, a broken bridge, leading nowhere, not traversing the Rhône; and if you have an enemy he could come with two men to the head of the bridge and catch the lot of you, like rats in a trap, for if you jumped into the water you would quickly be swept away and drowned in its smooth swift current. In Manila it comes to the same thing. You dance in a small air-conditioned enclave which a good security officer would condemn as dangerous because it is built on rent, and all around it, in the hot air outside, are the people who pay the rent but cherish the idea of possessing land of their own. Felipe's wife's diamonds were paid for with rent, and they were going to be reset with rent.

'Shall we take revolvers?' Doming had once asked, as we set out on the 45-minute drive round to Cavite, on the other side of Manila Bay. His tone of voice was the same as ours in London when we wonder whether or not to take umbrellas.

And one day too we went out into the country to take a look at some of Grandfather's land. It was a part of the province that had until fairly recently been in the hands of the Hukbalahap rebels and totally unsafe for Manila landlords. Things were much better than five years ago; the Government was bringing the Huk problem under control. But when we reached the village there were discussions as to how far it would be safe for each of us to go. It would have been nice to see the view from that hill, but this would be unsafe. We could go as far as the end of the village, but no farther. And Grandfather had better not even come as far as the village.

We were escorted by the *teniente del barrio*, the village head. In the village itself there were young men cleaning rifles, and I was told they were village guards. The *teniente* was the head of the guards.

'Then, with all this armed might around,' I asked, 'why can't we go and see the view from the hill?'

'Don't you see?' muttered Doming under his breath. 'The *teniente* is the local Huk leader.'

And Grandfather owned most of the land.

Stray thoughts—we were hotting up towards the end of a paso doble—Nati danced like a sylph—stray thoughts that wandered in and out among the dancing couples, that crept inside saxophones and were rumoured out of trombones, that sat in the expressionless eyes and fixed smiles of people concentrating on steps and movements, wearing shoes purchased with rent—stray thoughts. But things were much better. Five years ago there were no trains running, and when we went to Baguio the cars travelled in convoy at top speed all the way, stopping nowhere, not even for the ladies. Yes, things were much better now. All the same, every time we swung round and I saw those tall windows in the upper floor where we danced—but one's imagination sometimes becomes too vivid—I wondered if Madame de Lamballe's head might be about to appear, on a spike.

I boggled at the cha-cha. I had no wish to look like a penguin. After dancing for quite a time and drinking a liqueur—one of the social joys of the Philippines is that people do not, as in China, press you to drink more than you should—we reached the moment when convention allowed us to go home peacefully to bed.

I should add that, having met still more people in the ballroom, we ended up being twenty-two, which, bearing in mind that we started with three, may be classed as a moderate Manila evening.

(vi) *Western lights and oriental shadows*

We were home. No one had a key so we had to wait in the street while Doming called softly to rouse a servant without waking the whole street. Mercifully it had stopped raining.

In all the years I have known Doming and Trining, no one has ever had a key. Instead, at no matter what fearful hour of the night, someone has to be dug out to open the front door. Perhaps this is another Spanish custom. Certainly, on the occasions when I have arrived unexpectedly at night and rung the bell the reception was decidedly Spanish: no movement at all till after three rings of the bell, and after that the almost imperceptible opening of an upper window in darkness above. This is the moment one raises one's face to the moon, so as to be seen clearly. Then, although there is still a long wait to endure, it is unnecessary to ring again. The servant has to find the master of the house, say who has arrived, and ask for permission to open the door. Usually permission is not given, because the master himself wishes to open the door—which means finding slippers and a clean shirt first—and finally—anyway, what warmer welcome?

After repeated soft calls, a dull-eyed maidservant opened the front door and we went in. Trining went to bed at once, worn out. I too was exhausted, but as we walked into the living room, and the tranquil atmosphere of their home surrounded me, I reached that state of combined exhaustion and contentment whch puts further movement temporarily out of the question. Doming and I collapsed into heavily upholstered armchairs, really too hot for the tropics.

From somewhere an iced beer turned up on a small Spanish card table beside me. There was a long silence.

At either end of the tapestried sofa on which Doming was spread out were two low standard lamps, Chinese porcelain figures of Kwan Yin set into European tables and with the lights coming out from the top of their heads. The shades were small versions of those used over billiard tables, and the light they threw was subdued, projected downwards on faded Persian rugs, low Chinese tables inlaid with mother-of-pearl, and the gleaming red-tiled floor, in which, as one walked across it, sometimes a tile moved slightly. From the top of the shades, light rayed out over the wall in the shape of two fans, displaying a landscape by one of the country's most famous artists, using the European technique of a generation ago, but with a mastery and vitality that gave it complete conviction—a stream with bamboos beside it, and a country girl leading two buffaloes down to drink. In the far corner was a radiogram, near me a small table with a rest in which a number of weirdly shaped pipes hung without any likelihood of being used. No one smoked pipes, but pipes were friendly to have around. The window bars were of decorative wrought iron, and the leaves of a creeper were coming in through a window which someone had not closed properly. Outside, the sky had evidently cleared. Moonlight threw into relief the meaningless patterns on the frosted glass panes.

On my left, across the room, two low steps led up to another part used as a dining room. From where I sat I could not see what I was looking for. Even by opening my eyes and looking round I would not be able to see anything but the dining table and some pictures on the far wall, unless perhaps just the end of one of the two antique dressers could be seen, with a glint of pink in cut glass caught in the low glow of the Kwan Yin lamps. But I was too sleepy to look round. It was just as satisfying to stay with my eyes half-shut and be comfortably aware of what was round the corner out of view: the dresser shelves filled with early English porcelain imitating Chinese styles, and later Chinese porcelain imitating English styles. That amusing and decorative collection was the final clue that re-created the illusion of being at home. It was one of Doming's eccentricities—so were the pipes, so was trying to make me feel a fool because I could not dance the cha-cha.

Oriental people are outwardly more strait-laced than we are.

There is little room for eccentricity in oriental life, and as a result, when eccentricity comes to the surface it often does so uncompromisingly, like a jet of water bursting through a small hole. In the West we set a higher value on eccentricity. We make room for it, and as a result it breathes in comfort, doing little damage and a lot of good. It is integrated into our way of living.

Doming's eccentricities were like ours. The fanatic despair which often accompanies oriental eccentricity was entirely absent from this house. The peculiar bowls and dishes, which no one else would bother to collect, smiled beneficently from their shelves, irritating the mind like a discordant note neatly contrived into a subtle piece of music. The irritation did not hurt or offend; it simply made one's belly shake, pushing up a tremor which, because we were very tired, ultimately issued forth like the grunt of a small pig.

'What's wrong?' asked Doming.

The silence broken, we became aware of each other again and sat up.

'Nothing at all. I'm suffering from my usual incapacity to believe the evidence of my senses. We are in Europe, and we are cousins, or something like that.'

He laughed slightly. The room and the city were still.

'You don't like Felipe, do you?' he said thoughtfully.

'I wouldn't say that. I think he's been over-indulged all his life, and I find it difficult to talk to people like that. Besides, he doesn't seem to have much sense of responsibility. If he's scared of going back to his lands because he might be kidnapped, why doesn't he sell out to the people who need the fields for their own use?'

'Did you ask him that?'

'Of course not. How could I? I hardly know him.'

'You could, you know. He could take it.'

I sat up still further.

'Doming, there's some bond between you and Felipe. What is it?'

He lit a cigarette.

'Nothing special. We were in the same outfit during the Japanese occupation. We were imprisoned together by the Japanese in Fort Santiago.'

Filipinos, their critics say, are flashy, spectacular people without

137

much depth. They cannot be relied on, and would be risky allies in war.

'What sort of outfit was it?'

'Nothing really. Organizing sabotage and passing out information to the Americans. There wasn't much else we could do.'

Spectacular people who have rendered service to their country generally like to talk about it. I had known Doming a number of years, and this was the first time he had ever mentioned the matter.

'How were you caught?'

'By pure chance. The Japanese police were searching the house of one of us in connexion with something quite different. In the house they found an American tabloid magazine. It didn't mean much to them, but they took it away, and of course at their headquarters someone must have spotted the date of the magazine, which was recent. From just that one slip-up they knew we had some means of contact with the Americans.'

'What happened?'

'Oh, they were clever. We felt they must be after us, but when day after day nothing happened we weren't sure. In fact, they were waiting for us to make the first move. Against Felipe's advice actually, we moved—it was a scheme we'd been preparing for some time and it did quite a lot of damage. Our show went off all right. They let it. From it they learnt the mechanics of the thing, and within a few hours we were all arrested.'

In spite of the late hour I could not let this moment slip by without enquiry. 'I understand Fort Santiago was bad enough under the Spaniards,' I said. 'Presumably the Japanese added a few distinctive touches of their own.'

Doming looked down at his feet and said simply:

'I don't know what the Japanese were like in other countries, but it was the most terrible experience of my life. . . . You want another beer?'

There are terrible experiences which are recounted at noon after a week's acquaintance. There are others that are not told till after five or more years of friendship, and then only at half-past two in the night.

'If there is one,' I replied.

'Ricardo!' he called quietly.

There was a movement in the kitchen beyond, as another of the servants, a sixteen-year-old lad from Doming's father's province, staggered to his feet and came sleepily into the far end of the dining room.

'*Cerveza.*'

We could have gone quite easily to the refrigerator in the kitchen and taken it out ourselves, but that was not the way. The only revolution the country looks back to is the overthrow of the Spaniards.

'Yes,' he went on, 'it was tough.' I said nothing, waiting for him to continue. 'The prison was just a small stone room. There was no window, but during the day a little light filtered through from somewhere high in the ceiling. We each had our section of the floor where you sat with your knees up, in rows facing each other. No one was allowed to move, stand up, or speak, and there were two Japanese guards at the entrance day and night. There was a single hole in the floor which we all had to use, but people got dysentery and couldn't control themselves. And if you weren't careful you got covered with lice. The man next to me had lice on him. At night he used to become frantic, trying to pick them off. Then he'd be delirious, and call out for the saints to help him, and for his mother. In the end he went mad, and they took him away.'

'How many were there in the cell?'

'Thirty-eight to begin with. But if a man died you were allowed to call to the guards, and in the morning they'd send an orderly to look at him and have him carried out. There was one man begging his neighbour to strangle him. He'd had enough.'

'And Felipe was with you.'

'Yes. If it hadn't been for him we might have been worse off. He kept a sort of control over the others. When the guards changed, or when they were half-asleep, we could talk in undertones. Felipe kept faith alive in that place. And he got it worse than any of us. Again and again he was taken out for questioning. He was horribly beaten. He was given the water treatment. They just flung him back in again afterwards. But somehow he stood it.'

'I suppose you thought you'd never get out.'

'It varied. Sometimes for several days you had hope. After that there would be days of no hope. And days when there was hope which you kind of manufactured but which you knew was just a delusion.'

'How long were you there? Can you remember?'

'Of course. That was the one thing we all knew. I was there for eighty-three days, Felipe for another week longer. In the end we were all released, though why we none of us know to this day. But if it hadn't been for Felipe I don't think any of us would have come out alive. I think we'd have killed each other, scrapping over food and water, and with the others we thought were filthier than ourselves.'

As he spoke, each feature of the room, each single item of comfort and good taste, seemed to grow larger and more important. A deeper harmony pervaded everything, as if it were of itself some silent but absolute reply to the evil that had preceded it. Even Felipe's wife's diamonds, in retrospect, sparkled with a less chilly allure.

'I sometimes think the Japanese must have been worse to the Filipinos than to any of the other Asian people they conquered,' I said.

'I wouldn't know. You may be right. We didn't fit into their scheme of things. They got us all wrong from the start. Most of the ordinary Japanese, the soldiers and police, hated us because they thought we were aping the Americans. They didn't seem to be able to understand that we don't ape anyone. We behave as we are. In some ways we're very Spanish, in other ways very American. Shouting political slogans at us won't change that.'

I finally got to bed at three, and shortly after five there was daylight and the claxons of hurrying motor cars and no curtains on the windows because that would have made the room too hot. I pretended to myself that I was still asleep, until at six the boy Ricardo made a mistake and brought the morning coffee which had been ordered for eight. But what was the use of complaining when if one did not really rather enjoy it one would never go to Manila anyway?

(vii) *A thumbnail sketch of Philippine history*

Unlike other Asian territories that have been colonized by western nations, the Philippines have no great traditions to look back to before their colonial period. In their pre-Spanish history there is no Asoka or Akbar. It is even probable the entire island group was only united for the first time under a single effective government during the American period, for the Spaniards, although nominally in control of all the islands, held only a shadowy sway over the remoter parts, the people of which, provided they did not interfere with Spanish interests, were left much to their own devices. The Philippines today are an adventure in nationhood, and because of the country's unusual historic background it is an adventure of exceptional interest.

The original human material of the Philippine nation is not unlike that of Indonesia, Borneo and Malaya. The earliest known inhabitants were Negritos, some of whom still survive. About two thousand years ago migrant visitors began to arrive by various routes, tribal people akin to the Malays, possibly driven out of what is now South China by the expansion of the Chinese nation during the Han dynasty. The later arrivals had a fair degree of culture; the earlier migrants were more primitive and are the probable ancestors of some of the tribes that still live in the wilder parts of the archipelago.

Trading contacts with the Chinese, and a small amount of intermarriage, probably go back to the first centuries of the Christian era. The first important association with a superior civilization, however, occurred during the great period of Indian overseas expansion between the second and ninth centuries. The Philippines became part of the system of related Hindu and Buddhist states loosely known today as Further India, which stretched across the whole of South-East Asia from the Bay of Bengal to Formosa. There was trade and probably some intermarriage with Indians.

Whether the Islands were actually ruled by Indians is more doubtful, but certainly the culture of the trading towns was Hindu, possibly also influenced by the declining institutions of Indian Buddhism. The Islands were evidently administered as a group of small kingdoms, some of which may have been little larger than private estates, dominating hardly more than the ports, rivers and easily accessible hinterland. By the early fifteenth century there were probably substantial Chinese trading communities in most of the principal centres.

The Arabs had traded for centuries in South-East Asia. When they accepted Islam as their religion, they emerged for the first time as a political factor in the region's affairs. In the early part of this millennium they began to undermine the Indonesian Hindu and Buddhist states, unobtrusively spreading their own beliefs and fomenting local palace revolutions, until the whole of civilized Malaya and Indonesia, with the sole exception of the island of Bali, came under direct Muslim rule. By the fifteenth century the movement had reached the southern Philippines, of which Mindanao, the second largest island in the group, became what parts of it have remained to this day, a Muslim zone. Without doubt the movement would have continued until the entire archipelago was part of Islam.

At this juncture came the irruption of Europeans into East Asia, led by the Portuguese, who, within fifteen years of Vasco da Gama's epic voyage to India, put an end to the mercantile power of the Arabs. The frontiers of Islam in South-East Asia ceased to expand and have hardly altered since.

The Islands' first contact with this new era in Asian affairs was the arrival in 1521 of a Spanish expedition led by the Portuguese adventurer Magellan, who had deserted his monarch and taken Spanish citizenship. Under the Treaty of Tordesillas, which confirmed the extraordinary division of the world by the Borgia pope, Alexander VI, into Portuguese and Spanish spheres of influence, the new-found islands were claimed for Spain. Some years later they were imposingly named the Philippines, in honour of King Philip II, and it then only remained for Spain to conquer them.

This King Philip set about doing in 1565. The conquest was an uncompromising affair, the classic example of sword in one hand and Bible in the other. The islanders were forcibly deprived of power and offered Paradise instead. The early conversions, we are told in the chronicles of the Church, were wonderful. As the Spanish priests did not at first understand the islanders' languages and the islanders knew no Spanish, one can see what they mean.

Hindu and Buddhist beliefs and traditions were stamped out. The zealots were determined to extinguish even the memory of the past, which partly accounts for the present lack of historical information concerning the pre-Spanish period. They next set about their real job, to build their own version of the Kingdom of Christ on Earth, which, like all human systems carried relentlessly to logical conclusions, produced only a realm of asphyxiation.

The first puff of fresh air to blow in was an indirect result of the otherwise unedifying British conquest of Manila and parts of Luzon in 1761–3, part of the Seven Years' War. Another and far more important freshening influence was the growth of liberalism in nineteenth-century Spain, which inevitably now and again brought to the Philippines civil administrators of liberal outlook, and which in time permitted the growth of a Philippine liberal nationalist movement among Filipino students and others resident in Madrid. This last, in which Rizal figured, had a powerful influence in the Philippines, stimulating progressive and revolutionary thought.

Aware of the danger of these developments to its power, the Church in the Philippines did its utmost to defend the kingdom it had wrought, and which had hitherto remained so satisfyingly motionless in an era of change. The defensive measures included suppression of all criticism of Church or Government, censorship of the Press, the opening of private correspondence, the banning of scientific subjects in schools, and a prohibition on the import of any literature concerned in the slightest degree with modern scientific or political concepts. At the same time the fervour of the devout was stimulated by reports of miracles and what was little short of a manufacture and sale of sacred relics.

English visitors in the later part of the last century have left descriptions of the last and most hideous phase of the Church's kingdom of perfection. Due to its immense ownership of land and its political hold over the people, the Church was in effect more powerful than the civil government. The judicial system was a mockery; people were imprisoned and even executed without consideration of any pleas of defence. On the merest whim, the Church would dispossess and engineer the imprisonment or deportation of any whom its members feared or disliked. In addition to censorship there was a spying system which reached into the interior of many homes. Some of the priests seen in the streets bore marks of syphilis, and their places of assignation and the nature of their arrangements in this respect were an open secret.

Finally, in 1896, a revolution broke out, led by extremists in the movement for national liberation. Because of censorship and the remoteness of the country, it is not easy to find reliable information about it. It was a clash between oppressed exasperation and last-ditch arrogance, conducted with brutality on both sides, and it appears to rank with the Indian Mutiny as being one of the most violent expressions of anti-European sentiment in Asian history. It happened to coincide with a war between Spain and the United States, in the course of which an American fleet was sent to take control of the Islands. After negotiations with the Filipino rebels and the Spaniards the Americans ended by undertaking the reduction of the rebellion and the acquisition of the country for themselves.

They were quick to rectify this somewhat questionable intrusion into Philippine affairs, and by 1902, when internal order was finally restored, they set the country on the road to modern nationhood, thereafter introducing a succession of liberal measures which by 1936 had brought the Filipinos a large measure of independence. The Church came to its senses, and in doing so produced the principal miracle in the history of its mission in the Islands—the fact that the Philippines is still today a predominantly Catholic country.

After the war the Americans spared neither money nor effort to put in hand the tremendous work of rehabilitation rendered necessary by the damage done, particularly to Manila, in the last phase of the Japanese defeat. On 4 July 1946 the Philippines became fully independent. Since then they have had economic ties with the United States which have somewhat isolated them from their neighbours in Asia. The rectification of this position, which has come to seem somewhat unnatural, is one of the changes which presumably lie ahead.

(viii) *A choice of culture*

Doming's family reflected some of the change and much of the enduring quality in the Philippine nation which are the two principal features of the country's last sixty years. His grandfather, who died between the two world wars, was one of the few Filipinos to hold a relatively high public office under the Spaniards. Though sympathizing with the more liberal patriots, such as Rizal, he was opposed to the activities of the Katipunan, the secret society from which the revolution of 1896 was kindled. He was absolutely opposed to the Americans, and when they assumed power he retired from public life. His feelings on the matter became more personal when his son, Doming's father, learnt English and ran away to the United States. The father disowned his son.

The son, however, was not entirely impressed by what he saw of American life, and having made his way in the United States by his own industry, without support from home, he travelled to Europe, where in Spain he found a mental climate more suited to his outlook. When he finally returned to the Philippines—and was reconciled with his father—he had found in his own life the balance between two different national cultures imposed upon a tropical Asian temperament and physique which is in fact today a true expression of the Philippine nation. By temperament he became a member of the small but influential section of Manila society which sought to preserve cultural ties with Spain in the face of the rapidly increasing americanization of the larger and less-well-off social classes, who under the Americans were finding greater freedom and opportunity than they ever had under the Spaniards. In Doming's personality this same balance was reproduced.

But the influences were not as simple as this. In families of this kind it is the custom for each child to have its own nurse, from whom, quite naturally, it learns its first language. Trining, for example, told me that as a child her nurse was Chinese, and until she was about fifteen she herself was fluent in Amoy dialect. For their own children Doming and Trining had employed only Filipina nurses, but these spoke a variety of languages. Their eldest daughter had had a nurse from Albay province, and the little girl's first language was thus Bicol. Two of the boys were brought up mouthing Tagalog, another Visayan.

As soon as they were older and coming more under the direct influence of their parents, the children all learnt Spanish. As soon as they started going to school, mixing with children of other families, going to the cinema and looking wonderingly at newspapers, English was added. In other words, they started life with a fair load of languages, with the possibility of not learning any of them really well. Trining struggled against this by minutely supervising their homework, but not every parent, I knew from experience, was as conscientious as she.

(ix) *The complications of an alien folklore*

The cultural parts played by the two European languages are interesting in relation one to the other. Spanish is the Philippines' main cultural link with the mature civilization of Europe and with the Catholic Church. Though it is probably spoken less than it was fifty years ago, there is an undeniable sentiment that it is the language of a gentleman. English, on the other hand, is not a link with Europe. At the present time, for example, it is not possible to buy a single British magazine from any of Manila's newspaper vendors. English is an exclusively American link, a material influence as much as a cultural one (the language of refrigerators, television, automobiles and bars), and chiefly because it is the language of the main newspapers and radio stations, it is also the principal channel by which political thought enters from outside.

It does not mean that the Philippines are politically a suburb of the United States. Far from it. Asian and Spanish influences innate in their manner of thinking make this unlikely. They have too individual a background. Where the American way of thinking really registers is in anything directly concerning the Philippines. The country is an unusual example of a nation which sees itself in some respects as another nation sees it. Certain catch phrases, repeated doubtless by two generations of Americans, and possibly by the Spaniards before them, have become part of the national folklore, as inevitable as the answers in a catechism.

The folklore is entertaining and easy to learn, but as an outsider I have to admit to being unconvinced by much of it. The Filipinos, so runs part of it, have a champagne palate and a coca-cola pocket. In other words, they spend their money before it is earned, and make a display of prosperity on borrowed money or by not paying their debts. Presuming this to be true, is it particularly a Filipino failing? Does the same not apply to their neighbours, the Malays, the Thais and the Burmese? It is a characteristic of the high-spirited energy and bonhomie of the South-East Asian peoples to spend up to the hilt, and sometimes—by accident, of course—a good deal beyond it. As for setting too much store by outward show, let us not be too hasty. When in Europe we wish to build a house we also borrow money, but we give the transaction an air of respectability by calling the people we borrow it from a building society—

which takes good care, incidentally, that we make no default in our payments. If there were no building societies, we would just borrow, and be in a safer position to make excuses about not paying up in time. We are inclined to overlook, too, that climate prevents us from investing in the same things. Our ideals might be a stone or brick house (hot, damp and expensive), good furniture (too much anxiety about bugs; rattan is more practical), books (need constant attention for fear of white ants and damp), and a piano (yes, but they soon wear out). The money spent on these items would in South-East Asia be more likely to go on fine clothes (instead of expensive furniture), a large and powerful car (instead of a stone house), and jewellery (like books and a piano, a pleasure, but also an investment). When we see for the first time people owning American limousines but living in very simple oriental wooden houses, we often leap to faulty conclusions. In fact, the expenditure involved is determined, like our own, with one eye to common sense and the other to prevalent fashion.

Filipinos are lazy. This is a fundamental item in the folklore. It is repeated with infuriating frequency by the majority of Europeans and Americans who have anything to do with the Islands. It is the proverb which ends discussion. After it, people fold their hands and wag their heads. Yes, what is there that even the best-intentioned friend can do? Filipinos just are lazy.

It has been demonstrated in this century that if you repeat something with sufficient emphasis and often enough, even though it is untrue, people will end by believing it. Most Filipinos have ended by believing this part of the folklore. They hotly deny its truth, of course, especially to outsiders; but quietly, inside themselves, they have a disquieting feeling that it really is true. As an assumption it informs a great deal in public life. Everyone should work harder.

A day or so after my arrival a friend drove me out for the day to Tagaytay, one of the great bowls which are a feature of Philippine geography and which were evidently once the craters of enormous volcanoes, such as can be seen in France in the neighbourhood of Le Puy. It was a sunny morning, and the countryside wore its most colourful aspect. After passing through a cool forest of coconut palms we entered a level open scene of rice fields, their flatness broken by occasional groves of bamboo, beyond which, in the distance, the noble form of Mount Makiling rose dark grey-blue, with a single white cloud clinging to it half-way down.

As everywhere in South-East Asia, the people supplied an indispensable ingredient to the beauty of the scene. In England we climb hills to get away from man and his works. Only man is vile, we say. It was hard to have any such sentiment on the road to Tagaytay. Men and women were working here and there in the fields, almost all of them dressed in bright colours, a sky-blue shirt here, a red skirt there, a yellow-and-purple check farther on. The women wore cloths over their heads, the men high straw hats, and along the road we kept on passing them, riding buffaloes or tough and well-fed ponies. Some of them were going to market their goods, which were hung against their horses' flanks in fibre baskets slung from a light cloth saddle. In their gay clothes and high hats they looked irresistibly jaunty, smoking cigarettes or odd-shaped pipes, calling out to their friends as they passed, and winking at young girls. Their curiously European features helped a stranger to identify them. Here came the local Don Juan on a grey pony, here a buccaneer on a buffalo, here a young fellow who liked Westerns, here an older man respected for his fair dealing—the actors in a Spanish rustic drama, but with exaggerated make-up, giving them an added simplicity and liveliness of character. About two-thirds of the people in the fields were men.

'I can hardly believe it,' I said.

'What's that?' my friend asked, concentrating on steering past the ungainly buffaloes.

'Men!' I said.

'Men? So what?'

'Men working in fields,' I said. 'You go into the countryside around Hongkong and there are many villages where you'll never see a man working except for a day or so at planting or harvesting.'

'Is that so? How does the work get done?'

'By the women, of course. They do everything: plough, tend the fields, open the irrigation channels, carry water to the village and nightsoil to the fields, cut grass for fuel, carry stones and tiles for house repairs—and have babies.'

He was interested now.

'What do the men do?' he asked.

'Oh, mostly you can find them in the villages, playing mahjong, gossiping, or else just standing around under a sunshade with the youngest baby strapped to their back.'

'H'm. Easy life,' he commented with a chuckle. 'You'd better keep that quiet over here—mustn't give us ideas. People usually say we're a lazy bunch.'

Far be it from me to criticize ancient wisdom, but I certainly do not think that I myself could work as hard as the people I saw in such a changelessly warm climate.

As for Manila, things move faster there than in any other city of tropical Asia, with the exception of Hongkong which is only just in the tropics and is stimulated by enjoying a winter. Compared with Bangkok or Rangoon, the pace of affairs in Manila is that of a typhoon, and the scale of Filipino business is very much larger than that conducted in South-East Asia by any other than Chinese or Westerners. Perhaps to American visitors it seems slow, and that people do not pull their weight. The clue is, I think, that the delays which occur in transacting business in Manila are not the same as American delays. Filipinos are by temperament more complex than Americans. Steady driving bores them; they prefer to go now fast, now slow. They have ideas of face which are somewhat Chinese. They have difficulty in combining in partnership. Like other Malay people, they crave personal independence. Like the Chinese, their deepest loyalties are personal, rather than to institutions or ideas. These features form a special pattern of existence which, because outwardly their behaviour is extraordinarily western, strangers do not immediately identify and make allowances for. When mysterious delays occur, which by the stranger's standards seem unnecessary, when at the crucial moment of concluding a contract the Filipino business man is found loafing about for several days thinking about something else, the irritated stranger quickly condemns him as lazy. In fact, the Filipino's partner has perhaps not given him full and proper credit for his conduct of the negotiations, with the result that all his zest for the deal has evaporated. Life is more personal than in a western city, but every whit as active.

A third item in the folklore is that the Philippines have a griev-
ously low standard of living. Ministers make references to it in
their speeches. At international conferences the Philippine delegate
may be expected to describe his country, at some stage of the
proceedings, as poor and underdeveloped. This is not a mannerism.
Foreigners, ranging from economic experts to casual visitors, have
told them so, and they believe it. Government policies are framed on
the assumption that this is a correct description.

Well, I know a man in Bulacan province who is a barber. He
lives in a village of moderate size, and when he is not cutting
people's hair he is tending chickens, of which he has about two
hundred, laying eggs for the Manila market which, thanks to the
transport of the local co-operative society, is within reach. He has
a wife and four children, and he lives in a wood-and-fibre house
standing on stilts, like all the other houses in the village, as a protection from rain flooding. His chicken-houses are built on the
same principle. He speaks mostly Tagalog, but can manage a simple
conversation in English. He went to the local elementary school,
where Spanish was not taught. He is a simple country type, honest
and hard-working. Round his house are some banana trees, and in
a good year he can make a little extra selling bananas. He has no
other sources of income. In the village he is considered to be of
average means, though more industrious and steady than some of
his neighbours.

His house is too small to have separate rooms within. The
steps up to the verandah level are solid, but once on the small
verandah and into the house's single room the floor gives slightly
as people move about, and the impression is somewhat similar to
living in a wooden basket with a roof over it. A plywood partition
gives some privacy for himself and his wife. The children sleep on
a flat square wooden bed in the inner part of the room. Cooking
is done in an annexe at the rear, on the same level, and beyond the
kitchen is an enclosure with a wooden door, used as a lavatory, with
a shallow ash-pit in the ground below it. The contents of the pit
are used as fertilizer on a few beds of vegetables.

His way of living is simple. His food is the same as that of
other villagers. There is a small cinema in the village, but he does

not encourage his children to waste money on it. He keeps one good suit of clothes for going to church or to any social events where a suit is required, and for his occasional outings to the nearest big town, Santa Maria Bulacan. To have a haircut, one must go to his home. There is another barber in the village, who has a proper shop and does things in a more fashionable way. My friend cannot afford the outlay for this. His clients are mostly farmers and the less well-to-do.

He keeps a mirror, a shelf for his scissors and clippers, bowls of water, soap, and an ordinary chair, all on the verandah. If wind and rain come together and the verandah gets wet, the whole outfit is moved inside. There we find his more important possessions. Like other houses of the same kind in the village, he has electric light, on which he runs a refrigerator and a good radio set. His wife has a Singer sewing machine and a full-length clothes cupboard with an inset mirror. There is a dining table and enough chairs for the family, two rather worn armchairs, some religious prints in frames, Japanese cheap crockery and glasses, and underneath the house two bicycles, one for himself, the other for his eldest son. When I last saw him he was saving up for a television set but doubted whether he would be able to afford one for a long time to come.

Not every village Filipino is as well-off, industrious and fortunate as he. His children are clever and have had few illnesses. His family worries have been slight. But he is the poor man's barber, not considered in the same class as his more swanky rival, who gives shampoos and can curl the hair of those village youths who require it.

Comparing him with second-class village barbers in other countries, one would hardly conclude that the Philippines had a low standard of living. With barbers in India and China he could not be compared at all. An Indian village barber would probably think a description of his home was a vision of the life hereafter. A Chinese barber would make enquiries about migrating to the Philippines. A Greek, Turkish or Portuguese village barber would say he lived pretty well in luxury. Even an English village barber, though he might not care for the idea of living in so flimsy a house, would probably admit he was doing all right.

Once again, perhaps the only true comparisons are with other countries of the same region. The average Malay, Indonesian or Burmese barber would say the Filipino was a good deal better off than they, but they might be expected to say enthusiastically that that was the sort of living they hoped to achieve. They might already have sewing machines themselves, and bicycles, and some of the furnishing and crockery, but with no electric light in the village it would not be much use thinking about a refrigerator, unless it was a kerosene one. A radio set would be nice, but re-charging the batteries would present problems. And of course the wooden house on stilts is already theirs, with the bananas, the vegetables and (though not so carefully looked after) the chickens.

On consideration, they might in fact say that the rural standard of living which the Philippines in some places already have, and which in others they are actively aiming for, was materially the goal for which the rest of South-East Asia should strive.

(xi) *Seeing oneself through someone else's spectacles*

The first person I expressed these thoughts to was a young Manila newspaperman, one evening at Doming's home. He looked at me with an air of disbelief.

'You really think they would?'

'Of course,' I said. 'Why not? You have the highest standard of living of any country in South-East Asia.'

'You're kidding,' he said, watching me intently to see whether in fact I was.

'Of course I'm not,' I replied. 'You travel around for yourself. You'll see. Go to Borneo, Java, Burma, Thailand, anywhere you like—and then come back and see what you think of the Philippines. The trouble with you people is that the only country you really know anything about outside your own is the United States, and you look at yourselves through spectacles made in America. Take them off. Look at yourselves with the strength of your own eyes, using your own mind instead of other people's clichés.'

His continued reaction of surprise intrigued me.

'I never heard anyone talk like that before,' he said slowly.

And of course he did not believe me. How could he be expected to believe a stray European wandering around Asia, presuming to tell him the exact opposite of the folklore?

But I do not think I was telling him a falsehood.

This is one of the most curious examples to be found in Asia today of the effects which western thinking has on that continent. People may irritatedly say that they do not believe what the West says on this or that subject, but the West speaks so loudly and effectively that, even if they do not believe, they sometimes act as if they did, producing a double deception. Before they know where they are, they find themselves acting parts in a play of the West's invention. And how can it be otherwise, when one of their principal means of finding out about their own continent is from American and European magazines, and from newspapers chronicling events reported by American and European news agencies? In Europe and America we would have a strange view of ourselves if our daily newspapers depended on Indian and Chinese news agencies operating internationally from Delhi and Peking, no matter how unbiased they tried to be.

(xii) *Champagne and incense*

Permitted every comfort except sleep, I somehow struggled along for the next few days, dropping off to sleep occasionally on short car rides or when left momentarily in peace in an armchair between two engagements.

I had morning coffee with Francisco Lim, American-educated Fukien proprietor of a drugstore.

'No, I can't say I'm worried by any so-called anti-Chinese legislation they like to introduce. I've kind of established my bona fides here. They like the look of my face, I guess, and I don't mind theirs. We get along.'

.   .   .   .   .

Don Evaristo, grey-haired, brown-skinned, distinguished-looking senior government executive, gave a *merienda* consisting of Philippine sweets, Chinese tea served in little bags, American style, with champagne and cigars.

'We farmers . . .' he said at one stage, with a gesture that flashed a superb diamond close to my face. 'We are simple country people,' he went on later. 'Our wants are those of poor men all over the world—a little shelter, food and clothing. We want enough to make us believe we are human beings.'

.   .   .   .   .

Eating land crabs beside an inland lake with Eugenio, a college teacher, delightful new items were added to the folklore.

'But because you're British it can be no pleasure to you to know that this is the most advanced democracy in Asia.'

'Why not?'

'Hell's teeth, it's not your policy, is it? Don't you still control India?'

'We certainly do not!'

'Well, that's not what we've been told.'

.   .   .   .   .

With an urbane Spanish Franciscan, speaking fluent English, we drank beer between Angelus and supper in a centuries-old priest's house built like a fortress, cool stone and tiles within.

'They've changed, those friars,' said Doming as we left. 'When I was a boy you had to kneel and kiss their hand before you could speak to them.'

.   .   .   .   .

At home in Manila, drinking fragrant glasses of *calamansi*, the Philippine lime, glamorous fashion-writer Concepción suppressed a bored sigh.

'Of course every writer wants to write novels. But who for? Nobody reads anything but magazines.'

.   .   .   .   .

At dinner in the garden of his California-style home, Manila politician Benedicto warmed up on his favourite theme.

'He threatened me with assassination, just called me up and spat it out over the phone. But I didn't even make a report to the police. I don't believe in bodyguards. An honest man has nothing to be afraid of.'

His sons and daughters served us as we sat at table.

'That's one thing to be said for the big family set-up,' said his wife, fanning herself. 'There's always someone handy to fetch things and answer the telephone. We're not like Americans, washing their own shirts and socks.'

.　　.　　.　　.　　.

On my last evening there was actually a gap of three hours for which nothing had been arranged. I was just about to retire upstairs to sleep when Nati arrived.

'Say, I'm bored. Doming, let's all go to a movie.'

What it is to be the wife of a public figure.

But Trining refused to go out.

'You go together,' she insisted. 'I must stay with the children. Unless I watch them they'll never pass their examinations.'

Trining being adamant, Nati being determined to drag us out, Doming being assailed by a conscience which insisted he had not done enough to entertain me, and I being so sleepy from over-entertainment that I could hardly pay attention to anything, it ended by Doming, Nati and I driving off to the cinema, leaving Trining at home.

As we passed the Church of El Nazareno the car drew up and Doming stepped out.

'Just a minute,' he said to me. 'You two wait here.'

Nati and I sat in semi-gloom.

The street was not one of Manila's brightest. It had been raining, and there were few people about.

'It's Friday,' said Nati. 'He always has to stop off here on Fridays.'

At first I did not understand what she meant. Looking in the direction in which Doming had gone, I saw that he had crossed the street and was walking up to the wall of the church, which was unlit within, its massive doors already bolted for the night.

'Why?' I asked, suddenly curious.

'Didn't you know?' she replied. 'When he was imprisoned by the Japanese his mother swore an oath that if he ever came out alive she would go once every week for the rest of her life to pray at El Nazareno. When she was dying she asked Doming to carry on the vow.'

'And he's always kept it up?'

'Sure. He's the type that can.' And at this point she made a revealingly European reaction of embarrassment. Her voice hardened slightly, reverting to a more sophisticated tone of tolerant disbelief, as she added: 'It's quaint, isn't it. But one has to respect these things.'

I looked again towards the church. Doming was now standing motionless, facing the aged stone wall, his head slightly bowed. Near him was an old woman in a similar attitude of humility, and as we watched, a younger woman, poorly clothed, holding by the hand a gawky undernourished boy, came to the empty space next to Doming. They stood thus in a row, each in their own field of silence. It began to rain again gently.

'Of course, he only goes out of respect for his mother,' said Nati, for whom the wait was becoming irksome.

Glancing by chance at the driver's rear mirror I noticed he was looking at me carefully in it, trying to gauge my reaction in the gloom. As my eyes caught his, I read in them his own respect for this pact of the spirit, and, sensing mine also, he smiled slightly as he looked away toward the church.

The rain was becoming gradually heavier. Slowly Doming turned away from the church wall. At the kerb he waited, unconcerned about the rain, for two cars to pass. As he crossed the street towards us, slowly, as if thinking deeply of something, I realized he was unaware that it was raining.

Back beside the church wall the old woman, raising an umbrella, continued her devotions. The mother and son stayed for a moment more, then ran for shelter.

Doming got into the car. It was only then, in the dry interior, that he became conscious that his clothes were damp. With a little jerk, such as we sometimes unconsciously make when shifting our thoughts from far to near, he took out a handkerchief and wiped the rain off his face and hands.

Talking of other things, we drove on to the cinema.

IV

(i) *Monsoon flight*

The rest of my journey lay westward. A four-engined plane took me as far as Bangkok. As we reached the mainland of Asia we ran into the great clouds of the south-west monsoon, now nearing the end of its season. They rose up around us like huge white floating towers, with blue spaces between them. Sometimes we plunged into one, gloomy grey inside and filled with hostile energy that made the aircraft shake and rise and drop sharply. After a few minutes we would be out the other side in an interval of blue calm before meeting the next.

At Bangkok I changed planes, taking a smaller two-engined craft, an elderly Dakota operated by the Burmese national airline and piloted by a skilled Australian who, like a dancer, gracefully guided us round the great white towers, keeping always in the blue. Occasionally, passing close to a cloud, we would have a bump or two, but on the whole the journey, though slower, was more peaceful. It was a pleasure to watch the pilot's careful advance through the lines of this huge atmospheric army.

The latter end of the monsoon is the part I like least. In the earlier months, when the cloud is denser, at least one sees the sun less. But towards the end, when short downpours are followed by suffocating periods of sunshine, during which the whole earth all but issues forth steam, the Indo-Chinese peninsula starts to be hard to endure. Looking down, I could see drenched villages, saturated fields, lying in shadow, and a mile or so away a scorching expanse of rice lands caught in brilliant light, from which men were doubtless praying for the next cloud to protect them.

There are important differences between the impression obtained of these countries from a map and from the air. On a map, the whole area is coloured according to national divisions; green runs on to a certain point, where there is a black line, beyond which everything is mauve. From the air, there are two main types of landscape, the level and lower land, which is irrigated and planted, and in which there are villages, and the upper and hillier land, which is unbroken jungle, stretching for miles and miles. From the air, one thinks of a new kind of map, with the lower land coloured and described as countries, and the upper land left vacant white. Each country is a gradual encroachment into the virgin jungle that still surrounds it. Pressure of population will have to become heavier and a hundred years or so pass before customs officers will have white gates and hoist flags a hundred yards away from each other. The colours will take years to move out into the white.

Another difference concerns names on the map. For European countries three sizes of type may be used—ten-point for the capital, eight-point for large cities, six-point for prominent towns. The same treatment given to the Indo-Chinese countries does not convey a relative impression. To do this, the capital of each might be in ten-point, and the rest of the country, with the exception of perhaps two six-point towns, might be left blank. Apart from the capital, the unit of real importance is the village, each in its green ocean of rice land, through which, three times in as many hundred miles, a road passes, a phenomenon so outstanding that the passengers in the plane peer at it out of their windows and discuss it with their neighbours. An old town, famous in history and dignified with eight-point lettering on the map, turns out to look like a somewhat larger village than the rest, its past stamped on it in the shape of a great square that once enclosed a royal palace. With any knowledge of history or government, one's first thought, at the sight of these peaceful landscapes, is of sympathy with the rulers of such countries in their detached capitals, from which they cannot swiftly despatch men to do their bidding or post soldiers along strategic lines of defence. For each head of a cabinet there must be times, one thinks, when he has the frustrating sense of being no more than chairman of an urban council.

(ii) *English Kyaung*[1]

Within twenty-four hours of arriving in Rangoon I called on Uncle Ba Yin, who told me that our mutual friend, U Prajnananda, had recently died. The unexpected news brought me a sudden deep sadness. It was not merely that U Prajnananda, with his stimulating conversation, gift of prophecy, and immense knowledge of Buddhism, was one of the people I had been looking forward to seeing during my stay in Burma: with his passing yet another link between East and West, though a strange and hardly recognized link, was severed, and might be left unreplaced.

After drinking tea and eating pomelos with Uncle Ba Yin in his garden—he himself was fasting that day—I strolled round to the hillock not far off, on the top of which, surrounded by trees and sheltered by a rough hedge, U Prajnananda had had his cell.

It was in a suburban, almost rural, part of the outskirts of Rangoon. Near the main road were suburban houses in English style, adapted to the tropics, occupied by small well-to-do Burmese families, with here and there a Chinese or Indian home in the same style, which is one of Britain's cultural bequests to Burma. The path to the monk's cell which, due to undulating ground, seemed remote from the houses, although it was less than a hundred yards from the nearest of them, was becoming overgrown with long grass and weeds, flourishing in this season of rain and heat. At the entrance a wicker gate lay with its back broken against the now unruly hedge. Fixed to the gate a piece of wood bearing the name of the place still had some paint on it, and the name was still legible— ENGLISH KYAUNG.

Within the plain earth compound, in the middle of which the simple wood-and-thatch cell rose like the hut of a wild man of the forest, there was still the air of desolation which follows departure of any kind, in this world or from it, and which pullulating vegetation had not yet had time to conceal. From the top of a bent pole planted beside the hut, the last brown tatter of what had once been a Buddhist white flag shivered slightly in the wind. At the door of the cell the piece of sacking that had once given protection from rain and wind lay in a dark damp lump on the ground, like a pat of cow-dung. Bending down, I passed through the entrance and,

[1] Pronounced *chowng*=monastery.

with something akin to a sense of sacrilege, squatted down to look around inside.

There were two old cooking pots, and part of the earth floor was still black where the monk had formerly lit a fire. Uncle had taken away the few books that had remained; the bed, made of packing cases, was not worth anyone's while to remove. On one wall was a torn Burmese calendar, rotten with damp. The roof of the cell had fallen in slightly, letting a glimpse of sky show through. From a cultivators' village in the valley nearby came the soft bells and gongs of Burmese music, while a light wind made the leaves of one of the trees brush the roof, a cold dry sound without rhythm.

It was here that I had sat in earlier years, on a packing case or low stool, listening to U Prajnananda, and reckoning the depth of his knowledge and the strangeness of his life. But the cell was now void of him. Nothing of him lingered about it. There was only emptiness and the natural face of the world, with its earth and trees and grasses, and the realization of how small is the mark upon it that a man can make.

I had known about U Prajnananda some time before first meeting him, and ten years ago, finding myself a near neighbour of his, I had asked Uncle Ba Yin to take me to see him. Coming with Uncle, who was one of his closest friends, I was well introduced, and with the additional circumstance that U Prajnananda and I were both English, the monk talked without reserve, and the way was opened for other meetings.

Like all monks of the Hinayana Order of Buddhism, he wore saffron robes and shaved his head. His possessions were those of an ordinary monk: three robes, writing materials, a razor, a needle and a begging bowl. In addition, because he lived alone instead of in an established monastery, he possessed books, cooking pots and stools. He sat on an old newspaper spread out on the earth floor of the hut.

Despite the brown skin of his bare arms and head, he was recognizably European. His face was so cadaverous that his chin protruded from its features as in a bare skull; but his small deep-sunken eyes were fiery with life, displaying an aggressive, argumentative temper. This was in absolute contrast, however, with the lines round his mouth, which showed a set resignation, a final and utter pointlessness in his attitude to worldly existence. In the inner conflict between the man of the eyes and the man of the mouth, the second had mastered the first; but both remained graven on his expression. When Uncle and I came upon him it had just been raining and the monk was cold. On the ground in front of him was one of the huge volumes of Arthur Avalon's *Tantra Shastra* which he was tearing out page by page and burning on a small fire for warmth.

'I've no use for them any more,' he said, when I mentioned that it must be hard for him to tear up even his own books. 'Even these are attachments.'

It did not take more than a glance at these and his other books to see that he was an erudite reader in the subjects that interested him. His small library contained many of the key books to a knowledge of Hinduism and Buddhism that have appeared in the English language. He spoke of attachment, compassion, action and inaction as one in whom Buddhist precepts and doctrine were ingrained as part of every thought and word.

In the course of conversation he spoke of his early wanderings in India and Tibet between the two world wars, and his final coming to Burma and taking of the yellow robe. He spoke of timeless things, timelessly. He told how at first he had lived in Burmese monasteries, until laxity of discipline and bickering among the inmates had forced him to the conclusion that he had best live alone. He explained the difficulties of achieving any advanced state of mental calm and understanding while living in houses or buildings that have been formerly occupied by others, the echoes of whose thoughts remain behind. He spoke of celibacy, and of the means whereby the human body can be completely controlled by its wearer.

But on that first visit it was not so much this, the timeless aspect of him, that intrigued me, as the other, more mundane, aspect which, like a contradicting limit, rooted him in time and place.

To the end of his life he would never be able to conceal, had he indeed any wish to, that he was born in London. He spoke with a dry, whining, complaining Cockney accent. He discussed material affairs with the nasal intonations of an aircraftman complaining that he got sausages for breakfast when he wanted bacon. When discussing Buddhism, his words were of themselves so interesting that one's preoccupation with his accent lessened, and on one occasion when I attended the annual lecture he customarily gave in Rangoon, at which he prophesied concerning the future of Burma, and sometimes of Asia and the world in general, what he said was so absorbing that to this day, though I remember the scene well, I cannot recall the sound of his voice in the hall—only what he said. (It was late in 1945, and he spoke of the coming triumph of communism in China and the rise of that country as the dominant force in East Asian affairs, an announcement which his audience found strange and unlikely.)

Then, in his cell, he would switch suddenly to domestic subjects and say, like the keeper of a Bermondsey boarding-house:

'I loathe bananas. But almost everybody brings me them. What do they think I am—a monkey?'

Like all wearers of the yellow robe, he begged for his food, being largely dependent for his cooked food on the households near his cell. These families were his principal support, acquiring merit thereby according to Buddhist doctrine. But additionally it was the custom for people visiting his cell to bring food with them.

Had he had a neutral English accent, the sense of timelessness around him would have been far more pervading than it was. His accent impelled speculation on his origin. Had he been dumb he would have belonged to the world. Because he could speak he might still belong, by right of mental conquest, to the world, but by birth he belonged to a certain social class in a certain part of London, a link which years and the Sutras, a shaven head and yellow robes, had not effaced.

It is as useless to advise Englishmen not to divide their own people into different social classes as it was in Japan to announce that there would be no more peerage. English and Japanese people, each with a tight insular civilization with inner relationships peculiar to itself, naturally regard their own people in this way, placing them mentally in the sphere of society to which they seem to belong, and treating them accordingly. The Japanese peerage might be abolished by the stroke of an American fountain-pen, but the way people thought in terms of their own society remained. The same would be true of us were a similar writ made. Instinctively, and whether one likes it or not, I placed U Prajnananda in a social class.

And having done so, I respectfully asked him about his early life. He responded without concealment. Out of one of the packing cases, which he used as a cupboard, he took a tidy package of papers wrapped in neatly-folded thick rice paper. Opening the package, he took from it, as if it was a passport, an English newspaper cutting, about two column inches in size, and dated, I judged from the context, about 1917. It told of a gunnery officer, a young Londoner who, in the trenches on the Western Front, read in his spare time the gospel of peace in the Bhagavadgita and other Hindu works, and wished after the war to go to India to study these books further. I do not remember if the item bore the officer's name. If it did, it was a fact which my mind did not retain. The name existed no more. The man was Prajnananda.

Through the spirit of Buddhist non-attachment surrounding him, I thought I denoted a faint indication of western pride as he took the cutting back and replaced it in the paper package. He had been in the newspapers.

Later there was another hint of the same thing when he explained how, after the war, wishing to leave for the East, he had sold the two houses which he owned in Mayfair and which would now be no use to him, using the money to finance his journey to India and subsequent travels there and in Tibet. He named the street in which the houses were situated. From personal knowledge as a Londoner I knew that at that time the street in question was one of the most fashionable as a place of residence, and that the houses, if well sold, could have fetched a substantial sum.

If what he said was the truth—and it was improbable that he would practise any deception—how was it that a man of the class in which I had placed him should own property in this Mayfair street, with marquesses and millionaires as his neighbours? Although not from the so-called officer class, it was not unlikely, during the First World War, that he should have become an officer. The location of the two houses posed a more mysterious problem.

From what he said, I gathered that it was not until coming to Burma that, having earlier explored other religious schools, he adopted Hinayana Buddhism and took the name Prajnananda. He had no passport, no documents tying Prajnananda to his English name and position. In fact the newspaper cutting was now the only tie between the two, and even that might be doubted by some.

I fancy that one of the reasons why he later forsook monastery life in Burma was that so many of the Burmese monks, prior to the Second World War, were taking part in political activities, most of them of an anti-British nature. When the Japanese occupied Burma he was interrogated and afterwards left in peace. The Japanese however had special letter-boxes in most of the Burmese towns, in which citizens could post confidential accusations to the Japanese police against their neighbours. At some stage of the occupation U Prajnananda was in this way accused of being an Allied spy. There were no grounds for the accusation, which was probably prompted by monkish jealousy, but this time he was more closely interrogated. He appealed to the senior Japanese authority and was granted an interview. Although the official concerned was not entirely convinced of his innocence he ordered his release—possibly having Buddhist leanings himself—and subsequently visited him at his cell.

(iii) *Weaknesses in East-West relations*

Among the Burmese U Prajnananda was not a showpiece. No westerner who becomes absorbed into eastern life need be, unless he desires it. Entering a Burmese home he was greeted as if he were a Burmese Buddhist monk, believers prostrating themselves before him, thereafter discussing religion or their personal problems in a natural way.

But to my way of thinking, his life was a symptom of an important feature in the relations between West and East. He was one of the few westerners who, during the colonial epoch, came to the East to learn rather than to preach. By and large in East-West relations hitherto, the West has preached, and the East, willingly or unwillingly, has listened. Now that this phase has ended, we have reached the time when we can be wise after the event, and two of the defects that are beginning to appear are that our teaching was too exhaustive, and was too much of a one-way affair. Instead of sticking to the broad fundamentals of the indisputable gifts it had for the East, allowing the East to work out the details in its own way, the West sought to impose details which, though suitable for itself, were often unsuited to oriental life. If the popes of the seventeenth century had been less concerned with the detail of whether Chinese ancestral rites were or were not compatible with Christianity, China would in all probability today be a Catholic country. If European administrators in the last century had been less determined to impose the details of their own laws and institutions of government on the countries they colonized, these countries would today feel that they had something noble to defend in the great ideological conflict of this century, instead of being divided on whether what they now have is worth defending or not.

In a variety of ways the West has, with good intentions, confused the East. It has achieved many great and wonderful changes that have allowed the foundations of a new world to be laid, but it came to the East like a bull in a china-shop, breaking useful things which it did not notice or understand. Some of those broken pieces have now to be picked up and glued together again, and Asia's problem is to decide which.

While Asians in the colonial period might soak themselves in western thought, social difficulties stood in the way of Europeans acting conversely. Such conduct did not fit into the pattern of the colonial *mission civilisatrice*. Some tried it, and as a whole they are a varied and fascinating band, ranging from mystics to buccaneers. Many of them are unknown, and most of them were in their time spurned and misunderstood by their own countrymen. But colonial society developed attitudes so stiff and self-protective in the East that it soon became physically incapable of containing anyone who did not adhere minutely to its limited social canons.

The very people who could have been used as the channel through which a more balanced relationship might be reached between the West and the East were bundled contemptuously out of the western fold, to do as best they could, without influence or respect from their own people, among the easterners whose ways they outrageously seemed to prefer to their own. As people used to say with depressing unction in India under the British Raj, you either ran with the hare or hunted with the hounds.

The existence of this peculiar choice—and I can say from my own experience of those days that it was a very grave choice—has had its own distinctive effect on contemporary Asia. The westerners whom the East knows best are those, of whom U Prajnananda was one, who chose to run with the hare, and who, whether in social or religious work, or in other capacities, chose to make their home in the East and become part of it. Despite a century and more of colonial rule, and in spite of thousands of westerners having come to India and Burma during the war, personal ties between Indian and Burmese families with families in the West are very few. The percentage is probably higher with Burmese than with Indians. Incredible as it may seem, it is only rarely that one meets English-speaking Indians in India today who have ever really sat down and conversed with an Englishman.

One might be inclined to accept this with a philosophic sigh were it not that in the Philippines it is an ordinary occurrence, in town and country, to meet Filipino families who correspond with Americans from all parts of the States, even the most remote, whom they first met as soldiers at the end of the war or as administrators before it, and who have a home for any of them who may perchance go to the States one day. That is one of Asia's pleasant surprises, a forerunner of the type of international relations which should in time stretch all over the world, in the new age into which we are painfully moving.

In this new age we speak hopefully of good relations between West and East. It is well to ask first of all: what does Asia know of the West? Books, magazines and movies are useful, of course, but the best books are men and women, and of them how many does the East know? The bond between Asia and the West is a slender, tangled thread, weakened by a hundred years of missed opportunities, prejudice and disdain.

As I squatted alone in U Prajnananda's cell, its emptiness filled me with foreboding. For although, because he ran with the hare, his own society ejected him, in his own strange way Prajnananda was one of those who kept something alive between two very different civilizations, and the emptiness he left behind him was not confined to his gradually collapsing hut. It was an altogether larger kind of emptiness that has somehow to be filled, not, as in the past, by men and women who soaked themselves in the East partly out of protest to hunting with the hounds, but by those who will make a voluntary contact, out of goodwill and a desire for learning.

The problem of the personal touch, vitally important in all that concerns the East, is now more difficult than it used to be.

While the need becomes yearly greater for East and West to be familiar with each other, the severing of colonial connexions, coupled with the restrictions on foreign commerce which some of the newly-independent Asian states feel obliged to impose in their own interests, have resulted in a serious lessening of opportunity for making personal contacts. The thread is becoming thinner than ever, at the very time when more strands should be added, and twisted into strong rope.

.   .   .   .   .

Who was Prajnananda? If he had told me he was three hundred years old and was about to reincarnate in Tibet, I would have believed him. But he had said no such thing. There was nothing so extraordinary in his story, and he was a Cockney.

The story that I have fabricated round what he told me—and it may be completely wrong—is that his father was an ex-batman servant to a high-ranking military officer of good family, who owned two houses in Mayfair and had seen service in India, where he had developed an interest in oriental religions. The military officer was a bachelor, or else he was childless and a widower with few relations, and when he died he left his property to the servant who had looked after him faithfully for many years.

The servant's son was already at school, but the sudden increase in their well-being, due to renting out the houses, meant that he was able to go to a better school. Although the second part of his education was thus better than the first, he never lost his Cockney accent. Furthermore, he had the run of the old officer's library, in which he made his first acquaintance with Hinduism. He became deeply interested, and when, an officer himself, he was sent to the Western Front in the First World War, he took with him from the library a copy of the Bhagavadgita. His father and mother died during the war, and when he returned to London at the end of it, determined to go to India, the houses had devolved upon him, providing the wherewithal for the journey and for his subsistence thereafter for a few years. The rest was as he told me.

Perhaps there is a flaw in it. Anyway, I think it must have been something like that.

There was another reason why I was sorry not to find him still in the cell. I owed him an apology. Some years before, on a very short visit to Rangoon, I had come with a Burmese friend to see him.

'We had better buy him some fruit,' my friend said, as we drove to the nearest point on the road from which we could walk to his cell. 'We must not come empty-handed.'

We stopped at a roadside stall, and the driver quickly got down, bought some fruit, and put it beside him on the front seat. When we got out, my friend carried the fruit as we ascended the hillock to the clump of trees and cell at the top.

To our disappointment, U Prajnananda was not there. There was naturally no means of finding out where he had gone. There was nothing to do but wait or return. As it was beginning to rain, we decided to return.

'In any case,' I said, 'we might as well leave the fruit.'

'Yes, by all means,' my friend replied, and it was only then I noticed that the driver had bought a very fine bunch of bananas. I had forgotten to warn him that the monk did not like them. In fact, it was only as I took them from my friend that I myself remembered.

How difficult it is to please the great and the simple in this world, and what foppish, silly creatures we seemed, afraid of getting our shirts and trousers wet because we had a luncheon appointment, beside the gaunt life of this solitary man burning his books for fuel. But there was nothing else for it. A heavy shower was coming, leaving us no time to obtain more acceptable fruit and return.

I shall never forget the acute sense of sorrow that filled me as I leant down and laid the bunch of bananas at the foot of the sack across the door, foolishly laying them there gently and reverently, as if to do so would make them less unwelcome.

The next time I came he had gone away for ever.

(iv) *Burma's background and situation*

Each time I have been in Burma I have found Rangoon a depressing place. Before the Second World War it must certainly have been one of the best-looking cities in Asia. Its flat lower section, containing docks, banks, commercial houses and large

Indian and Chinese residential quarters, had been developed according to a town plan, grouping the principal buildings on streets converging on the small golden Sulé Pagoda, in the heart of the town. This was the only part of Rangoon that was entirely urban in character. Passing from the river through the town zone, one quickly reached undulating land beyond, in which excellent metalled roads, bordered by magnificent trees, reached out in easy and irregular patterns to houses in large gardens, covering an area larger than the commercial zone and giving Rangoon the reputation of being a garden city. This part, when I knew it, was chiefly occupied by the British and the Burmese. Delightfully picturesque lakes broke up any pretensions the area might have to being part of the town, and on the highest of the many hills, approached by a fine road guarded on each side by stone *chinthés* (Burmese lions, or dragons), arose one of the great sights of the East, the Shwédagon Pagoda, over three hundred feet high and entirely covered with gold leaf, the effect of which in sunlight is almost dazzling, with at the top its *hti*, or umbrella, of precious stones encrusted in gold.

At the end of the war, the Shwédagon and Sulé Pagodas remained—Allied bomber crews were carefully briefed to avoid damage to pagodas and monasteries throughout Burma—together with many houses in the garden city, and the skeletons of what were once first-class roads. But in the commercial zone the damage was overwhelming. In one important quarter there was not a building left standing, and the place generally wore an air of devastation. Roads were a mass of bomb craters and pot-holes, not having been repaired during the Japanese occupation, pavements had been ripped up and become slushy pools of pale brown mud, marks of fire scarred the walls of the buildings left standing, and hardly a window had glass in it.

In this shattered place, in the last days of the war, Indians, Chinese and Burmese (during the colonial period the Burmese were the least important in their own capital) began creeping about, opening shops and stalls, repeating like ants in a broken nest the behaviour followed before the breakage occurred.

'It would take *us* twenty years to rebuild it,' a British business man said to me, 'and if they make the country independent I doubt if it'll ever be rebuilt.'

. . . .

Before the British period, what is today united as Burma was ruled by kings. Sometimes the country was united, sometimes divided. Mahayana Buddhism and spirit-worship became established at an early stage, but during the Indian classic period of colonization, by which Lower Burma was affected, other ideas took root, including Hinayana Buddhism and some Hindu concepts. Handwriting was also derived in this way from India. By the eleventh century Hinayana Buddhism had clearly become the principal religion, subsequent contact with Ceylon, the true home of the school, purging it of much of its earlier Hindu accretions, until by the fifteenth century it was beginning to look more or less as it is today. Though Hindu influences could be removed, however, spirit-worship proved more enduring; and Burmese belief today is thus an intriguing compound of Buddhism in its most austere form, atheistic and nihilist, and spirit-worship in its gayest and most practical form of making sure that the guardians of trees, wells, bridges, houses, rivers and fields are kept happy and contented. Reincarnation is an accepted belief.

During the Yuan (Mongol) dynasty in China, attempts were made to conquer Burma, and in 1287 Kubla Khan's grandson invaded and sacked Pagan, the ancient capital in Upper Burma. There was a series of Burmese wars of conquest with Thailand, Burma's traditional enemy, and as a result of Burmese onslaughts on the Mon kingdom in Lower Burma many Mons migrated to Thailand for safety. The Mon language, the Sanskrit alphabet of which is the script of the Burmese language, is thus spoken on both sides of the Burma-Siam frontier. Another attempt by the Chinese to take territory in Burma occurred in the middle of the eighteenth century and was repulsed decisively by the Burmese in 1770.

The Burmese monarchy, unless the reigning king was a forceful character, was an organism of endless intrigue. By tradition the king had many wives, a traditional pattern of intrigue being the machinations of rival queens to have their sons declared heir to the throne. The life of a named heir was in constant danger, and as a precaution some kings declined to name an heir, sometimes until too late. Once the heir succeeded to the throne his position was often insecure until he had organized a massacre of his nearest relatives, including his half-brothers and the queens rival to his own mother. Any who escaped massacre were liable to set themselves up as pretenders, and a change of reign classically involved a period of anarchy until the new monarch had established himself.

When a king was energetic and not too involved in wars, taxes were collected, but there was no tradition that the money so raised should be spent on public works. Education was a monastic responsibility, and most towns and villages organized their own public works when necessary. By far the most stabilizing influence in the country was that of the Buddhist Church. Life revolved—and still does to a great extent—round monasteries. The monks educated the people, compiled the law, and exercised a profound moral influence in every branch of life. There was a disciplinary head of the Church at the capital, and care was taken that in monastic appointments men would be chosen fit to maintain the Church's important traditions.

With its difficult frontiers of mountain, jungle and sea, Burma had little contact with other lands. Buddhist learning was essentially traditional. It did not come sufficiently in touch with outside ideas to make it evolutionary. The kings occasionally cherished the concept, probably acquired from China, that their seat of government was the centre of the world, and believed that it would be given to their descendants to achieve invincibility and become lords of the whole earth.

Burma was one of the relatively few territories to become part of the British Empire entirely by conquest. The annexations were made piecemeal. In 1826 Assam and Arakan were acquired in the north, and Tenasserim in the south, among the main reasons being to curb piracy in the Bay of Bengal and prevent Arakanese disturbances in East Bengal. In 1853 the whole of Lower Burma was occupied, the kingdom now consisting of Upper Burma only; and in 1886, partly to prevent the French doing the same thing from their territories in Indo-China, the conquest was completed and the last king deposed.

The British found themselves responsible for administering a nation rooted in, and guided by, religion. They themselves were not Buddhists and had little understanding of Buddhism. Their ingrained respect for other people's customs—a feature of British imperial rule which has not been given its due—made them opposed to interfering with Burmese customs and beliefs, except where, as for example in the practice of obtaining evidence by torture and executing criminals by mutilation, there were obvious humanitarian reasons for doing so. Apart from such things as these, the British contribution to Burma was from the outset largely confined to material improvement. If Burma is to be understood today, this is one of the most important points to remember. Although under British administration modern roads, railways, bridges and buildings were constructed, river steamers ran up and down the Irrawaddy, and ocean-going ships called at Rangoon, although methodical production of teak and rubber was introduced, oil was exported and modern cities arose, although public health enormously improved, although with the maintenance of law and order and the proper administration of justice the country began to wear the face of progress and well-being, the real life of the people, which was pre-eminently religious, went into a chrysalis. Burma under foreign rule became a country of almost complete mental stagnation.

In the circumstances it is difficult to see how it could have been otherwise. Thailand, with less obstructing frontiers, a wider view of the outside world, and, at the crucial moment, a highly intelligent and capable monarch, retained her independence throughout the most aggressive period of colonial expansion. Burma had not these attributes of fortune. If it had not been ourselves, it would surely have been the French who would have occupied it.

In a sense, the colonial epoch brought Burma something worse than stagnation: the period was one of Buddhist moral decline. This arose from a far-reaching error of judgment made by the British administration when, after the last king's deposition, the disciplinary head of the Buddhist Church was deprived of his legal powers, in particular those relating to appointments and expulsions from monasteries. No longer the repository of the law, the monasteries still remained the principal educating influence in the country, but the moral and intellectual standards of the monks themselves declined appreciably. Riff-raff of all kinds hid their activities under the sanctity of the yellow robe, until in certain instances the monks became a positively corrupting force.

Imperial rule thus unintentionally loosened the foundation of society. What did it do to strengthen the foundations once the weakness was perceived? Burma was the outer fringe of a vast empire controlled from Calcutta, Delhi and Simla, where little attention was paid to it. The machinery of administration and law as it existed in India was introduced into Burma. It was only vaguely appreciated at the Indian capital that Burma was an entirely different country demanding different treatment. Various forms of local self-government, on Indian models, were among the first of Britain's positive attempts to make life move forward again. Not being designed to meet Burmese conditions, they were not a conspicuous success. The law was another contribution, and though it did not, as it did in India, spread like a scourge, it confused as much as it enlightened. In the long run the most important contribution was the introduction of western education through Government and Christian missionary schools. Through these schools, though Christianity did not spread, modern western ideas of democracy and politics did. Burmese people learnt to think in a new language.

But even if, in the two decades before the Japanese invasion, Burma advanced considerably towards the political goal of becoming a self-governing democracy within the British Commonwealth, the air of spiritual stagnation did not change. The educated knew what the political developments meant; the rest understood little. The country remained under the so-called steel frame of an alien civil service, while the process of transferring responsibility for the country's welfare from ecclesiastics to laymen, and from dispersed to centralized authorities, continued.

Then came war, a phenomenon which invariably invigorates the spirit and can only destroy what is material. The destruction which the war caused in Burma was on a very large scale, and what was destroyed, being material, was precisely Britain's chief contribution to the country. The roads and bridges, the river-steamers and railways, were smashed to pieces. Ironically, too, it was we ourselves who destroyed the most, unavoidably, in the latter years of war, when the Japanese were being driven back the way they came. A material civilization preaching material things (for that is Indian and Burmese man-in-the-street opinion of the rôle played by the West in Asia) was obliterated by itself, as Buddhist and Hindu wise men in Burma had for long said it would be. As Burma emerged from the war, so too did the sense of justification that they had not after all been wrong about the West. It had its good points, but it was a self-destructive dynamism of which in future the country would do well to stay clear.

What is the score now? The Burmese people's standard of

living was high before the British came (much higher than that of India and China) and it is still high. Except for the Karens, they have not taken to Christianity. Their faith in Buddhism and spirits is tempered by a certain modern reserve, but it is not challenged or threatened. They have acquired a taste for various occidental products, western-style houses, cars, radios, the cinema, biscuits, cigarettes. The idea of a political democracy appeals to them, but there are great difficulties, chiefly temperamental, about putting it into practice. They have learnt a good deal about modern administration, although, had they not chosen to withdraw so hastily from the Commonwealth, they could have learnt a great deal more. Their civilization remains what it was before, a culture of villages and small market towns, but with the village as the most important unit. Their experiences under the Japanese have strengthened their love of national independence, a sentiment traditional in their dealings with their neighbours, the Chinese and the Thais. Through air travel, the port of Rangoon and the English language they have a much wider view of the world than was possible under the kings. They are unlikely to withdraw again into self-centred obscurity.

But from personal experience, in which the whole nation shared, they have learnt that the West is a warring entity, and that to be involved in the West's disputes is to risk being afflicted yet a second time by war on a grand scale, when what they actually need is generations of peace in which to set their house in order. It is Burma's special misfortune that this must be done at a time when the continent of Asia lies in the shadow of greater issues, which may at any moment reduce it to a new havoc.

(v) *The lingering smell of the Golden Foot*

After a visit to Rangoon in 1950 I came away thinking that the place reminded me of nothing so much as of Canton on the eve of the fall of the National Government of China. The Burmese ministers were all living in a single compound surrounded by barbed wire and searchlights. On the ground floor of each of the houses lived a gang of armed toughs from the particular minister's home village, for protection. None of the ministers went out without a heavily-armed escort. Every so often bandits cut the main water pipe supplying the city. Buildings, streets and pavements presented the same appearance of dereliction as in 1945. There is a loose pavement stone near the Bogyoke Market which looks secure but, if you step on it after there has been some rain, tilts down and flings brown water all over your behind. I had the misfortune to step on it in such conditions in 1945, 1950 and 1952. I now know exactly which one it is (so do all the market people). Private houses were heavily bolted, and the practice of keeping youths from the village as retainers, who might or might not be armed, was fairly common, particularly among prominent people. One had to be careful what one said and to whom. I would ask my host and hostess whether it would be convenient if I went to call on such-and-such a person, and if the answer was doubtful I ruled out the idea. At night, despite the heat, every window had to be closed, and my hostess explained that it would be as well if I locked myself in my bedroom; they did the same. Throughout Rangoon, as in Canton in 1949, there was an atmosphere of suspense, as if everyone were waiting for something to happen.

But on each subsequent visit the atmosphere was the same, except that the something people seemed to be waiting for did not happen. From month to month and year to year the Government somehow precariously survived, its writ running solely in Rangoon and the principal towns, communication between which was exclusively by air. Nearly the whole of the rest of the country was still controlled by rival organizations, communists of two varieties, one national, the other international in sentiment, Karen and Mon minority groups, and bands of ex-Kuomintang Chinese soldiers. Meanwhile the Government made impressive announcements about the inauguration of a socialist welfare state, its representatives attended international conferences in the name of the whole country, and a little later the Prime Minister paid goodwill visits to foreign capitals.

In some ways foreign visitors saw one of the worst sides of the Government, which in its grave situation could very easily be condemned by outsiders for devoting a disproportionate amount of its energy and intelligence to unnecessary details. Was it really necessary for such exhaustive enquiries to be conducted about foreigners coming to Burma, sometimes involving delays of three or four months before a visa could be issued? Was it really necessary for visitors to have to obtain permission from the Home Office every time they moved from one town to another, and give their reasons for moving? Was it really necessary for them to have police escorts everywhere they went, except in Rangoon, and for such a minute check to be kept on everything they did while in Burma?

Perhaps it was; but certainly other foreigners whom I have since met, and who have been through the extraordinary complications of a visit to Burma, did not think so. Most of them came away never wishing to go there again.

The Government could of course be described as being in a state of war, and obliged to act in ways that would be abnormal in times of peace. But even in times of war, distinctions are made between friendly and unfriendly aliens, and certainly between friends and enemies. In Burma there seemed to be no such distinctions. All aliens, unless on visits sponsored by the Government, ran the risk of being treated as unfriendly. Having many Burmese personal friends whose attitude was completely different, I was not particularly aroused by this treatment. But in brief moments of irritation I occasionally had to admit that I had never been in a situation where I was so hemmed in by rules.

It is of course true that the assumption of administration by the Burmese was rendered unduly difficult by their inexperience, the Rangoon government offices during the British period having been run almost entirely by Indians. These expatriate Indians returned to their own country when Burma became independent. More or less overnight, Burmese country clerks were called upon to run the vast offices of a capital city, at the speed which the modern world demands of a capital. It was certainly not easy for them, and one cannot expect to see the results of this sudden change disappear for several years yet.

I suppose some people would say there was poetic justice in a Britisher having humbly to ask Burmese officials for permission to do this and that, and being told to come back tomorrow or the next day. But as, for fifty minutes at Mingaladon Airport, officials pored over my documents, checking and cross-checking them and asking questions, as my passport was impounded as being incorrectly visa'd, and as I waited two hours in town for the third day in succession trying to get it back, it occurred to me that this

was very like, in modern dress, the treatment that foreigners sometimes received over a hundred years ago, when people prostrated
themselves beneath the Golden Foot, when the Golden Throne of
the Burmese kings was the centre of the world. A lingering smell
of that famous foot wafted about the dismal Rangoon office.

(vi) *Moulmein under siege*

Dependent on being allowed by the Home Office to leave
Rangoon, I was permitted to buy an air ticket to Moulmein, and
after going to the Home Office and being a thorough but polite
nuisance to the officials concerned, I obtained the necessary permission within the remarkably short space of forty-eight hours.

The third largest town in Burma, Moulmein was the scene of
the principal disturbances of the Karen-Mon rebellion which broke
out in 1948 on the question of the Government's refusal to grant
autonomy to a Karen-Mon State. Formerly a quiet straggling
market town, its horizons broken by the cheerful pinnacles of
pagodas and monasteries, it had now become an armed enclave of
government authority, with entirely new down-at-heel quarters
of refugees and squatters from the surrounding bandit-ridden
countryside.

Twenty minutes after reaching my host's home we were visited
by the police, a well-spoken inspector and a corporal. Who was I,
what was I doing, and where did I intend to go? On this occasion
the painfulness of the situation was mitigated by the courtesy with
which the duties were carried out. I explained that I was on holiday
visiting friends. That was of course too simple to be believed.
Everyone knows that foreigners do not move about unless they
are up to some mischief. It was allowed to pass at this first interview,
however, and with a warning that I must on no account attempt to
leave the centre of the town without a police escort they departed.

The restrictions turned out to be less hampering than I expected.
To see the sun set over the Salween river from the Ridge at Moulmein is one of the things one is supposed to do. But the Ridge,
though only twenty minutes' walk from the town centre, was
considered dangerous, and the police inspector had particularly
mentioned it. It was the custom for bandits to sneak in among the

monastery buildings along the top of the Ridge and kidnap people (Kipling would have thought the end of the world had come). Accordingly we telephoned for an escort, and at the requested time the same two men came to accompany U Mya (my host) and myself. By the end of this excursion a friendly situation had been created, my absence of ulterior motive was established, and there were hints that a few inconveniently long journeys into the country would be a welcome relief from police station routine.

After a week in Moulmein I had to conclude that the police protection system was not as one-sided as it looked. Though the police discovered from it a good deal about my contacts and interests (it would be amusing to know what conclusions they reached), I was able to go where I wanted when I wanted, with the comforting safety of an armed escort in what was undoubtedly a dangerous place.

All social engagements were by daylight. At the first sign of dusk, guests started home, and on the outskirts of the town it was clear from the behaviour of the people I met that every night was an anxiety. In the centre of the town every door closed at nightfall and would not be opened to anyone, whether the voice calling outside was known or unknown. It was even considered unsafe to pass from one house to its neighbour after dark.

Moulmein is one of the few large towns that has a substantial Mon-speaking percentage of population, and in the country around it are several areas where the Burmese language is seldom heard. Elsewhere in Lower Burma, however, the tendency has been for the Mons, once the dominant community, to identify themselves completely with the Burmese, forgetting their own language and traditions in the process. It is only a minority of the existing Mon population of Burma who still hold to their own language and ways, a minority whose homelands border the country of the Karens, without whose larger and more important demand for autonomy it is unlikely that the similar Mon demand would ever have been noticed.

But although, among the dissentient voices in contemporary Burma, that of the Mons is the weakest, in view of the cultural contribution which this particular community has made in the past to what we know today as the Burmese nation, it is in some ways the most interesting, and the most demanding of sympathy.

The Mons once had their own kingdom covering all Lower Burma. At times it was more powerful than the Burmese kingdom to the north of it; at times it resisted encroachments as an equal. But the Mons were—and still are—a gentler people than the Burmese, less pugnacious, more given to the finer aspects of civilization. Their ultimate defeat by the tougher and more ambitious Burmese was almost inevitable.

Lying as it does between the two vast cultures of India and China, Burma unavoidably represents a mixture of both. Chinese influence on Burma, however, has been comparatively superficial. In matters of food and costume there are affinities with China. But on the general subject of Chinese influence one has to tread warily, because certain things in Burmese culture which appear to be derived from China were probably originally adopted by the Chinese themselves from the tribal people they ousted or intermarried with as their own civilization expanded, and those tribal people included the ancestors of many who are today Burmese. Thinking of Burmese development throughout the country's history, the influence of India must be admitted as of greater significance.

It was via the Mon kingdom that Indian influences penetrated into Burma, and amongst the Mons that they first found expression in the country. Handwriting, the growth of literature, architecture and other arts, the Buddhist religion and philosophy, most of the prime features of the Buddhist state of Burma, were derived from Mon connexions with India and Ceylon. Furthermore, when Burma finally settles down to peace, after the birth pains of creating an independent, self-governing nation are over, it is to be expected that, as so often in the past, the Mons will be among the foremost contributors to the intellectual and artistic life of the country.

Mon participation in the Karen rebellion arose from the Burmese Government's intransigence in refusing to give financial aid or any official recognition to schools in which the Mon language was to be the medium of instruction. But with the rebellion arose the more grandiose demand for an autonomous Mon region. As the Mons are scattered widely across Lower Burma, the definition of such a region presents serious difficulties, and having already conceded autonomy to the Shans, the Kachins and the Chins in the north, the Government was not prepared to discuss seriously another division of the country which threatened to leave it with direct control over no more than an ill-defined section of Central Burma, the only area where the Burmese are indisputably the majority community. The greater number of Mons have for generations been Burmese-speaking, and it seemed pointless to alter this process of complete cultural integration. When this hitherto quiescent segment of the community, peaceful but persistent, demanded special recognition, it was a problem of exceptional difficulty for a young government to handle, and intransigence cost dear.

In Moulmein the dust had settled over the act of rebellion, but among the Mons I met there was a deep-seated sense of malaise. An election carried out some time earlier, at which the Mon community had put up a large number of candidates, was openly spoken of as having been rigged by the Government to discredit the Mons. Mon officials in government service intimated that their chances of further promotion were negligible, due to Burmese distrust. Numbers of well-educated people whom I had met in 1945 had escaped when the rebellion was suppressed and were living in the country, where they were said to be organizing their own administration independent of any form of government authority. Moulmein was surrounded by a danger zone lorded over by bandits, but beyond this zone, it appeared, was a large and peaceful area under local control, with its own village guards, schools and even courts, an area which some people spoke of favourably by comparison with the dangers of existence in the bandit-surrounded town. By virtue of controlling the principal areas of cultivation, this independent administration could continue to subsist without difficulty, probably for an indefinite length of time. Only a genuine change of heart on the part of the Government, and concessions giving Mon political representation, recognition and financial aid to Mon schools, and guarantees that local administration would be conducted by Mon officials, could—or so it looked—bring the area once more under Rangoon's authority.

(vii) *Rendezvous with a patriot*

One of the people I particularly wanted to meet in Moulmein was a young Mon friend of my own age named Chit Hlaing. We had first met just after the war, but since leaving Burma at the end of 1945 I had not seen him again. He had, I knew, played a prominent part in the rebellion, after which he had disappeared and was said to be imprisoned. By chance in Rangoon I had met a mutual friend who had given me news of him. After three years' imprisonment he had recently been released, and could be contacted in Moulmein.

On my first evening there I asked U Mya if he knew where Chit Hlaing was.

'He's in prison,' he replied.

'I heard he'd been released.'

He shook his head.

'He's in prison.'

Which was U Mya's bluff way of saying that he did not propose inviting him to the house.

From another friend, however, I found out that in fact Chit Hlaing had been released, but was under police surveillance of some kind, being obliged to report to a police station every other day.

'Could I have his address?' I asked.

My friend demurred.

'I don't think that is the best way,' he said. 'I will arrange something and let you know tomorrow.'

I was by this time familiar with the stage-pieces that recur in what should be normal social life in Burma today, and made no protest. Two days later my friend returned with a rendezvous arranged. I was to go to a certain monastery at a certain time the following day and ask to see the abbot.

'But does anyone in the monastery speak English?' I asked.

'No,' he said with a grin. 'But it doesn't matter. A friend will be expecting you. Sit down where he tells you, and wait. Oh yes, and when you see Chit Hlaing it would be better not to show you know each other. Even in the monastery—one cannot be sure.'

He then explained exactly which monastery and which building in it I was to go to.

I did as I was told. On the following day, putting on a fine silk *loungyi*—I was calling on an abbot, after all—I arrived at the monastery and approached the building my friend had indicated. It was a plain wooden structure raised above the ground. As I mounted the steps to the open door the place was so silent I feared

I might have come to the wrong house. But as my head came level with the floor a young monk seated within, reading a book, hastily rose and ushered me in. He had clearly been waiting for me.

Motioning me to sit on the floor, he brought a glass of drinking water and a palm fan, appreciatively fingered the silk of my *loungyi*, and began to make conversation in Mon. He was a jolly country lad, and could not have been long in the Order. I offered him a cheroot, which he declined with amusement, finding a match for me to light one for myself.

I looked at some of his books, and by picking on the illustrations managed to conduct some sort of conversation with him, mixing English with my few words of Burmese and Mon. This continued for ten painful minutes, while I wondered whether perhaps I had not made a mistake and this unknown youngster was baffled by my visit but felt it his duty, according to Burma's high code of hospitality, to entertain me.

Then Chit Hlaing's head and shoulders appeared, coming up the steps. I was by this time so thankful to see him that I nearly forgot my instructions and stood up to greet him. But as I did so, the sight of worshippers passing across the precinct below to the main temple reminded me. The monk rose, and they spoke for some moments in Mon. Chit Hlaing was then invited to sit, and more water was brought.

'We are waiting for his Reverence,' Chit Hlaing said in English, making sure I understood the situation. 'He will be coming back soon.'

As the monk placed a glass on the floor beside where Chit Hlaing sat cross-legged, I took stock of the change that had come over him since we last met. I doubt if I would have recognized him in the street. He was wearing a European white shirt and a plain green cloth *loungyi*. Of medium height, sturdy, with broad shoulders, a tough square-shaped head, close-cropped hair, and rather small sharp eyes, he was, like most people in Burma, agile and alert, with an obviously quick sense of humour. But in seven years his features had hardened; his expression was dry and tense. Sympathy was there still, but he had acquired a tautness of character. Once a small-town lad whose ambition was to marry a pretty girl and be the happy father of a family, he now had the dignity of a man set apart, with a dedicated life that few others would care to share. He had come noiselessly up the steps; as we began to speak his words were quiet and measured; and soon he would noiselessly depart.

From him I learnt more than from anyone about conditions in the large parts of Lower Burma over which the Government had no control. But, listening to him, the impression formed was not so much of that outer area as of our own immediate surroundings. To him the country was a peaceful place where, with hard work, the life of the people was being improved, better standards of village hygiene were being brought about, education was developing on lines suited to the nature of the community, trade was prospering (there was evidently boat trade with Rangoon), and the leading monasteries were co-operating. But to him the country had the beauty it has to men in a besieged town who know well the fields around them, which they can no longer reach. To me, with little such knowledge, his words brought only more consciousness of the twilight of suspicion in this government town, with its disintegrating society, its spying and distrust. The palm trees in the monastery precinct began to grow silently hostile, the gay pagoda eaves laughed with a sneer, and I found myself brooding, as one does in a besieged town, of that impossibility, an immediate escape. Ten minutes seemed too long to wait.

He continued talking quietly, and thus I listened, although had it not been for the heat of the day I would have felt cold.

'I would like to go abroad,' he said wistfully. 'I need more experience. I should like to study how government works in your country.'

'Why not?'

He laughed slightly.

'The Government would never let me go.'

We talked of the old Mon kingdoms and their struggles against the Burmese, and as we did so I pondered on the strangeness of how this ancient conflict, submerged during the British period, now re-emerged with the participants speaking English and thinking in terms of western political balances. The essential had not changed.

From this insignificant conflict, one among dozens such throughout the continent of Asia, a single fact unexpectedly stood out by itself, large and general, much larger than the actual issues we were discussing about schools and administrative boundaries.

The weapons may be modern, but the conflicts are mediaeval.

When Japan entered the Second World War, she took the field with the full panoply of western armament, yet her concept of territorial conquest belonged to the age of bows and arrows. Though China wears a mask of communism, he does not need to be much of a philosopher to detect behind it the classic aim of restoring, in republican guise, the Central Flowery Kingdom, the exclusive source of all enlightenment. The Burmese communist factions, created from personal disagreements and based on personal loyalties, are, with slight dialectic trappings, the counterpart of those pretenders who so often, at the death of kings, reduced the country to confusion, until captured and killed. Every year some breath of mediaeval Asia is wafted into our daily newspapers—misunderstandings between Thailand and Cambodia, Philippine territorial claims in North Borneo, Tibetan resistance to Chinese pretensions, differences between the people of East and West Java, contemptuous Burmese remarks about Thailand, and, on a smaller scale, Karen and Mon resistance to domination by the Burmese, the depth and significance of all of which can only be understood by delving far back into the past.

Is it reasonable to expect it to be otherwise? The colonizing powers were not in Asia for long, and though they wrought many superficial changes, and some fundamental ones, there were many things they had no effect on at all. Old conflicts and aspirations were suffocated by other temporary rivalries motivated in London, Paris, The Hague, Madrid and Lisbon. Now the pressure on the blanket is withdrawn, and the patient is getting up, stretching his legs, and remembering what happened long ago, before he was put to bed.

We are too inclined to look back on the age of the Pax Britannica as to a desirably normal phase of human existence, whereas in fact, in the long context of history, the peace and security which Great Britain imposed over the greater part of the whole earth was a decidedly abnormal period. It was, in fact, unique. Normal human existence, as history shows, is an endless tumult of conflict, with stability created here and there for fifty years or so, until replaced by disintegration and more conflict. It resembles far more closely the state of the world as it is today than did the age that has just gone.

Yet, at the moment of re-engaging in its multitude of conflicts temporarily assuaged by the Pax Britannica, Asia is threatened by a far greater conflict than anything the world has known. Sitting within the doorway of the raised wooden monastery building, we watched worshippers coming and going, in their colourful silk *loungyis*, with flowers and paper sunshades. Small bells along the monastery eaves tinkled silver in the light breeze. How far away, unreal and unimportant that greater conflict appeared in this setting, talking with this man of my own generation who had dedicated his life to the conflict that really mattered to him, a conflict nearer, more real, and no less difficult to solve.

'Supposing, for example,' I said, 'China were to invade Burma. Your present divisions as a nation are a standing invitation to her.'

He thought for a moment.

'If that happened, I think we would probably all unite, as we did against the Japanese, but . . .'

—and he concluded with a remark that showed shrewdly that he did not expect India to welcome any development that might bring the Chinese frontier to the Bay of Bengal.

'So until something like that happens, you hang on in your struggle with the Government. Is that it?'

'Yes,' he said quietly. 'What else? It is now—what do you say in chess when——'

'Stalemate?'

'That's it. Stalemate. We cannot eat them, but they cannot eat us.'

(viii) *Cold war in the monastery*

Something like a tremor among the people in the precinct—a movement of respect and attention—indicated the abbot's return. We rose and went down the steps to await him just as his yellow-robed procession came in sight. He was accompanied by two other monks, and by two boys doing their customary period of instruction and discipline in the monastery. All were shaven-headed and robed, and one of the boys held a sunshade over the abbot.

He greeted us warmly, even to the unusual extent of shaking hands with me. We had not met for seven years. In a moment we were once again seated in his room, while lacquer betel-boxes and spittoons were produced and Chit Hlaing proceeded to prepare betel-leaf, nuts and lime. The abbot was in his early forties, a tall jovial man with large Mongolian eyes, rather dark skin, and the perpetual rumour of a disarmingly well-informed smile. His shaven head made him look slightly older than his years, and laughing lines cut deep around his eyes and mouth.

With Chit Hlaing acting as a rapid interpreter, we discussed the fate of some of the monasteries I had visited and abbots I had met in the Mon country on my last visit. From his suave treatment of the situation it was clear that he too was party to the arrangements concerning my meeting with Chit Hlaing.

After ten minutes or so a young boy delivering circulars—he looked like a Sino-Burman—mounted the steps, handed one of the circulars to a monk, and quickly left. The monk, after a glance at the addressee's name, in Burmese, handed it to the abbot, who, to my surprise, without opening it, threw it on what was evidently a pile of scrap paper in the corner of the room.

'Please don't let me interrupt your reading,' I said hastily.

Without interpretation he understood.

'I seldom read such things,' he said in Burmese.

'What sort of circular is it?' I asked Chit Hlaing.

'Haven't you seen one?' he said, and with the abbot's permission, and slight signs of amusement from the monks, he fetched the document from its pile of neglect, tore it open, and showed me. 'They're issued by the Chinese.'

Amid an undertone of chatter which I could not understand, I glanced through the publication. It was in Burmese, but from the pictures it was easy to see what it was about. There was Mao Tse-tung on the front page, an illustrated article about the Dalai Lama in Peking—'Illustrating freedom of religion,' Chit Hlaing commented, repeating his words in Mon, which provoked laughter—pictures of happy factory girls in appalling padded overalls, factory chimneys in the background, a description of a mammoth irrigation scheme, and the usual pictures of happy processions, happy dancers, happy commissars, and happy people shouting slogans of peace.

'And do you mean to say they even send this round to all the monasteries?' I asked in amazement.

'Yes,' the abbot replied, venturing a word of English, then added something in Mon to Chit Hlaing, who laughed.

'His Reverence says that in any case paper is always useful in the monastery.'

'Oh, of course, of course!' I said, handing it back quickly to the abbot, who chuckled and flung the publication back to its corner pile.

Conversation shifted to other subjects, and I could not be sure how long it was—about twenty minutes perhaps—before the postman called, delivered some letters at the head of the steps, and left.

This time, of course, more attention was paid to the articles delivered. Letters were sorted, and one of the novices ran off to deliver them to other buildings in the precinct. But as the abbot saw what he himself had received he cast a wry look at Chit Hlaing and held out yet another printed circular for my inspection.

This time I tore it open, while the others, knowing what it was, whisperingly awaited my reaction. As I unfolded it and found the Stars and Stripes on the front page, I hastily suppressed a desire to laugh out of sheer surprise, but was too late. My reaction was observed, and there were titters all round, not loud, and with a suggestion of embarrassment in them. The two publications had arrived within half-an-hour of each other, and apparently they nearly always did. Perhaps, the expression of one of the monks implied, it was not a suitable subject for levity, but, if people like myself thought it funny, it had to be admitted that . . . And one to another, they joked more freely and with mounting voice and energy, glad to liberate into the easy sphere of absurdity something which had till now been a problem to them, something which was evidently important somehow, to some people, somewhere, though why it was important was hard to say.

Seeing that I was examining the magazine, one of the monks, breaking away from the chatter, said something to me in a serious tone. Chit Hlaing interpreted.

'This monk says everyone wishes to be friendly with Burma. The nation is more important since independence.'

The monk nodded at me sagely as Chit Hlaing reproduced his words.

Inside the American publication were pictures of happy Burmese shaking hands with happy Americans, current news items concerning America in the East, a happy American family watching television at home, and—no, as one turned over the pages, one realized it was not just that. There were articles of general interest, some on simple scientific subjects, and at the end there was a section in English which was a combined article and language lesson. It was certainly in a different class from the other.

I handed it to the abbot, who glanced briefly through it, and threw it loosely over to join the Chinese one in the corner.

(ix) *Myself servile and afraid*

'You had better go first,' said Chit Hlaing when the time came.

With the same display of casualness with which we had greeted each other, we now said goodbye. The abbot kindly rose to escort me to the foot of the steps, but Chit Hlaing stayed in the shadow within.

'Don't go back to the country, Chit Hlaing,' I said.

He smiled—a tense, taut smile.

'We shall meet again,' he said.

Already outside on the steps, and without looking back at him, I echoed it.

'We shall meet again.'

The abbot and the monks were shaking hands and smiling, their robes richly coloured in the declining afternoon sunlight, and in another moment I was making my way by nonchalant detour back to the house in which I was staying.

When, the following day, I stepped into the Rangoon plane and waved farewell to my kind old friend U Mya and the police escort I had a peculiar sense of relief. Good as it had been to meet many friends again, the mental affliction of living in the calm surroundings of intolerably strained nerves had begun to tell on me, even without my having been aware of it.

In Rangoon, after the usual delay, I obtained the Government's permission to leave the country, and it was only then, as the plane bearing me to Calcutta rose on the last section of its flight, and the landscape of Burma receded finally into distance, that I understood the full depth of my own inner feelings. As Akyab fell back and was lost in endless green jungle, and as even this gave way to the freshness of the sea, I faced point-blank the fact that I was thankful to be out of the country. The aircraft could not fly fast enough for me. Like an escaping prisoner, I searched the pale morning mist for a glimpse of the shore ahead, imagining a variety of horrible incidents that might occur to convince the pilot he should turn back.

Though unreasonable, even ridiculous, such is the cumulative effect of having constantly to ask permission from petty functionaries to do what in other countries may be done freely. Without being conscious of it, one's spirit sinks into a state of servility and fear.

It is this human trait that communist and other dictatorial governments have exploited with such skill. The citizen is aware that the government is more demanding of him, but he is not aware to what it is actually reducing him. He does not feel servile or afraid. It is only when coming away into a freer atmosphere that he realizes, with surprise, how his lungs are deeper than he thought, his step lighter, his prospect better, and the whole world, including himself, larger and infinitely more interesting.

Apart from this—and it may well be that an alien sees more of it than a Burmese citizen—it would be misleading to suggest any other comparison between Burma and a communist country. Burma is not a communist country, and on this and later visits I came away thinking it most unlikely that she would ever become one, unless invaded and occupied by a communist power, or infiltrated by international communism, as opposed to the present personal factions wearing communist badges.

Since independence, Burma has been going through one of those periods familiar to the country before the imposition of the Pax Britannica. The king has died. He was a great king. His reign was long and his rule good, and his death has been the long-awaited opportunity for rival ambitions to air themselves and engage in a struggle for power. Gradually the heir must increase his strength and impose his will; for he is the strongest, and if he gives evidence of ruling well there is no reason why he should lose his power. Only combined could his opponents threaten him, but the very nature of their opposition makes them incapable of combining. If the new king is persevering, one by one he will humble them. After that is done, he will reach the greater problem: how to prevent the same thing occurring upon his own demise.

Burma's first republic has had certain measures of wisdom forced upon it. Its lack of military strength has taught it to yield, instead of taking measures to suppress—and only by yielding can there be eventual unity. Where it has considered it unwise to yield it has not been ruthless in success. It knows the spirit of this softer age in which we live, in which the razing of a few villages can arouse the same bitterness as, two hundred years ago, might not even have been roused by the public mutilation of a thousand rebels.

The sea beneath us began to look brown, showing that, though no land was yet in sight, we were nearing the Ganges delta. Ahead was haze. Over Bengal it was evidently a peaceful day, with the first stillness of autumn giving rumour of the enchanted season ahead.

The brown water changed to long issues of mud, the mud to dark green banks of waste, the waste to a million rice fields, with villages, ponds, small groves of trees, waterways, thin roads and bridges, a landscape instantly recognizable as that of a great and ordered civilization. After half-an-hour or so we came in sight of the huge grey oval of Calcutta, metal in the midst of an immense flat vegetation, with the Hooghly river passing across it like a veined flaw in a piece of pale green jade.

But when we landed, the anxiety generated by my stay in the land of barred windows and bolted bedroom doors had not been dissipated. In the waiting room I watched anxiously as the Burmese hostess handed my passport to her Indian opposite number, and as my luggage was transferred from Burmese to Indian hands. Surely now there could be no more questionings, body-searchings and suspicious undertone conversations in Burmese.

'Would you step this way, please.'

It was the Indian woman airport official who had spoken. With the relief of a child rediscovering the parent it has lost, I pushed my way to the front of the passengers and followed directly behind her.

V

(i) *Calcutta and a greater orbit*

When I first entered India, in 1944, I found the act of doing so an extraordinary spiritual experience. It was as if the sky was not sky at all, but a heavy pall, in the gloom beneath which the only expressions heard were of lamentation and suffering. The initial impact was of a land of woe.

It was impressive; there was a poetic grandeur about it; and in those days I often wondered what was causing it to be so. The sun shone brighter than in many other parts of the world, yet in retrospect it was gloomy. There was orderly government, almost all the facilities of the modern world, and, except in nationalist politics, the same degree of personal liberty as in Great Britain. Yet it was a lifeless, tormented land. There was a great deal of jollity in personal relationships, yet in retrospect only sorrow.

I do not know whether British people long resident in India noticed it. I assumed, as many of my companions also did, that India was like that and one must make the best of it. But, at the same time, a fervent believer in Indian independence, I harboured the idea that there were limits to this assumption, that under other circumstances the pall would lift, laughter would be heard, and the listless become active.

Returning now, on my first proper visit since independence, I awaited eagerly the initial impact of arrival. A Hindu concept, and one in the efficacy of which I personally believe, is to judge people at the first instant of meeting, and by the first words spoken. The same can certainly be applied to cities, and sometimes also to countries. When travelling to places one has not seen before it is interesting to note down such first impressions and re-read them a year later when one is more familiar with the place concerned. They often hit on truths which, with familiarity, one has overlooked.

As we approached the coast of Bengal my mind moved out in search of the first indications of the pall. I knew it so well, it was like an old friend, that dark, brooding, sorrowing spirit. Instead, however, the normal atmosphere of the plane cabin remained unchanged. A Burmese passenger smoked a cheroot (are Burmese aircraft the only ones in the world in which cigar-smoking is permitted?) and I wished that, thinking cigars would not be allowed, I had not packed mine deeply away.

I then thought that perhaps aircraft are not the proper places in which to detect atmospheres. The air in the plane, after all, was still Burmese—or so my unscientific mind said. But after completing formalities at Dum Dum Airport (they took four minutes, compared with Mingaladon's fifty) and embarking on a somewhat bumpy busride to Calcutta, I decided that the air in the plane had been Indian. It had happened. There was no more pall. Out through the bus windows Bengal still presented its classic appearance of respectable decay, pediments still crumbled, gay tropical herbs still sprouted from imposing porticos, cows still sat on Doric verandahs (until gently invited by servants to move), and the Bengali seated next to me in the bus still began explaining his country by insisting that Indians must not be looked down on because they have brown, or chocolate, skins (when his own was the colour of old ivory), but . . .

It was fresh. It was also ordinary, like arriving in Belgium or Italy. It was the normal, undifferent world. Yes, cows sat on verandahs. But they were ordinary white Indian cows on ordinary, stucco, gently collapsing Indian verandahs. And it was fresh. There was no woe, no lamentation, no heavy funereal sky. It was like revisiting old familiar places, but in another incarnation.

Calcutta, when we reached it, looked slightly cleaner, and the centre of it a great deal cleaner, than when I last saw it, overcrowded during the war. Pompous statues of British gentlemen in uniforms and academic robes still adorned the fringes of the Maidan. Government House looked as imposing and well-kept as ever. Some of the old landmarks—Clive Street, for instance—now bore Indian names. But Calcutta remained what it always was, an extraordinarily successful freak of British and Hindu ingenuity, the combined effort of two delightfully illogical peoples. Really, we ourselves have underrated Calcutta. Walking in early morning down Chowringhee, with imposing old buildings on one side and the great trees and grassy expanse of the Maidan on the other, is to see a city conceived of in noble terms, despite scavenging crows picking an open dustbin or two that someone has omitted to empty.

Arriving in Calcutta, I have the same sense of ease as when arriving in London. This is a city I understand well enough to feel at home in. It breathes security of the type a Londoner is accustomed to. Like London, it has personality, as opposed to beauty. It moves at a smooth, unruffled pace. An Indian demands of Calcutta the same somewhat disinterested helpfulness that an Englishman demands of London—and gets it. Again like London, it is not an immediately inviting city (in the sense that Rome and Paris are). It needs knowing. But, once known, it arouses faithfulness in its patrons.

My taxi drew up outside the great arched doorway off Chowringhee where Ramen-da[1] lived. I was expected. A servant took my baggage, and following him I mounted an imperial-size flight of stairs within the immense building, on the upper floor of which Ramen had his office, studio and apartment combined.

A brief, effusive greeting, the allocation of a room, the provision of Bengali clothes while my laundry was done, a bath with water pouring out warm and comfortable from a roof tank in which the sun heated it, and there I was in the vast high-ceilinged living room, with tables and desks littered with half-read books and journals, walls hung with portraits finished and unfinished, corners congested with easels and canvases, and out of the windows the calm trees of an interior garden, and a faint roar of the Chowringhee traffic somewhere beyond.

Tea and Bengali sweetmeats—lolling comfortably with feet up on low tables—a sudden sense of calm, tradition, continuous civilization. One of India's most distinguished artists, and principal of what must be one of the largest art schools in the world, Ramenda sat on a wicker sofa and talked as if I had just returned from an hour's walk in the town. Short and rather bald, with fine Brahmin features and sensitive lips and hands, he gesticulated slightly in conversation, in Bengali fashion. But the way he sat with one leg over the other, and the shrewd, tolerant, affectionate way he discussed people and things, belied his flowing white Indian garments.

[1] *Da*=Elder Brother.

In his humorous oval eyes, from which he occasionally removed and dried his spectacles, glinted an ineradicable cosmopolitanism acquired from extensive travel in India and the West.

It was difficult to believe that earlier in the day I had been in the unsettled, anxious surroundings of Rangoon, with its water pipe cut by bandits for the second time in six weeks. The gay bustle of Manila was like a far-away trivial dream; and Hongkong, with its struggling millions faced with the problem of the age in its most revealed, naked form, was on another planet.

Yes, there were communist students in the art school. They had organized a strike to coincide with an official visit by the Governor of Bengal. And Ramen-da explained the effective but subtly oriental way in which he had dealt with the situation and ended the strike threat.

But these were transitory matters in a great, settled scheme of things. Within half-an-hour we were away into anecdotes, reminiscence, tales of friends, politics, travel, religion, changing customs, India and the world. And the warm afternoon sun fell on the unruffled trees in the garden as it does in Europe on a summer day when life slows down for an hour or two, awaiting coolness and dusk.

Tonight there would be no ceremonious Chinese dinner to wash the dust from the new arrival with many viands and too much wine. There would be no Manila dance-band or gay smart women. Nor would there be any strained tea-ceremony etiquette, or folding up little pieces of soiled paper and drawing silk cushions out of noiselessly sliding drawers. It was fun to have experienced all these things, but after being out in the typhoon one must sooner or later come to shelter. To savour the world's diversity is only bearable if each journey radiates out from a central point of silence and tranquillity. And in Ramen-da's studio was the first hint on my homeward journey that I was leaving the zone of storm and divergence, entering the silence, the unity.

Here there was no effort to adapt ideas and expressions so that they meant something in the context of Japanese or Chinese concepts and prejudices. Here human reaction did not have to be gauged or guessed at. Here once more was the world of childhood, in which we know the way.

Lying back deeply in my chair, my mind and limbs felt heavy with the weariness that unexpectedly comes over us at the end of a prolonged mental effort. In Doming's house I had the sense of being at home—the sense which brings on this weariness—but it was a home surrounded by dancers, cars driven too fast, bandits, and the question of whether or not we should take revolvers. It was like a bird's home in the top of a tree in a high wind. Here among the easels and canvases was a home with strong walls and a placid garden, the finality from which we start and to which we return.

The greatest joy of that first day in Calcutta was being able to talk once more on any subject with the certainty of being fully understood. Chinese conversation, when at its best, is more like a game than a striving to express thoughts. It is an arabesque of puns, riddles, proverbs and classical quotations. Or if it is not, it too often tends to be the drab recital of prices, values and material amounts. Chinese thought, though wonderfully succinct, hilariously down-right, fabulously subtle, lacks the particular brand of inventiveness which we of the West prize in our intellectual life. Rather than frame new ideas, it prefers, with extraordinary aptness, to apply old formulae to what for a moment seemed new. It looks at the world from a standpoint of profound antiquity.

An hour or so after my arrival, several friends whom I had not seen for eight years or so called to give greeting. But even with them there were no elaborate invitations to meals, no ceremonies of return to be undergone. The Hindu mind, a quiet cool organism in the immense heat of the tropics, does not think much of years or miles. A friend went away yesterday, he returns today. He went out, he comes in. We talked, drank tea, discussed the latest books, the latest philosophy. What did I think, for example, of the most recent developments in existentialism? My jaw dropped. Had there been any? I had been busy with Confucius—oh, and Karl Marx—anyhow, old-fashioned stuff.

Old-fashioned. This was something unexpected. Living in the Far East one does not feel old-fashioned. On the contrary, one often has the impression of sitting on the spearhead of the world's affairs. Yet, talking to my Indian friends, I was conscious of being out of date with that quality in the world which is constantly moving towards new ideas, that quality which created, and continues to nourish, civilization. And I observed for the first time, as if it were an undreamed-of revelation, that contact with the West was synony-mous with contact with that creative, evolutionary quality, while loss of contact with it meant being stuck in a morass of static thought which is out of keeping with the pace and needs of this age. Seen from Calcutta, the Chinese conflict appeared to lie between two outmoded forms of thought, each stiff with age and claiming, like religions, to be all-embracing, neither of them associated with the real spearhead of the world's advance, which, if it can be said to be of metal, is of a substance soft, malleable, subject to change, its thrust tentative, exploratory and unconvinced.

My Chinese friends, menaced by communism, took refuge in Confucius, quoted classic sayings of the Han dynasty, or else buried their bothered heads in the Church, which consoled them in a medium that was not quite their own, but was at least alive, real and belonging to the twentieth century. My Indian friends, after discussing communism in China and the East in general, moved on to the more congenial subject of the latest developments in European philosophy, literature and art, and their relation to current Indian thought. My Chinese friends had arrived at a full stop of utter uncertainty, where for my Indian friends there was not even a comma.

(ii) *A new master in an old house*

Before reaching India I had written to my elderly friend, Devadas Basu, at whose country house in Bengal I had often stayed during my first year in India. To my surprise there was no reply. Then, two days after my arrival in Calcutta, a short note came from Devadas' son, Prakash, telling me that his mother was dead, his father recuperating from a serious illness. The same day, in the afternoon, I went round to the house near Alipore where Dev Babu[1] was staying.

The tone of Prakash's letter had prepared me for a shock. Seated in a wheelchair on the verandah, Dev Babu, clad in his customary white dhoti and punjabi, was hunched down in silence, alone. I first saw him in profile, the strong leonine profile I remembered so well from happy times in the past. He looked at first unchanged—the intellectual brow, rather dark skin, greying hair brushed loosely back, heavy-rimmed glasses.

[1] *Babu*=polite form of address in Bengal.

At the sound of my coming he turned slightly, a hard, cold look of enquiry, the challenge which I saw at a glance he now threw out to all unknown people who came near him—I had never seen such a look in his eyes before. Then he recognized me.

'It is you. Come and sit down near me. I am not allowed to get up.'

He did not smile, not even in the eyes. But from his voice I knew he was glad. As I came to his side and saw him full face, I realized why he did not smile. The profile had deceived me. The full face was shrunken and one-sided, the eyes unnaturally large and cold, the chin . . .

'I have cancer, Austin. In my jaw, you see. But they have performed an operation.'

The voice too had lost its fullness; the tongue functioned with difficulty. It appeared that the left jaw had been entirely removed.

Because the lion is king, his fall into sickness and age is to us more tragic than the fall of dog or fox. Dev Babu, though unknown to the great world, was a king among men, proud under attack, humble in friendship, as a scholar never dogmatic, as a master never unjust. To him, more than to any other single individual, I owe the fact that today I dare put pen to paper and write of Asia. It was he who first invited me to live in an oriental home, as a guest who ended up almost as a member of the family. It was he who opened the indispensable door which, closed, permits the stranger to hear only the banter of the market, the chatter in the street, the philosophy of beggars at the temple gate.

'My wife died ten months ago. They say I should go home, to have quiet. My daughter-in-law could look after me—Prakash is married, you know—but I do not wish to go back now.' Without the expression of his shattered face changing, he gave a short, caustic laugh. 'I am deadwood.'

After he had told me other family news, I took charge of the talk, so that he might rest. I led him to what I judged would interest him, to Chinese art, to the Japanese temples and monasteries I had seen, to the influences of India in classic Japanese sculpture, to Hindu philosophic influence in the Far East.

At the end, silent for a while, he stirred slightly.

'I did not understand that Hindu ideas had travelled so far,' he said deeply, in a tone that was unfamiliar to me.

'Neither did I,' I said, 'and, of course, the influences are in fragments. But there they are, all the same.'

'What is the use?' he said sharply. 'It achieves nothing.'

Before there was time to ask him what he meant by this, Prakash turned up, conversation switched, and I was left for the moment with the problem unsolved. After some more discussion, Prakash and I left to take the evening train down to the country.

The train trundled peacefully out, as it always used to, stopping at every station, off-loading commuting clerks and business men. Prakash, too, had not changed in appearance, but, symptomatic of the new India, his ideas had been broadened by opportunities which before the war were non-existenct. He had been to Australia for two years on a British Council fellowship, and was about to leave for the United States under the Fulbright scheme, to study university librarianship. Strangely enough, there were people in our compartment who remembered me from eight years ago—the same people, living in the same homes, working in the same offices, with the same interests but, in their various ways, with a broader view of the world, now that the colonial curtains round India were lifted.

The stationmaster was the same. There were greetings. We drove through the dark village with its lotus ponds shimmering in dark gold autumnal moonlight, just as before, bumping along over brick roads, over humped bridges, in a tricycle ricksha pedalled by a lean youngster with a sweat-rag on his shoulder.

Prakash and his young wife, Kamala Dévi, were now master and mistress of the great old country house, built in the colonial style, with colonnade and Corinthian stucco, dating back to the days of Warren Hastings. But for me it was hard to imagine what it would be like without Dev Babu and Bo Dévi, Prakash's parents, for it was as their home that I remembered it.

There was still no electric light in that part of the village, but pressure lamps had replaced the old oil-burners. We mounted the stone staircase, just as decayed as it always used to be, and pushed open the double doors at the top, leading into the long verandah room with its red polished floor and glass windows inserted between the pillars of the colonnade. Following the old routine, I let my sandals slip off before crossing barefoot within.

'Oh, don't bother,' said Prakash, walking in with his *chapals* on.

It was the first sign of change.

In the house itself there was no longer the old sense of spaciousness and quiet order. There was more furniture, more decoration, more homely disorder. Distant relatives, refugees from East Pakistan, had had to be sheltered. There were obvious signs of the house having more occupants than the authoritative and independent Dev Babu would ever have allowed. His idea had always been to keep as much as possible out of family affairs. Prakash, despite his foreign travel, tolerated a more oriental state of family botheration —provided that for the greater part of the year he could live away from it, his place of work being in another part of the province.

Kamala Dévi, recently graduated from Calcutta University, was contributing as much as, perhaps more than, Prakash to the subtle changes going on in the house. Kamala was attractive and intelligent. With the frankness that is between young men who have known each other as bachelors, I commented when Kamala was out of earshot:

'A good choice, Prakash!'

And for a moment the dark house rang with laughter.

The details of the evening—the dinner, the provision of fans, the stoking of the pressure lamps, the arrangements for washing—did not proceed as smoothly as they used to under the kindly guidance of Prakash's mother. Bo Dévi, though she had never been abroad and spoke no English, was an experienced wife and hostess. To Kamala these duties were new, and, on this occasion of entertaining her first foreign house-guest, she was a little nervous. But after dinner, left alone with me at the table, she found that it was easier to use her hesitant English when Prakash was out of the way than when he was there, liable to correct her.

'You see we're having mutton,' Prakash said at dinner, with a hint of wickedness. 'Father would never allow us to eat it before, you remember?'

I would have been just as happy with Father's restrictions, but the item had to be put down as another emancipatory change.

In the bathroom, before we went out to the cinema, I found another. In the old days when I was staying in the house, the window shelf was the repository of a collection of nim sticks—small twigs of the nim tree which have been used for centuries by Indians with which to clean their teeth—and one toothbrush, used by me. As, unpacking my things, I put my toothbrush in the immemorial place, I noticed that there were still a few nim sticks on the shelf, but in addition there were now eight toothbrushes and numerous tubes of toothpaste. Dev Babu considered nim sticks superior to toothpaste, and did not encourage the use of toothbrushes.

In the room outside the bathroom, where the slow drip of water used to be heard all night, falling from pot to pot in an ancient system of filtration through charcoal and sand, the wooden frame and the pots had been removed.

'We don't use that old thing any more,' Prakash told me when I enquired about it. 'We use well-water now. Much more hygienic and better to taste.'

Perhaps he was right about hygiene, but the water at dinner was certainly not so good to taste as the old filtered water. That is modernity, though, to please the doctor more than the epicure.

When I returned to the living room there was another item to be added.

'What about the python in the garden?' I asked. 'Is he still there?'

'He is!' said Kamala fervently. 'Horrible thing.'

'Oh, surely not,' I protested. 'I always thought he was rather pleasant.'

He was, in fact, a pleasant feature of the garden. He lived in a hole in the lawn, and was very large and well-fed, about seven feet long. He moved about without disturbing anyone, and Dev Babu and Bo Dévi never considered there was anything frightening about him. The only precautions that were ever taken by us were not to walk in the garden at night without a torch, lest one should accidentally step on him, when of course he would be likely to bite in self-defence. He lived on frogs and all kinds of insects, one of his favourite occupations being to crawl down some fence-posts in the garden which had become hollow with age and provided homes for an amusing assortment of beetles and centipedes. He would enter from the top of the post, and if the hunt was successful he would go right down to the bottom, leaving only his tail waving vaguely out of the top. The dog was the only member of the household who worried about him. Sometimes, as the snake was passing along, the dog would bounce along sideways, keeping close to the snake's head and barking furiously. But he never dared touch the snake, a fact which the snake was aware of, for when the dog became too tiresome he would swerve his head out towards it, with the humorous intention of seeing the dog scuttle backwards in fright.

To Dev Babu the snake was at least inoffensive and at best sacred. The Lord Siva had a cobra, the goddess Kali a cobra's hood. In the triune Padmanabhan, Siva's cobra spread his hood as the reclining god's pillow.

'Pleasant!' exclaimed Kamala. 'Not when he comes into the house! I have a young baby, remember.'

Yes, that was a much more understandable reaction—less imaginative, of course, but is that not also a part of what we call modernity? It was not a carbolic age that produced Hindu philosophy.

In the inner central room of the house, where the family idol of Sri Krishna had his abode, I observed even more unusual developments. In the old days the room was by decree kept empty, used occasionally by the women for sewing, or in the evening for reading or music. Now it was full of refugee family members' beds and mosquito curtains. There were no fresh flowers before the idol, no room in front of it even to permit the ceremonies of worship to be performed.

In sum, the home which I had come to regard almost as my own in India was now much less different from my real home than it used to be. Its reactions, its sentimentalities, its pretensions, its inner laws were gravitating slowly westwards, without conflict or falsity, without rebellious assertion or escapism. It was changing without giving any impression of change. Prakash was surprised when I reminded him of former days. He had forgotten that they were different.

It is not possible to grasp the full significance of this without knowing something of Bengal's background. Like the Japanese, the Bengalis have in their character rival strains of conservatism and desire for innovation. Bengal was the first province in India to take seriously the adaptation of western innovations to Indian requirements. Conversely, at a later date, Bengal was the first to develop the brand of conservative nationalism which bore the Indian independence movement forward to success. During this later period, Bengal has been the most conservative of all the more accessible provinces of India, at times insisting almost to the point of pigheadedness on the maintenance of a pure national culture. To

Bengalis of this turn of mind, the westernized citizens of Bombay were spurned as renegades from the Cause. It is thus possible to say in this context that when Bengal changes, India changes. The anchor chain may incline, but not till the anchor itself drags will the ship noticeably move with the tide. (I should add that to say such things as this in provinces other than Bengal is to incur protest and derision; but as an outsider from provincial rivalries, such is my opinion.)

.   .   .   .   .

At the cinema—the family owned it—I met Prakash's uncle, Pradip, older, fatter, more grey, but just as full of anxieties and family worries as ever. For Pradip Babu, Bengal was the centre of the world, the only really decent place that any right-thinking man could dream of living in. Seeing me, he promptly assumed that I had after all decided to settle in Bengal, and congratulated me on my good sense.

'Why are you not wearing dhoti?' he said, looking down severely at my white trousers.

'I do sometimes,' I said lamely—but in fact, now that to wear Indian clothes was no longer a sign of nationalism, I found so many of my friends wearing trousers instead that I had put my Indian clothes away.

There were changes in the cinema too. Eight years ago the women all sat upstairs, men downstairs. Now a section of the circle was reserved for ladies who wished to sit there; apart from this, men and women sat where they liked. In the seats in front of us were a young couple with shoulders discreetly touching. In the old days, not so long ago, there would have been cries of scandal and in-decency. Now, few even noticed it.

Walking back from the cinema, Prakash touched on the subject of his father.

'Did you notice how he had changed?' he asked.

'In what way?'

'Mentally.'

I remembered the curious challenging look as Dev Babu first saw me, before he recognized me, and his unexplained remark about Hinduism.

'Yes, I noticed something.'

'Before her death my mother became terribly worried about him. My father, you see, became an atheist. Yes, there are atheistic schools of thought in Hinduism. He became more and more interested in them, and we could none of us convince him of anything else. Now it is depressing to see him. He has absolutely no faith. He thinks death is the end of everything. It makes it so much harder for him, now he is sick.'

We walked in silence for some time.

'It's strange when you think,' I said, 'that your father taught me about as much about Hinduism as anyone I have ever met.'

'I wish you could talk to him,' Prakash said.

And it lies on my conscience to this day that, as a traveller moving from place to place with a time limit, I left his request unanswered. It could certainly have had little chance of doing good, but the thought of old Dev Babu, sick and alone, facing into vacuity, has power to haunt.

(iii) *Benares*

Two days later I resumed my westward journey. Taking the best train of the day, I left Calcutta at eight in the evening, travelling all night and into the following morning. By the time it was daylight we had left Bengal and were passing through Bihar, across countryside characteristic of the Ganges valley, an immense landscape changing so slowly that, were one to sleep for an hour or so, to wake up and look out of the window again one might think only ten minutes had passed.

It was now the first part of October, the rains were over, and the landscape was already looking brown and dry, with its innumerable huge trees, its small squared-off fields, the finality of its rich flatness. Here and there groups of men sat beneath trees, waiting for the day's heat to end; buffaloes basked in muddy and slowly-drying-up pools; a small boy perched on a gate played a pipe; and always, as the train passed, white paddy birds rose in flight.

Round about eleven in the morning we reached Benares, just within Uttar Pradesh, the former United Provinces, and I left the train. Though still fairly hot in the sun, the weather was cooler and less humid. Benares lies in the shape of a sickle moon on a bend in the Ganges, with a flat landscape of grassy banks and dunes on the opposite side.

'You should certainly go there,' said Ramen-da, when I suggested it. 'Benares belongs to no time or place. It is a city of dreams and improbabilities.'

That was not exactly the reputation it had acquired in my mind from reading English books about India. There it figured more as a city of sex-worship, Hindu and Muslim rival fanaticisms and strange cults of the dead—an exciting but horrible place.

I found, however, that Ramen-da's description was possibly nearer to the truth today, although of yesterday it was hard to believe that Benares' sinister reputation was not justly earned.

There are not many main streets in Benares, a great part of the city consisting of a labyrinth of narrow stepped alleys and passages among the temples and houses near the river. I found a good hotel on the most central main street. As it was a Brahmin establishment, serving only vegetable food, there was a certain flutter when I asked for a room. The manager's assistant was on the point of refusing, when the manager himself, a tall tough middle-aged Bengali, arrived, and showed me to a room at once. He had served as a sergeant on the Western Front in the First World War, and was glad of a chance to reminisce about his experiences.

It is a significant fact that once you are inside an oriental hotel, and particularly when people see that you are familiar with their eating and washing customs, you are accepted as an ordinary man of the country. If difficulty arises, it is over the initial business of getting in. Oriental people who complain about racial distinctions in hotels in the West do not always realize that something of the same kind also happens to occidentals in the East. People tend to be suspicious of a westerner travelling alone, and afraid he will be a cause of objection among other guests. Whichever way round, it is a natural feeling. Westerners who in the East stay only in the gloomy respectability of first-class international hotels do not encounter this difficulty. It is only when travelling cheap that distinctions have to be overcome.

It is a Bengali saying that in Benares one must beware of steps, bulls and widows (*shiri, shar, rari*). The steps, in the labyrinth, need no explanation. A casual glance to look up at a beautiful tree rising from a crack between two house walls and spreading high and wide enough to shade a temple courtyard, and before you know where you are you have tumbled down five or six steps and landed in the arms of a smiling temple panda who offers to show you the inner mysteries of Hinduism and very delicious sex statues. The bulls are certainly a terror. White, well-fed, and with splendid pointed horns, they wander at will through the labyrinth, the passages of which are so narrow that when a bull is coming it is often safer to retreat than risk being jabbed by a horn. For the bulls are like traffic police clearing the way for a procession: you get out of the way, or else. . . . Benares is one of the very few places in India where the sacred animal is aggressive.

As for the widows, their presence in such numbers is linked with the fact that one of Benares' most important trades is death. In India, and particularly in Bengal, old-fashioned people believe that certain ways of dying are better than others. It is better to die, for instance, in the open air than under a roof. It is good if, before dying, one can drink a sip of water for each member of the family. And it is a good death to die in Benares.

Although Benares is far from Bengal and the landscape around it is typical of Bihar and Uttar Pradesh, Benares is a pre-eminently Bengali city. Travelling westward across India, it is the last pronouncement of the riverine, deltaic culture of Bengal which, on the journey, slowly yields to the drier, sandy culture that gives forewarning of the desert. Bengalis are Benares' principal patrons in its capacity as a centre of religion and tourism.

For generations devout Hindus have come to Benares to die, and the provision of good deaths has become a local industry. Nowhere in India are funerals better organized. Whereas in Calcutta the barefoot mourners bearing a corpse trot distractedly through the streets, occasionally crying out the names of the gods, in Benares they march fiercely past shouting in strict rhythm 'Rama Nama Sattva hai! Rama Nama Sattva hai!' (In the Name of Ram is the Truth.) The air reverberates with the rhythm. Ten or so funerals may pass under the windows in a morning. The tourist soon finds the words and the dull thud of bare feet that accompanies them ingrained in his mind.

With the men who came to die came their wives. The good death accomplished, they were left to return to their homes as widows. But in former times the life of a Hindu widow was far from pleasant. By tradition she was no longer of any account in her own house. She had to wear a man's clothes, and remain in perpetual mourning. Even though young, she was not permitted to remarry. It thus sometimes came about that, rather than face this grim future, widows preferred to stay in Benares, making there a small home of their own. Sometimes, naturally, they felt lonely; and sometimes, among the many tourists, they met pleasant Bengali gentlemen on holiday, escaping momentarily from the tedium of being married to women who did not understand them.

I think that is what Ramen-da meant when he called Benares a city of improbabilities.

     ·   ·   ·   ·   ·

The steps, the bulls and the widows were still there, although as the treatment of widows improves in India the possibility of improbability lessens. The erotic sculptures—nothing spectacular—radiated encouragement at odd turns in the labyrinth. The market for silk, brocade and every kind of fine cloth remained one of the last brilliant sensations of Asia's departing mediaevalism. The funerals still passed every few minutes (*Rama Nama Sattva hai!*), and when there were many to be cremated at the burning ghats beside the river it was still true that, where no mourner stayed to see the final consumption of the body by fire, the remains were sometimes dumped into the water before being completely destroyed. Being an industry, death is a matter of commercial values and time-saving, like any other industry.

But after a few days in Benares, I began to think that some element of savagery had gone out of it. Though remnants of its insalubrious past were still evident, it was clearly in the process of becoming a quiet, respectable market city, with a university and a residential suburb in the former British cantonment. I concluded, rightly or wrongly, that the reason for the change was the departure of a great part of the Muslim population to Pakistan.

When the Muslims conquered Upper India, Benares was the scene of ghastly atrocities. The Muslims were genuinely horrified by what they found of phallic and idol worship in this sacred Hindu city, and in various ways, depending on the personality of different rulers, they tried to stamp out the hated cults, either by massacre, forcible conversion to Islam, or the banning of music and religious celebrations. In the heart of the city, on the site of one of the greatest mediaeval temples, they built a mosque, one of the tall, thin minarets of which is still Benares' landmark for miles around in the plain. But they could not succeed in stamping out Hindu practices. It was left to a later century, and to our forefathers, to expunge the worst of them, such as widow-burning and thuggery. Instead, in the dense congestion of an ancient city, Brahmin and Mussulman jostled each other in an atmosphere of tension liable to explode for any trivial reason into appalling bloodshed. Each felt his religion threatened by the other; each became, as is usual in such circumstances, a purist, an extremist. Archaic features of both religions were thus artificially kept alive long after the time when, with the coming of western influences and the development of liberal thought in India in many other directions, they might have been expected to be modified and rationalized.

This situation continued, strenuously kept under control by efficient policing during the British administration, until India achieved independence and was partitioned into India and Pakistan. Then at last the pent-up hatred of fanatics on both sides released itself in one of the grimmest butcherings in history, when throughout Upper India Hindus and Muslims slew each other with a fury that intelligent men on both sides found incredible. Hundreds of thousands of Hindus fled from Muslim areas into India; equally enormous numbers of Muslims fled from Hindu cities into the newly-created Pakistan. Thousands were murdered on the way.

In Calcutta, though I heard many eye-witness accounts from Hindus and Muslims of what happened during those weeks of nightmare, and saw, at such places as Sealdah Station, some of the thousands who were still homeless, living on railway platforms, it was not until reaching Benares that the effect of what had happened started to come home. Calcutta is a commercial city, Benares a religious one. Calcutta was left virtually unchanged, so far as its fundamental ways of life are concerned, after the terror and partition. Benares, I felt without having been there before, had changed radically.

Benares, the Hindu orthodox animal, had shaken itself after the fray, cleaned itself up, and set to work again as usual, only to find—yes, it was hard to face up to—that the old way of work had unexpectedly lost some of its savour. There was no longer the fervent excitement of heading processions as near to the great mosque as the police would allow. They could now march right past the mosque entrance. Who cared? The sacrificing of goats by the slow slitting of their throats, to which Muslims strongly objected, ceased to represent a principle. It uncomfortably began to appear for what it really was—a degraded cult of cruelty and filth. There was no longer the challenge, the danger, the self-justification. Everybody agreed these days, saying yes, certainly, do just as you please. Life was not so exciting as it used to be.

In the transformation thus taking place, the old will slowly assume new forms. The steps will stay—they are picturesque, provided they do not interfere with drainage. The bulls will have to be kept under control—they are bad for the tourist traffic. The widows—well, Prakash had no interest whatever in good and bad deaths, and he is not unusual as a representative of his generation, so I suppose the funeral industry will slump and there will be no more widows.

In a way it is sad to see an exotic culture fade away, drained of its *raison d'être*, but as I came out of my hotel door and boarded a ricksha to take me to the station—

> Rama, Rama, Rama, Ram!
> Rama, Rama, Rama, Ram!
> Rama Nama Sattva hai!
> Rama Nama Sattva hai!

—I decided that, on points, I preferred this new age of carbolic.

(iv) *More washing than wickedness*

It was not, however, until completing the next phase of my journey, and reaching Lucknow, that I became more certain of these vague, general sentiments of change.

Whereas Benares, with a large Muslim population before the partition, was culturally a Hindu city, Lucknow, with a large Hindu population, was essentially a centre of Islamic culture. Once the capital of the Nawabs of Oudh, it boasted the best Urdu spoken in India, and was noted for its music and dancing, arts which in Upper

India, for various social reasons, had by the beginning of this century become largely an Islamic preserve.

Like other cities, it had its cantonment of British bungalows in large gardens, its colonial-style church, its modern commercial centre and its old city. In addition it was dignified by the Nawab's palace, designed by a French architect, and by important mosques and schools. But its main attraction, distinguishing it from all other cities in the world, was Chauk, the principal street through its old city.

Entered beneath an arched gateway, which led from Lucknow's sedate exterior into its astoundingly different interior, Chauk was a fairly narrow street, with dark shops raised two or three steps above the street level, and with a long row of balconied upper storeys on either side, from which women gazed seductively down, holding your glance while someone picked your pocket. Like Delhi, it abounded with the spectacular and the terrifying. Every passage through it was an adventure. Every type of turban, beard and knife, every known variation in the villainy of the human physiognomy, every deception, every cunning, could be seen in Chauk. As a matter of course, if one settled down to drink some horrifying beverage in one of the shops, panders would politely enquire whether one would like a girl—later in the evening perhaps? of such and such an age and (for an extra fee) never had by man before—while from the balconies bangles clinked, fans waved, and swooning eyes indicated from which particular house the panda operated.

Had that been the whole story, Lucknow would have had little originality. The real fact was that, as with the geisha of Tokyo, many of the women combined the cultivation of physical beauty with lively and witty conversation, and with an art, usually either singing or dancing. It was possible to go with a group of friends in the evening to one of these houses for the pure enjoyment of some of the finest dancing and musicianship in India. A maiden aunt, escorted on such a visit, would have been enchanted and come out none the wiser.

Here in this extraordinary half-world, Indian royalty, escaping from the suffocation of viceregal formalities, a dwindling treasury, and the stagnation of life as a cipher, escaped into the solace of arts perfected in generation after generation by training and tradition, not least among which were arts of physical love. Sustained by the rich and idle, music and sin inseparably thrived, catering in their numerous ways for every taste, from the unimaginative to the connoisseur's.

Naturally I wanted to see what Chauk was like after the partition. My host in Lucknow, however, a young South Indian Brahmin scientist, recently married, did not encourage me. We visited South Indian friends, government officials, and even mosques. We cycled out into various parts of the country to see what were in themselves revolutionary happenings: the slow process of starting co-operative farming in villages, and a wonderful and painstaking extension of village irrigation. But I had already decided that the key to what I wished to see would be found in Chauk.

It eventually dawned on me in the course of conversation that, though my friend had been in Lucknow three years, he had never been to Chauk, and was not quite sure where it was. As he later confessed to me, Chauk might have traditions, but so too did South Indian Brahmins; and something inside him refused to contemplate anything so outrageous as a visit under the famous arched gateway. There was nothing for it but to get him in by accident.

One day, passing the gateway, I swerved my bicycle round towards it, shouting:

'This way, Krishna!'

As I expected, he swerved round with me. But when he saw the name of the street, he braked his cycle.

'No, not in there!' he shouted back.

But by this time I had already shot through the arch and well into the street beyond, under the balconies with—well, what was the world coming to?—washing hanging out to dry from them. Finding a suitably dirty-looking tea-house, I came to a halt and dismounted.

I looked back. No immediate signs of Krishna. Evidently he was still outside the gate wrestling with the conflicting claims of Brahmanism and Indian duties toward guests, even troublesome ones.

Ordering tea, I looked about me. The fierce Muslim faces of the old Chauk had gone. Everything was quieter. There were a few women on the balconies, I now saw, and the inevitable panda was approaching, a local Hindu, not one of the bearded strong-man types of which Chauk used to boast so many. And as he reached me, Krishna emerged through the gate, looking sheepish and pedalling very slowly.

'I've ordered tea for you,' I said as he came up, 'and now would you please help me talk to this gentleman, who is doing his best to be of assistance to us.'

Krishna looked disdainfully at the panda, and with Brahmin innocence asked him what he wanted.

That did not take long to explain.

But if Krishna was surprised by the speed with which I had, as it were, settled down in Chauk, the panda was no less surprised to see a South Indian Brahmin. Though informed that we were not customers, he could not tear himself away.

'Ask him how business is,' I begged Krishna in an undertone. 'It's a perfect opportunity.'

As far as South Indians can, Krishna blushed, and asked the man something different.

'No,' I said, 'ask him straight.'

'What? Just like that?' my host queried perplexedly.

'Sure! Why not?'

He did so, and an air of misfortune crossed the panda's expression. In fact, business was not at all good. None of the old clients came to Lucknow any more. There weren't any good singers these days, and as for the old custom whereby rich men maintained their own favourite girl musicians or male dancers, well—no one in India seemed to have any more money. He glanced at me as he spoke—the stranger was British?—yes, things had been better under the British.

Somewhat disconcerted by the broad laugh which followed Krishna's translation of this, he smiled furtively and moved away. From a balcony opposite, three unprepossessing girls withdrew from view.

It was as I thought. Even Chauk was turning into a quietly respectable Hindu street. The linen hanging from some of the balconies betokened, without need of words, the presence of placid shopkeepers' families inside. The modern unspectacular world was moving in among the ghosts of the old. There were shoe-shops now, and shirtmakers, a radio store and a brassware merchant or two.

But as we cycled out of the street, Krishna was smiling.

'Thank you,' he said. 'You've emancipated me from one more of my Brahmin taboos.'

When we reached home his wife was waiting for us, with lunch ready.

(v) *Cantonment hotel*

From Lucknow I moved southward, to various places in Madhya Pradesh, from there going westward till I ended up in an old fortress city on the fringe of Rajputana. It was Dipvali, the autumn feast of lights, when in most places doors, windows and rooftops are decorated with hundreds of lights, ranging from electric ones to candles and wicks resting in saucers of oil. The streets of the city were full of brightly-lit stalls selling goods from all parts of the country round about.

There was only one hotel, in the old cantonment area outside the town. It was a single-storey building with a long verandah from which each room led directly, with swinging horse-box doors and curtains behind them. The dining room was distinguishable by its full-length door of metal gauze, like a meat-safe.

When I came, no one was about. But after I had rung the bell several times, a thin elderly Indian waiter, or bearer, came, in a white uniform and turban, with a metal plaque with '1' written on it on his chest. He explained that the sahib, the owner of the hotel, was away in Simla, and that he, the No. 1 bearer, was in charge. He conducted me to a room, later bringing the hotel register for me to sign. What time did I require dinner? What kind of breakfast would I like, and when? Would I like some warm water for my bath?

Involuntarily I smiled.

'Not many English guests these days?' I asked, noting the expert way in which the old fellow set about things.

'Ah, sahib,' he complained. 'Very few. Mostly Indians today. Things are not so good now as in the British time. These Indians— well, I tell you—they give very small tips.'

'Perhaps they don't get paid so much.'

'They get paid all right, but they never give a tip like a British tip.'

With a kind of fascination I watched him unpack my case, setting out my things just as my own bearer used to in the days of the Raj, according to the immemorial pattern which was the same for every Englishman. The pattern was the same because to bearers all Englishmen were the same, as indeed, in their response to the absolute service and loyalty their bearers offered them, they were.

The master might be a liar and a drunkard, or a man unused to power, 'dressed in a little brief authority', but because of his responding respect for his bearer's loyalty the *mystique* of the Englishman remained about him. When he came home tired after work, he sat back with iced whisky while his bearer took off his shoes and socks, and washed and dried his feet; and when he came home drunk the bearer undressed him and put him to bed. Everything in his domestic life was managed on the assumption that to remove a shoe or look for a tie was beneath the dignity of an Englishman. The bearer decided what clothes he would wear, and which tie with what suit. The sahib must never be bothered with such matters.

Yet, and it was the secret of the relationship, there was no humiliation in such service. It was service freely given. Among British families with long connexions with India, father served father, and son served son. It was a common occurrence for a newly-arrived subaltern to find a young Indian calling on him in his first days, saying, 'My father served your father, sahib, and I have come to serve you.'

The bearer's loyalty was such that he could quietly tolerate his master's every foible; his service was such that his master tolerated all his. The bearer might be a liar and a cheat; but to others, not his master—apart from routine cheating, also part of the pattern, on all purchases at the rate of ten per cent. It was a relationship of unspoken understanding, with at its base a mysterious equality—the perfect master and the perfect servant.

In the actions of the old hotel bearer was a contented sense of familiarity in making me comfortable. With the Indian officers and others in the hotel he never knew where he was. Sometimes they would not like him to unpack their belongings, or they wanted things this way, not that—whereas all Englishmen were the same, wanting the same things. He was clearly happy when he had done his work, but as, going out, he glanced back at me, there was also sadness.

'You worked for army officers before?' I asked.

'Yes, sahib. Long time.'

'A colonel?'

'Colonels, generals, field marshals—all of them I work for,' he said expansively, and with a hint of irritation at my not having recognized the fact at once. 'Before, this was a big place. Every night parties and dancing and new men coming and going. I was the No. 1 bearer then—very busy, plenty things to fix up.'

As I went out in the evening to see the trade fair and the lights in the city, some of my fellow-guests were on view on the verandah, two English missionary ladies, an Indian major and his family, quietly discussing the little happenings of this dusty garrison town. They were evidently residents.

Returning after a visit to the city, I pushed open the meat-safe door and entered the dining room, a high room, the height of two storeys, with fans and few windows. Coloured prints of Highland cattle, in gold mounts and frames, hung between antlers and the horns of wild buffalo. At the far end, in the most prominent place, Christian Virtue (also in a gold frame) triumphed over the Heathen (the Hindu, I fear). An English couple, visitors from another town, conversed in low tones, and looked askance as I came in. But when I gave them good evening they responded. Apart from them, the place was empty.

The table was laid with a heavy array of knives, forks and spoons, the plate of which was worn and yellow. There was a typewritten menu with words on it peculiar to the half-world of the old Anglo-India. A clear soup came first, made from beef, which because, having stayed with Hindus since arriving in India, I had not eaten for some time, gave me a feeling of nausea. An old dry fish followed, fried some time ago and kept warm, then rice with curried mutton and egg. Finally a heavy piece of cabinet pudding. No vegetables, no fruit—for the British in India were known as beefeaters, and would only be given vegetables if they were insistent about it. The vegetables might even then be out of a tin, part of the immemorial pattern being that memsahibs would never tolerate Indian vegetables.

Compared with the fresh and delicious meals I had been enjoying till now, this was the breakfast of a penitent. It looked sad and forsaken, like the bread and wine of a dead religion. It reminded me of other similar restaurants I had known in my first days in India, when bearers hurried from table to table, when the laughter of the drinkers could be heard outside on the verandah, and into each word penetrated the pretence that India did not exist, that this was another England, but with meat-safe doors and malarial mosquitoes. In those first days, in subdued loneliness, I had sat silent amid the hubbub, conscious only of the silence beyond it, the great world around, from which I was insulated by taboos more adamant than those of the Brahmins.

The same old bearer served the dinner. He seemed to do everything. Since entering the hotel I had seen no other servant.

'How many other bearers are there?' I asked him, looking at the metal plaque with 'I' on it on his chest.

He sighed.

'No more, sahib. All gone. Myself am the only one.'

No wonder, really. After the gods are buried, who will go to their ceremonies?

'Why don't you serve proper Indian food?' I asked. 'Why not make this a place Indians will come to?'

He looked shocked.

'No, sahib. Master-Sahib would not like.—Coffee outside, sahib?'

'Yes, please.'

At the entrance to the dining room, the restaurateur's licence hung under glass. The signature was an English name, with the word Major after it. The last piece in the puzzle fitted in. The owner of the hotel was a Eurasian, misguidedly, but with noble intent, preserving the trappings of his English ancestors, come wind come weather, with a reverence born of the oriental blood that was also his.

(vi) *The light of yesterday*

I had not written to Dibyendu for six years, and was hesitating whether to look him up. But as my way to Delhi lay through the city where he lived I saw in it the answer of the fates and broke my journey there.

Dibyendu was the son of a man who, when I last met them, was a very important person, believed to enjoy the Viceroy's confidence. They had a house in New Delhi and a great estate in what is now Uttar Pradesh. I never met the father; he lived in a cloud of glory. When people like myself visited the house, he was always either touring the provinces or unexpectedly summoned for consultations at the Viceroy's House. In addition, he was by way of being a religious leader, deeply interested in Hindu-Muslim accord.

I first met Dibyendu when we found ourselves sitting side by side on our suitcases on the platform of a country railway station, waiting for a train which was four hours late. He was a tall, lanky fellow, pale-skinned, with prominent cheekbones and heavy-lidded eyes that concealed the fire of his inner personality. No one could possibly have guessed that he was the son of so important a person. He wore a rough white shirt and khaki slacks, and travelled without a servant. He was a brilliant talker, with unusual personal magnetism. Counting the four hours' wait and the four hours' journey that followed, we talked on that first occasion for eight hours without stopping.

He lived apart from his father, partly in protest against being forced to marry a woman he did not care for, and worked as a contractor with, at that time, a number of important government contracts to fulfil. It was hard to find a subject to do with Indian culture or religion on which he could not talk with a vivid freshness. When the train arrived, we found two seats in a compartment that was then full, and his conversation electrified the other passengers. Beginning as a private discourse to me, it ended as a general sharing of experiences and opinions. It was one of the most enjoyable railway journeys I have ever made.

His personality was of that warm, pliant type from which leadership comes, with that essential negative ingredient that draws toward it the respect and support of the strong. But, as is often the case with men of this type, within the warm glow of brightness around him there was a strain of shadow. When he mentioned that he had studied deeply the lore of Tantra, the sinister side of Hinduism, the nature of this shadow became plainer. I had expected him, in spite of his father's position, to be interested in the nationalist movement for Indian independence. I seldom met in those days any young Indians of any originality or enterprise who were not interested in it, or actively campaigning for it. But when the subject of politics came up on the platform he lightly dismissed it, while in the compartment, in the presence of others, I did not like to mention it again.

Tantra is a cult akin to what we know in the West as black magic. By the achievement of an unusual degree of control over the physical body, its adherents are able to develop various powers of an occult nature which they can use in their daily lives to influence people to do what they want, without the people influenced being

216

aware that they are acting other than of their own volition. I should add that once one has some slight knowledge of the cult it is easy to recognize a Tantric at work and take precautions against him. It is a dying cult, probably found today only in India and Tibet, although in former centuries it was established in China and several countries of the Further East. Dibyendu, I discovered on subsequent meetings with him at his New Delhi home, was a Tantric adept, with considerable powers.

He professed to be fed up with the cult, and to have abandoned it, but in my mind's eye it appeared that his interest had originally been stimulated due to the peculiar emptiness of an upbringing in which, as the son of a public figure, he was encouraged to be interested in anything he liked except the subject dominating the minds of nearly every young man of his age and schooling—politics.

'Why don't you drop all this and join the Congress?' I asked him once.

'What's the use?' he replied. 'They'll never get anywhere.'

I expressed my doubts.

'You don't understand the Government of India,' he said. 'Gandhi will never succeed in moving it.—Try this sweet; I don't think you've tasted it before.'

And on this—as it turned out—instable foundation he continued to build his life.

.   .   .   .   .

We had not met for eight years. I gave my name slowly and carefully over the telephone on arrival in his home town.

'Oh yes,' he said. 'How are you?'

As I should have known, he was not pleased to hear from me.

He did the ordinary Indian thing of asking where I was staying, but after this we plunged into formalities remembered from the days of dealing with Englishmen during the Raj. The normal Indian reaction to an arrival after long absence is to fix a meeting at once, often regardless of office hours. Here there were to be delays. A day must elapse first. That was part of the ceremony maintained in the comedy of whisky-drinking bara sahibs becoming infuriated by oriental diplomacy and evasiveness. The following afternoon a car would be sent for me—oh, now, just a moment, would a car be available then?

'Never mind,' I said. 'I'll come by tonga.'[1]

I did so, and when, in his neighbourhood, I stopped the tonga to ask a passer-by which house was Dibyendu's, I realized that, in the excitement of independence, this once powerful family had been forgotten. The passer-by looked vague, repeated the name, and enquired of another pedestrian. Such a thing could not have happened eight years ago. Everyone then knew where they lived.

After some discussion I was at last given the directions I needed. But not till the servant ushered me in was I sure that I had reached the right house.

The living room was blinded and gloomy, and when Dibyendu finally came he was quite unnecessarily wearing dark glasses. He was still as thin as before, but gaunt and reserved. Briefly I heard of his family life. His father had died six years ago. The sons had quarrelled and parted company. His wife—the wife he married at his father's wish but never cared for—had died last year, and he was looking after his children unaided except by servants.

He spoke frequently of his eldest son, who was fourteen. He was good at cricket, but it was difficult to obtain exactly the kind of cricket boots he required in this quiet provincial town. They had to be ordered from Delhi.

He enquired about myself. I told him where I had been and what I had been doing since I last wrote.

'You have travelled a lot. You always wanted to travel,' he said. It was his only reference to the past, to what I had looked back on as one of the most stimulating friendships of my first visit to India. But it identified him, this wasted man, this empty vessel whose gifts had been offered at the wrong altars, with the bright, vital being that once was. Without that one remark I could not have perceived, through his cold reserve and the shield of his dark glasses, that I was in truth speaking to the same person.

What he was doing, I do not know; he evaded the question. No —in answer to another—he seldom went to Delhi and no longer had a house there. Tantra? He laughed self-consciously, as at a foolishness of youth; had he ever told me he knew anything about it?

'Your eyesight is all right, I hope?' I asked.

'Yes,' he replied, without removing the spectacles. 'But I find

[1] Pony-trap.

218

the light a strain. You must be very strong,' he added. 'I see you don't even wear a hat when you go out.'

No. Hats—topees—were part of the ceremony too. So was cricket. Dibyendu obeyed the rules of the ceremony. In the ceremony there was security. Without it there was only plebeian anarchy, the world that had slapped his face. I had hoped for that world. He had refused to believe in it.

I should not have come. In this house I was the traitor who returns to sup with the king whose downfall he procured. Silences fell between us, implicit in them this downfall, this treachery. Not till too late had I understood it. When I did, I was miserable.

I stayed the ceremonial hour, then announced departure. This time there really was a car.

Dibyendu came as far as the hall. Each of us made a statuesque goodbye. Before I was even seated in the car he had turned back into his familiar gloom. The driver started the engine. An inner door in the house closed.

Hapless Dibyendu! Born in the light, brought up in the light, in the end he had been dazzled by it.

(vii) *Taj Mahal*

When travelling in India, should your train happen to pass through Agra, it will stop, and you, no matter where you are going or what you are doing, must break your journey. That is one of the rules of life.

Having spent the night in Agra, you must rise before daylight. Do not wash or shave, or be preoccupied with any earthly affairs; this is not an earthly affair. Do not wear shoes or socks; they will be a nuisance. Wear sandals, which you can kick off and leave around (rest your mind, newcomer, no one will steal them). Wear a shawl over your shoulders; it will probably be cold. Having ordered a tonga the evening before, you will then drive in darkness out of the city and through a great park, till you reach the forecourt of the Taj Mahal.

It is unnecessary to tell the tongawalla to wait; he will, and both he and his horse will enjoy some more sleep. But you will walk under one of the great arches of the forecourt and descend into the garden, at the end of which, in grey gloom, you will see it. By this time your eyes will be accustomed to the darkness. You will sit cross-legged, or whatever other way is comfortable to you, on the edge of one of the fountains. Do not be disturbed by your own outlandish appearance. The great and the lowly have done as you are doing. Kings and clerks have sat where you are sitting. All were incognito. It was something that never happened.

Thus you will watch it. First it will be grey; then, as the light grows, blue. After that comes the pale pink that is sometimes seen in pearls; and, as the sun rises, a glowing pink that is eventually drenched into brilliant white as light assumes full command of day. If anyone is too old or too sophisticated for this, he has forgotten how to live. For this is one of the very few things on the face of the earth which only changes in such a way as to become on each revisitation more marvellous. This, I think, is because it is beyond the power of imagination to carry away in one's mind the full measure of what is here achieved. Despite a clear memory, and even adding the exaggerations of time, reality revisited shows memory to be a dullard, and exceeds every exaggeration. When people sometimes complain that Heaven must be a boring place if it is perfect, I always think of the Taj. As nearly perfect as anything that exists on earth, it shows already that perfection, when at last we shall see it, is a thing of undying wonder.

.   .   .   .   .

I have an excellent pale blue-green Bengali chaddar of thick homespun cotton, suitable for such occasions as a dawn visit to the Taj. It stretches twice my length from head to foot, and may be used as a shawl, a rug, an under-blanket and pillow, two blankets (one above, one below), or a bag for carrying possessions. At various times it has been used for all these purposes. Setting out before dawn, with the tonga waiting at the gate, I hastily put on white shirt and slacks, threw my chaddar over this for protection in the damp mist and dew, slipped into my Indian sandals, and was away.

I had already been sitting some time in the garden. It was a cloudless dawn, the light already strong, the sun up but still red, and the transforming miracle in process, when an Indian student settled down beside me on the stones I had chosen as the best place of vantage. For a time we watched in silence as the miracle continued. Finally, he began speaking to me in Hindi.

My own Hindi, such as it ever was, having fallen completely into neglect, I replied to him in English, in response to which he too switched to English, and thus our conversation proceeded, with a word or two of Hindi here and there. Every time he had a holiday, he said, and the weather was fine, he came here to watch the dawn break over the dome. Did I think there was any other building in India where such an effect of beauty could be seen in a man-made object? I mentioned a few—Humayun's tomb, near Delhi, the rock of the Penance of Arjuna, at Mahabalipuram in South India—and one by one we turned them down in favour of the Taj.

In the silence that followed, he looked at me.

'What part of India do you come from?' he asked.

When he had first spoken to me in Hindi it occurred to me that he had mistaken me for one of his countrymen, but when we switched to English I thought he must have realized I was not. Yet, of course, when I replied in English I was only acting as an ordinary Indian does when an educated fellow-Indian addresses him in a language he does not follow well. I had momentarily forgotten this.

Something inside me laughed, but I concealed it.

'Which part d'you think I come from?' I asked.

He looked me over carefully, my unshaven beard, my clothes, my sandals, a foot (slightly tanned) that protruded from beneath the folds of my chaddar.

'Somewhere from the North,' he said slowly, 'and yet you don't speak Hindi. Is it that you come from Kashmir?'

I laughed and told the truth. He looked at me even more carefully this time from head to foot.

'You don't believe me?' I asked.

'Yes, yes . . .' he said, looking in my eyes intently, 'I see now. I see it.'

He too laughed now, and as often happens on such occasions, conversation started from the beginning again, running over the same ground but in a different light. He breakfasted with me.

India was my first eastern country, and, in another sense, it always will be. It is pleasant in the East, after being monotonously distinguishable as a European every day of one's life, to find a country in which one can—even though only for a rare and fleeting moment—blend, and become part of the landscape.

There is a final point I omitted to mention about dawn visits to the Taj Mahal. Even dawdling on the way back, you still reach home long before breakfast time. It is then that you wash and shave, so as to appear as presentable as usual at the normal hour. The morning visit, as I said before, is something that never happened.

(viii) *The capital*

There are fellow-countrymen of mine who, making a short excursion from their islands and sniffing the streets of Southern Italy, say that the East begins at Naples. Coming from the Far East and moving westward towards Europe, the corollary may be added that the West begins at Delhi. It used not to, but it does now.

It is in Delhi that, on the westward journey, one first becomes conscious of an enormous number of people wearing trousers, as opposed to various types of oriental clothing—far more trousers than there ever were prior to independence. It is in Delhi that one first sees that oriental miracle, a bus queue, a sight filled with revelation for those familiar with the East. In Communist China, of course, there are also bus queues. In China there is the same overall movement towards carbolic civilization as there is in India. There is the same spring cleaning. But it is done upon the order of a task-master, who appoints the hours it shall be done in and the methods that shall be used, who makes universal rules that are applicable to some, inapplicable to others, that are easy for some, but bring hard-ship to others. People are admitting now that the cleaning was good, but they did not all enjoy the experience. In India there are no such taskmasters or universal rules. Each household follows arrangements suited to itself. There is no compulsion. The cleaning is in progress because the spring has come, and the spring is the time for cleaning.

To traffic police the old city of Delhi presents about as hard a problem as any place in the world. If it is humanly possible—but I doubt if it is—a traffic system has to be evolved to cope with lorries, cars, buses, pony-traps, bullock-carts, tricycle rickshas, hand-pulled rickshas, hand-pushed long wheeled barrows, trams, motor-cycles, hundreds of thousands of bicycles, and buffalo-waggons (they are the slowest). In the midst of all this a (sacred) cow may be determinedly trying to cross the road, regardless of the whole lot, and just as everything looks like moving on again the road unexpectedly turns into a flowing river of goats, hundreds of them, usually entrusted to a boy aged about nine, who looks respectfully frightened when a policeman curses his ancestors back to the seventh generation, but what can either he or the policeman do about it? What indeed.

The problem of cows versus traffic, like the problems of the monkeys of Lucknow and the bulls of Benares, is not, as it would be in China, a subject for government edict, followed doubtless by fines, imprisonments, public confessions, lectures and compulsory slaughterings. The republic of India is more civilized and subtle. It embraces all these matters in the single phrase: India is a secular state. From the moment of its inception it has, in other words, said: 'To decide what will live on in the new age, and what will die in the wake of the old, is too much for the wisest ruler to determine. In the shadow of this one general statement, therefore, let what is healthy in the old live on; let what is corrupt and rotten die.'

That is precisely what is happening. The monkeys of Lucknow, that scamper mischievously from roof to roof, stealing food, upsetting cooking pots, and attacking and scaring women, must still, by Brahmin custom, be given a public funeral at the cost of anyone who dares kill one. But from what can be seen of the younger generation in Lucknow, I would say that the monkeys' days are already numbered, not by edict, but by the slow, gentle movement of public opinion, growing in the shade of the device: India is a secular state.

As at Benares and Lucknow, the departure of so many of its former Muslim inhabitants had altered Delhi, and the arrival of hundreds of thousands of Hindus, refugees and others, for whom entire new suburbs were being built in all the outskirts of the city, marked yet another epoch in its rich and varied history. Many Muslims remained, and appeared to be doing well enough, but the violent animation that used to haunt the old city when they lived there in greater numbers had gone. Instead, the calmer Hindu spirit was infiltrating into the labyrinths and courts, a spirit more prudish, more smug, but more homely, steady and peaceful.

The change I had not expected to find was in New Delhi, that widespread garden capital designed as an expression of empire at the towering point of its existence. New Delhi—for its trees and airy spaciousness alone—was from the start a beautiful city, but it was by no means a convenient one to live in. All its shops were by law confined to a single area, Connaught Circus, on one side of it; public transport was scarce—the sahibs and Indian grandees who lived there did not travel by bus,—and if you accidentally returned from the shops without buying salt, and happened to live on the wrong side of the city, you might have a four-mile journey by bicycle (there and back) to repair your omission.

Independence and partition, which in a terrifyingly short time trebled the total population of Delhi, had filled up the emptiness of New Delhi. The pleasant open spaces and trees still remained—long may they do so,—but there were now frequent bus services, and houses that were once only occupied seasonally, during the legislative sessions, were now permanently inhabited, to the rooftops in some cases. Blocks of flats had gone up. The noble skeleton designed during the Raj now was a creature of flesh and blood. In its social life, too, the former insularity of Delhi had been surprisingly swept away by a more diverse society, a greater number of Indians from all parts of the country, a Diplomatic Corps, and foreign visitors from all over the world. Delhi had at last become, in fact as well as name, a capital.

(ix) *A modern Indian family*

Having found a remarkably good and cheap hotel in a distinguishedly filthy part of the old city, I telephoned to announce my arrival to a young Indian couple I had known before in London.

'No!' said Shankar's astonished voice at the end of the phone.

'Yes!' I replied.

'But you must come and see us at once. Can you come to dinner?'

Unfortunately I had an engagement.

'Then come to breakfast tomorrow.'

It was arranged. But when next morning I turned up at the appointed time I saw through a window that they had already started breakfast. Amid so many other things in their extremely busy lives they had forgotten their own invitation.

My arrival caused a tumult. Hand was clapped over mouth in horror, napkins were flung down, and a milkpot upset. Amid laughter and protestations I was conjured to eat the last piece of toast while more was prepared.

Nor was it only toast that came. A complete English breakfast was served—coffee, poached eggs (seasoned with Indian spices), toast and marmalade (made from Indian fruit)—while in animated conversation we caught up with each others' lives.

Shankar now held a responsible government appointment; Padma, his beautiful and vivacious Bengali wife (he himself was from South India), was on the staff of a newspaper. Yes, of course, Padma wore a sari in preference to any form of western dress, and, apart from an unvaried English breakfast tradition, Indian food was served. But the general *mis-en-scène* was familiar. As in England, newspapers and letters lay on the table between toast-crusts and butter-dishes. The telephone rang several times, and was cursed at as being a damnable invention. We were all deep in conversation when a car hooted outside in the drive. Good heavens, everybody was late! Padma's neighbour had already called to take her to the office, and Shankar must also leave immediately.

But the manner of my arrival—the forgotten invitation—ruled out return to the old city. No opposition would be brooked. I must move this very morning from the old to the new, and be ensconced in the house with all my luggage by the time they came back for lunch. We are not arguing, they said; we are telling you.

Thus to my experiences I can add an occasion when I went to breakfast and stayed for a fortnight.

The house was quieter when I re-entered it later in the morning with my luggage. Their little five-year-old daughter, whom I had seen earlier, was out somewhere with her aged South Indian nurse. In the servants' quarters the principal meal of the day was being prepared.

I was received by Abdul, turbaned, austere, eagle-eyed old head servant, who bore my things off to what was to be my bedroom. I did not follow him. Pleased to be once more in the comfort of a home, I relaxed in the living room, enjoying the ease of its English-style furniture, its wall decorations of coloured cloth in vivid designs from the Santal districts of Bengal, its Afghan carpets, decorated leather pouffes and gleaming Jaipur brassware. There was a Jamini Roy painting over the fireplace, and Shankar's graceful musical instruments were laid carefully in a corner. The bookshelves were themselves an expression of their owners' culturally diverse lives. Biographies of the great European composers stood beside beautifully-illustrated works on Indian art and music, printed in India in the English language, while from other countries were translations of Chinese poetry, Hardy's novels, the plays of Bernard Shaw, books by Indian authors published in England, books by European authors published in India, and the oddments we all enjoy, volumes of proverbs and quotations, books on conjuring, fortune-telling, popular superstitions and how to play contract bridge.

When I went through to my own room, Abdul was laying out my belongings in the immemorial way. Here was another field marshal's bearer. He made no delay about expressing his disapproval of the household in general. Delhi was not the same. It was impossible to find a good job these days. There was no alternative to working for a pittance for these Hindus—Abdul was of course a Muslim—from whom one never knew what to expect next. In all his born days he had never worked for such a family as this. Sometimes food was prepared and no one turned up. Sometimes there was no food and they (that was Shankar and Padma) would bring in eight guests for dinner. They spoke so many languages (English, Malayalam, Bengali, Tamil and Hindi) that it was impossible to know what was going on. There were endless callers and telephone messages, and when he complained that it was all too much for him they just laughed. There was no family life, said Abdul severely—only gadding about and enjoying themselves.

I am afraid the addition of myself to the household only augmented Abdul's disapproval. I fundamentally upset him in the first hour by sending him out to hire a bicycle for me, when I should of course have hired a car, and I too, like Shankar and Padma, seldom appeared when I said I would, and demanded food at unexpected moments when there was none. Each day he brought my morning tea half-an-hour earlier in the hope of finding me, as a decent Englishman should be, still in bed. But I was always up before him. It was humiliating. One morning he even got up before it was light. After this, with grim reluctance he accepted the disturbing irregularity of having, added to his many woes, a man who drank his bedside cup of tea on returning to the house after his first excursion

226

of the day (usually to call on friends who, like Shankar and Padma, had to reach their offices by nine).

A day after my arrival we were joined by Padma's young and charming Bengali niece, Shanti, come from Calcutta for a holiday 'to get away', as she explained it, 'from an emotional entanglement that was becoming stale'. On my former visits to India, young ladies did not have emotional entanglements. Marriages were decently arranged for them by their parents, and they made the best of them. Furthermore, for a chaperoning aunt and uncle to go off to work in the morning, leaving their unmarried niece at home alone with—my dear—an Englishman, was to court scandal and disaster, while for niece and Englishman to go out together to dine with mutual friends, and be seen in public in coffee houses or at the cinema—well, such things just never happened, except with *that kind* of girl. In Delhi as I now found it, such innocent associations were much more innocently regarded than before.

The presence of the Englishman on one occasion even served Hindu family purposes in a way the older generation would not have believed possible.

On her train journey from Calcutta, in a ladies' compartment, Shanti had received the attentions of a young Indian lieutenant who, each time the train stopped, came to talk to her through the window, and on reaching Delhi secured her baggage and a taxi in an off-season rainstorm, and with it, by way of reward, her address. His visit to the house was momently expected. Shanti, however, though escaping from an entanglement, did not propose to entangle herself again —not yet, anyway.

As all lieutenants should, he telephoned before coming, and it so happened that I answered the phone. When I told Shanti, on her return from an outing, that she might expect him any minute, she scolded me for encouraging him, saying firmly that she did not want to see him.

'You really don't want to?' I asked. 'I thought you were just pretending.'

'Really I don't,' she said.

'Never again?' I asked.

'Never. He bores me.'

'Then leave it to me,' I said. 'And whatever happens, don't let Abdul answer the door.'

The few words exchanged with him over the phone had suggested a way of dealing with this situation. At first he had thought, hearing my voice, that he had dialled a wrong number. But when I told him that Miss Banerjee was out, he concluded he was speaking to an Indian.

Towards the scheduled time, the bell rang.

'It's him! It's him!' Shanti called anxiously through to my room, and as I forestalled Abdul and went to the door, she dived out of sight into Padma's bedroom.

As I expected, my appearance at the door produced on the smartly-uniformed man outside an expression of utter consternation. He was baffled. What extraordinary sort of house could this be? Was I a relative, a secretary, or a lover?

I explained to him that unfortunately Miss Banerjee was not feeling well, and had retired to bed with a headache. The poor man dazedly said how sorry he was and that he would ring again later. With a last searching look at me, he turned smartly but resignedly away.

I closed the front door and went back to the living room. After a more than usually deep silence, thinking I heard the sound of a sari moving, I looked up to see Shanti peering cautiously in.

'Has he gone?' she whispered.

I nodded.

She clapped her hands delightedly and came in.

'But the poor fellow's self-confidence was radically shaken,' I said, 'and all his illusions about you have been shattered.'

'Why worry?' she said contentedly. 'Now I can enjoy my holiday.'

'Well, I only hope you don't change your mind about him,' I replied, curling up again with a book. 'Because one thing I'm quite sure of. He'll never call again.'

And I am told he never did.

(x) *The conflict within*

Abdul's tribulations reached their climax at breakfast time each morning. It was understandable that these Hindus should require an English breakfast—they had some pretensions to culture, after all—

228

but it was not understandable why they could not all eat their breakfast together. For well over an hour each day Abdul walked between kitchen and dining room, his mind concentrated on the poached egg situation. After one entry into the dining room he would return to order poached eggs. Upon his next return he would have to postpone the order. On the next he would be able to announce that poached eggs would be required in ten minutes. From time to time on this sentry-like patrol between two points a moment would come when he would actually carry steaming poached eggs into the dining room, only to find he had made a premature entrance, which would be followed a few moments later by a retreat to the kitchen bearing cold poached eggs. Yet when anyone actually sat down at the dining table they were invariably in a hurry and wanted their poached eggs immediately.

After this came the problem of how to obtain from his mistress her orders for lunch and other meals. Abdul would stand ominously beside her while she drank coffee and read a newspaper. He would make little coughs or move things about on the table. All to no purpose. No one paid attention to him, the family engrossed in newspapers and correspondence. Beaten by silence, Abdul would retire momentarily, only to find he had missed an opportunity. Suddenly, and for no known reason, the table would ring with nineteen-to-the-dozen conversation and shouts of laughter. Hastily he would return, but find it, equally unexplainably, once more silently absorbed and inattentive to him. This was not a family, he concluded; it was an asylum for harmless lunatics.

'Oh, yes, Abdul! Lunch,' Padma would say. 'Now, let's see. Will anyone be in?'

But before that could be determined the telephone would ring, or the First Secretary of a foreign embassy would arrive on a motor scooter. (What had happened to all these Europeans? Where was the world going to?) That might even mean more poached eggs.

By the time we again came round to the lunch problem, Shankar was in the living room interviewing a group of respectful people, and—

'Shankar, will you be in for lunch?' Padma called, without leaving her place at the table—for coolness in summer there was an inner window between dining and living room.

'What was that, dear?'

Padma's exquisite face assumed the swooning expression of one of Krishna's gopinis in a Rajput painting.

'I said, will you be in for lunch?'

Faint signs of irritation from the other room.

'Er—well, I——'

The telephone then rang again. Some of the callers began to leave, but as the door opened to release them, more arrived. Outside in the drive the neighbour's car hooted. Padma leapt to her feet, scattering newspapers behind her, while Shanti and I, left at the breakfast table, tried to hide our now daily amusement of being left between mounting commotion on one side and the lofty disdain of Abdul on the other.

No sooner did the car start than Padma would cry: 'Heavens! Stop! The lunch. Abdu—u—ul!'

As the car jerked to a halt, scattering pebbles and dust, Abdul would appear at the front door to receive his orders through the car window. Or at other times, when the car was well away before Padma remembered, orders would be telephoned from the office.

'Anyway,' said Shanti, as the tumult subsided and everyone left the house, 'how tiresome it is to decide about lunch over breakfast.'

.   .   .   .   .

It really was too much, however, for old Abdul, who in any case had never worked for Indians before, and, like many of his kind, had unfortunately learnt during the Raj to despise his own people indirectly, seeing them through his master's prejudices.

Passing through the servants' quarters, as I did daily to fetch my bicycle, I observed that the old man sought refuge in communism. Judging by the number of pamphlets lying about, he was a regular recipient of news-letters and so on from the Indian Communist Party and on Chinese affairs. One day I stopped and picked up one of these latter to look at. Knowing I had come from China, Abdul proudly tapped the page I held open.

'Now, there is a good country,' he said, 'where everyone gets good treatment, and . . .' The phrase he used meant that under communism there was no immorality.

'Do not believe everything you read,' I said to him gently. 'I have lived beside China for several years and seen things that are not put into papers like this.'

With the nearest I have ever seen to incivility in a man of his type, he gently drew the paper out of my hands, turned his back, and walked away. One unused to the East might not have noticed the subtle implication. I too was among the god-forsaken, the immoral, the topsy-turvy men of straw who were on top these days, knowing nothing except how to enjoy themselves.

Let not the fact that Abdul was a servant conceal the reality of this situation. Abdul was not one of the oppressed. He was the proud father of grown-up sons, who sent him money additional to his wages. For his age he was fortunate to be in steady employment, serving a household in which he was well treated. His simple material wants were provided for, and his shortcomings—those of old age—tolerantly overlooked by the family and their guests. In Shankar and Padma's circle, Abdul was an institution. As the Chinese would say, he was always given face.

But in this house he found himself face to face with a world of intellectual freedom which he had never seen before, a world which questioned established principles, approving and criticizing according to individual canons that varied from person to person. Nothing was laid down. There was no book of words.

To Abdul this new world was a disturbing and dangerous confusion. Its freedom was laxity, its movement instability. Living with it, he waited for the day when someone would cry halt, when immutable principles would be laid down for everybody, in the light of which a reign of morality would be established. This was the promise that communism gave.

(xi) *St. George and the Dragon in Asia*

It was the same promise that communism gave to China, and which in 1948 and 1949 the Chinese people overwhelmingly accepted. Should a day ever come when India is induced to follow Abdul's way instead of Shankar's, the effect on the household would be much as it was in similar households in China. Overnight, contact with the western world would be withdrawn. New York and London would recede into small dots in a mist. The newspapers and radio would give no inkling of their real doings and thoughts. Instead, the principles would be daily boomed forth, declaring with absolute confidence what was democratic (good) and what was bourgeois (bad).

In the family there would at first be resistance. This puerile nonsense could not possibly last. Indians are reasonable beings, and reason must surely prevail. But the booming would continue. Moreover, the most conservative elements in society, voices carrying great weight with the unlettered, would suddenly be heard again after long silence, declaring how communist principles were implicit in the classic books of Hinduism which the West had sought to destroy and would still destroy if it could, that archenemy of truth and virtue, with its loose morals and corrupt way of living.

After a time the family, by the sheer force and repetition of these declarations, would begin to feel ashamed. Cut off from the outer world, it would be doubtful of itself. Yes, it had done something desperately wrong. It must humble itself, and, in discussion meetings, publicly declare repentance.

This done, it would feel happier, at one again with the great world around it. It would put away its good clothes, remove the library from the living room to an unused back bedroom, or perhaps, with the wonderful emotion of expiating sin, burn the foreign books. Gradually it would realize what it had never understood before: how simple life can be, how free of worries, when one has only to tune in to the radio to hear how wonderfully all worry can be alleviated when there is a great government that truly represents the people. It is only in the western world that people, racked with headaches, continually complain how complicated life is. Life does not need to be complicated. It can become simple and beautiful.

Meanwhile the move towards carbolic civilization would continue reassuringly and at an accelerated pace. Westernization, on an up-to-date Russian pattern, would also be hastened. Even the most westernized would not be able to say there was not progress here. There might be less cars and bicycles, but literature, music and the arts would be encouraged as never before. Abdul would be able to go to splendid exhibitions of modern Indian painting in western technique, showing factory workers stoking beautiful red furnaces, and soldiers training to fight the enemies of truth and virtue. He would sometimes be given tickets to hear the symphonies of

Shostakovich, or to see very thin white women leaping about in rhythm with music, which is one of the great arts of the modern world—and Indian women too would be trained to leap in the same way, instead of cultivating their own demure styles, all of which were bourgeois, connected with temples and prostitution. Abdul's sons would learn to sing Russian songs and dance like cossacks. Life would be full of excitements and much more novel than before, but harmonized in the framework of principles and good conduct.

Thus it has happened in China, and thus it could be in many other eastern countries. It is important that we should not over-simplify the choice as it is presented to a sensible good-living man like Abdul. To him St. George and the Dragon do not appear as they do to us. The Dragon is a friendly Chinese dragon with four democratic claws (not the imperial five), while St. George is an English-speaking foreigner who is very rich, clever and powerful—the old landlord type from whose clutches the people of the East are trying to escape. Who would believe that the West is not deliberately misinterpreting the allegory, pretending that St. George is good and the Dragon bad, so as to deceive others? Who would willingly give loyalty to a rich, powerful, clever man unless, born on his estate, he owed his land and livelihood to him?

If the West were poorer, weaker, and—above all—more obviously guided by moral principles, it would have far more chance of being understood by Abdul and men like him. If it shouted the Ten Commandments or the Sermon on the Mount with the same force it gives to peculiar words like liberty and democracy, Asia would see more merit in it.

Yes, with Shankar and Padma it was like being in my own home. Seldom have I passed so happy a fortnight. But one of the fundamentals that made it feel homely was that in its moments of crisis this family was—as we are—morally in doubt.

Doubt is, in fact, the most profound of all the bequests that Europe and America have left in the East. We complain when the newly-independent nations of Asia do not readily align themselves with the West and what it stands for. We should look to ourselves for one of the reasons.

VI

(i) *The brothers who divided their house*

The second week of November had come. The days were warm, the nights misty and cool. If I was to reach home in England by Christmas I had to move on at once and not dawdle so much in the places I found amusing. The next phase of the journey was across the desert zone, through countries that lie close to the heart of Islam. It was an area new to me, where I had few contacts, and having now been living out of suitcases for several weeks I was tempted to fly straight over it into Europe.

Two considerations stood against this. Having encountered Islam in Indonesia, Malaya and India, I felt that a journey through the Near East would be instructive as showing the religion nearer its original setting. Secondly, this was a journey undertaken mainly to obtain what we called at the outset a processional view. With no time to linger and explore, the rest of the way would be no more than a series of fleeting first impressions. Nevertheless, however sketchy, I wanted those first impressions, in order to relate them to what I had already seen.

From the moment of reaching the decision to go ahead by land, I was embroiled in unforeseen problems. To start with, the Syrian authorities in Delhi, deciding I was a Jew, refused to grant me a visa. Hearing this, the Iraqi authorities explained that, though they were satisfied I was not a Jew, if Syria refused me a visa they regretted that they must do likewise. If I went to Pakistan I would probably have to rule out a visit to Afghanistan, since due to disputes between these two countries it would be difficult to pass the frontier from one to the other. Persia was in the midst of a dispute with Britain over oil, and the United Kingdom High Commission in Delhi did not advise my going there. If I wished to go to Israel, none of the Arab countries would admit me. If I even had the name of Israel anywhere in my passport they would refuse visas. I would require two passports, one for Israel and one for other countries. The problems of the Far East began to look relatively simple.

Telegrams at ambassadorial level were sent in various directions and a Syrian visa was quickly issued, although I only had it stamped on my passport in order to obtain a visa for Iraq, having by this time decided against a trip to Syria.

I had intended to travel on to Pakistan by train to Lahore, but there were no through trains. From Delhi one went as far as Amritsar, on the Indian side of the frontier—second class, this would cost 25 rupees. From there, for another 25 rupees, one took a taxi to the frontier, where one walked what was by repute quite a long way, carrying one's luggage, to the Pakistan side of the frontier. There, with luck, there might be another taxi (25 rupees) to take one into Lahore. The whole cost of this tiresome expedition, 75 rupees, was the exact cost of an airline ticket. I went by air.

The aircraft left Delhi at the first light. My last view of India on the ground was of the stars fading into a luminous green sky, with the great trees of New Delhi slowly becoming outlined against it, and, close to the perimeter, the graceful pumpkin dome of the tomb of Safdar-Jang. A little after nine in the morning, we landed at Lahore, capital of the Pakistan section of the Punjab.

There we were plunged back into the exasperations of that troubled, suspicious East which during my stay in India I had completely forgotten. A horrifying assortment of forms had to be filled in. All Indian rupees had to be declared, and could only be exchanged for Pakistan rupees at par, when in fact Indian rupees had a higher value. If one wished to consume any kind of alcoholic liquor, one was enjoined to apply for an addict's licence (for a foreigner these were easy to obtain). At the customs every piece of baggage in the entire plane was ransacked by women officials, and complicated inventories were filled in. As a last welcoming touch, this peformance took so long that the airline bus left half of us passengers behind.

Resigning myself to a new tempo of life, I bought an English-language newspaper and settled down to find out what Pakistan was thinking and talking about.

The Indian morning newspapers had reached the airport in time to be read on the journey. Among other items I had noticed a small heading low down on the front page of one of them, giving an account of a minor clash between Indian and Pakistan frontier police, in which a Pakistani had been injured. The Pakistan newspaper which I now opened carried thick black headlines right across its front page: BHARAT ATROCITY! Bharat, I knew, was an old Sanskrit word for India—Bharata-varsha—but I had not realized till then that this strange appellation was how India was described in the more fiery sections of the Pakistan Press. Reading the article that followed, it was recognizable as an account of the same minor frontier incident I had already read of in the Delhi newspaper.

Passing from India to Pakistan, or vice versa, one has to resist firmly the desire to make comparisons, to take sides in the tangle of disputes between the two countries. There is a quality of directness in the men ruling Pakistan that appeals to a westerner; there is a quality of sinuousness in the Hindu mind which, without close familiarity, perplexes him. The danger of making comparisons based on prejudice is so great that there is really no other way of looking at the two countries fairly than to compare the old united India with two brothers, with both of whom we were acquainted, sharing a single house. On an issue that concerned none but themselves, the brothers quarrelled, and divided the house into two parts, each living separately in his own. Whereas formerly we used to dine with both brothers at the same table, nowadays when we are invited we have to see them separately, and we will be a poor friend if we do anything—though it may be no more than a confidential wink or an innuendo—to exacerbate the misunderstanding between them.

At the same time, we need to know something of the mental background to their differences. I had not expected that a quick journey through Pakistan would show me anything about this. But the headline in the Lahore newspaper, seen within a few minutes of landing—the way in which the editors of two equally free presses presented the same news item in two completely different ways—read to me like a succinct message on a subject which might otherwise have taken weeks to appreciate.

In India, once the bloodshed of partition ceased, the Hindu animal, as we said earlier, cleaned itself up and set to work again as usual. In Pakistan it was different. The Muslim animal had won its deliverance by plunging loose through gorse and barbed wire. It emerged free, but shaking with the nervous emotion of the experience, its wounds smarting, filling it with anger and self-pity. Nor had its hoped-for freedom proved complete. Kashmir, with its Muslim majority, remained in the hated hand of Bharat, while the water needed to irrigate much of the Pakistan that verges the desert could only be obtained from rivers whose sources lay in Bharat, and whose flow Bharat controlled.

Kashmir, which in India, though a steady news item, figured in social conversation as a popular holiday resort, carried with it in Pakistan the sacrosanct spirit of an Alsace-Lorraine.

There was a certain fascination about this Bharat business. Wherever material from international news agencies was used in the paper, the word India had carefully been deleted by the editor and replaced with Bharat, giving the Pakistani reader the impression that this was the name which the whole of the rest of the world used when describing India. It produced peculiar effects: 'The Secretary of State warned Congress: "Bharat must think twice." ' American politicians had overnight, it appeared, become Sanskrit scholars.

(ii) *First night in Lahore*

Parts of Lahore, when we finally reached it, turned out to be hardly changed, except that even here, as in India, the separation of the two religions had brought a more peaceful atmosphere. The departure of nearly the entire Hindu and Sikh communities to India had lowered the political temperature. But in the older and once labyrinthine parts of the city was a scene of devastation, as if Lahore had been subjected to mass air-raids. In what was once a teeming warren-like quarter only a single high narrow section of a building, standing up like a bar of soap, remained in an empty field of brick and rubble, a gaunt reminder of the horror that accompanied partition.

As in India, so in Pakistan, the pattern of daily life followed without affectation the model set during the British epoch. But here there were more obvious difficulties. In banks and offices, clerks and salesmen were less sure of themselves. Transactions took longer. There was an air of experiment, of finding the way, such as I had not noticed in India. Please excuse these delays, Lahore seemed to say;

we have had to engage so many new men on our staff. The departure of the Hindus had had the same effect on Lahore as on Rangoon. Overnight, inexperienced junior clerks had found themselves in charge of large and complicated offices and routines which it would take them years to master.

Then there was the desert to be reckoned with. In dusty Lahore, for the first time on this westward journey, I was conscious of the closeness of the desert. Every vegetable and fruit in the market seemed, to a mind like mine, unaccustomed to deserts, the product of a greater struggle than in other greener countries, while the city itself was less like the mental centre of a surrounding countryside (as a normal city might be described), more like a ship within whose frame alone there was safety from the dangerous element around it. As the afternoon waned, the temperature began to fall sharply, and by nightfall it was cold enough to wear a European winter suit.

By the time I went to bed on that first evening, my impression was that to pass from India to Pakistan was to leave behind a country of frugal prosperity, contented by reason of its frugality, bent on a self-imposed mission of improvement, and enter a land with a similar self-imposed mission, but with a background of insufficiency, poverty and ignorance, a harsh, dry, bitter land that would draw a curse from the lips of the most patient cultivator. In each country the mission was one of struggle. But whereas in India there was confidence, in Pakistan that happier state had not arrived. The dominating spirit was of harassment, anxiety and dogged determination.

It was immediately obvious that the exodus of Hindus and Sikhs from Pakistan had been far more extensive than the exodus of Muslims from India. I cannot remember seeing any Hindus in Lahore, and I certainly did not meet a Hindu during my stay in the country. Whereas the Hindu and Sikh refugees in India included large numbers of educated and formerly prosperous people, the Muslim refugees in Pakistan consisted of a higher percentage of the poor and illiterate, many of their more prosperous co-religionists having stayed behind in India. From the start Pakistan had found itself saddled with problems of poverty and ignorance proportionately worse than in the old united India.

In the old united India, the mountainous North-West Frontier Province, the dusty plains of Western Punjab, the desert of Sind, and

238

the rocky wastes of Baluchistan, which today form the western and principal part of Pakistan, were strategic acquisitions. As a protective corridor they sheltered the rich but defenceless plains of India from invasion along its historic routes, from the West and North-West, the routes of Alexander, of the White Huns, the Afghans and the Turks. The corridor itself, a waste of anarchy and feud, was no ornament to add to the imperial diadem. But it was a void which a strong power, with the ability to organize stable government, could without much difficulty conquer and hold. Should such a power from the North-West occupy it, Delhi would be within bargaining reach. India would be at its mercy. To protect India both from being contaminated by the corridor's internal instability and from the designs of the states beyond it, in particular Afghanistan and Imperial Russia, the waste fringe which is now Pakistan was incorporated into the Indian Empire. During its time under direct British rule it settled down gradually to a more tranquil existence, while one of the largest irrigation systems ever seen extended the tilled area in the Punjab far out into what was formerly waste.

This difficult outer fringe of mountain, rock and desert, stretching from the Roof of the World to the torrid Arabian Sea, was what Islam received as its portion in the partition. It was as if, from a man's body, an arm were cut off and told, 'Now, arm, perform the functions of a whole body.' The arm would have had the same problems as the Government of Pakistan has had since the day of its creation. It would have had to develop a brain (a government), and means of locomotion and industry. Above all, it would have had to use its brain with great inventiveness and power of adaptation, to evolve a way of life suited to the peculiar needs of an arm living without a body. Few governments can have been born facing so arid a prospect, with so far to go to reach a green land.

A green Pakistan!—the very idea presented yet another of the country's peculiarities. Here was a desert country that was not inhabited by desert people. To those with no knowledge of deserts or their people, this may sound insignificant. Actually, it is a situation as precarious as that of a ship mastered and manned by soldiers, instead of sailors. The desert, like the sea, is another element that may only be used in safety by those schooled and traditioned in knowledge of it. To a desert people, such as the Arabs or the Central Asian tribes, Pakistan might well be described as a fair land, rich and abundant, but to people accustomed to land that is tilled and sown, the landscape of Sind is inimical.

As only a few casual conversations in the bazaar showed, the greater part of Pakistan's refugee population were those who, in British India, were known as Indian Muslims, settled city-dwellers or agriculturalists, knowing nothing of the desert or its ways. For them, if Pakistan was to be a land of promise, the desert must become green. They would not take to the ways of the desert. They must irrigate and limit it.

(iii) *Silver tea-set*

'The more laws and regulations are given,' wrote Lao Tze in the fifth century B.C., 'the more robbers and thieves there are.'

Confronted in Pakistan with rather more laws and regulations than usual, I found out how easy it is to become one of the thieves.

'I have to go to the bank to change some money,' I said to a Pakistani friend.

'To the bank?' he asked in astonishment. 'You don't want to change money there. Give it to me. I'll fix it for you at a better rate.'

Which he did.

Later in the evening the unexpected fall in temperature made me want a drink.

'Let's go to a hotel,' my friend said.

'But I have no addict's licence,' I complained.

'Neither have I,' he replied. 'Come.'

The hotel we went to was one of the old majestic type of British India, looking on the outside like a theological college, all turrets, castellation and ogive windows. As my companion confidently led the way in and we took a table on a dimly-lit terrace overlooking a garden, I came to the conclusion he was bluffing me. This was certainly no place in which to defy the law. And when the bearer came for our order, this conclusion was confirmed. My host tamely ordered tea.

Two prices were quoted, of which he selected the more expensive. Well, at least it would be warm. I resigned myself to a liquorless evening.

After a suitably long wait—it was after the normal tea hour and water would have to be boiled—the bearer returned, and there was at least the compensation that our tea was to be served with a grandeur belonging to a past age. On our table he set down a silver tray on which was a magnificent old silver teapot, with sugar-bowl, milkpot and cups to match—a distinguished relic of the Raj.

With some disappointment, however, I noticed there was no steam coming from the spout of the teapot, and putting a finger on the pot I found . . .

'It's not very warm,' I said.

My friend cocked an eyebrow.

'Would you prefer it warm?' he asked.

'Well, I—well, no, of course it's quite all right.'

Looking slightly worried, he poured out two cups of tea, handing me one of the ornate silver cups and saucers. The tea made a strangely frothy noise as it was poured out. I looked suspiciously at the contents of my cup.

It was beer.

'You don't really like it warm, do you?' he asked.

'No,' I said quickly. 'This is delightful. I didn't understand. I thought it was tea.'

'So it is, so it is,' he replied solemnly, lifting his silver cup to his lips, 'but at the more expensive rate.'

(iv) *By train across the Sind desert*

Although I began to make arrangements for onward travel on the day of my arrival in Lahore, such was the congestion on the trains that no sleeping berth could be obtained till several days after I was due to reach Karachi. In each train however, the hotel manager informed me, at least one compartment was held unreserved until the last moment, when, by payment of a bribe to certain railway officials, a berth could be obtained. Necessity dictating, I duly bribed and was given a berth.

The journey to Karachi took twenty-four hours, starting in the early morning. As the day grew hotter and the way went further out into the desert, the train became increasingly uncomfortable and those of us who had begun the journey together grew close to each other in companionship, providing for our common wants, sharing the food and fruit we purchased when the train stopped, exchanging books, and raising or lowering shutters and windows as the sun shone in now on this side, now on that, or as the wind blew into our compartment the intolerable dust of the desert.

My chief companions, also travelling to Karachi, were a Sindi business man and a young airport official, both wearing shirt and trousers and speaking fluent English. For part of the day we had with us also a student going to Multan. It was a harmonious company, and time passed quickly. Soon everything was covered in a film of dust. At each stop we shook what we could from our clothes, but whenever we lay down to sleep for a while it penetrated beneath shirt and vest until there was no relief from it.

The airport official laughingly shrugged his shoulders as for about the ninth time we shook out our books, rugs and towels.

'What's the use?' he said. 'This journey is always a torment.'

Alone among the travellers, one man made no contribution to the mobile, temporary society we formed. He was a heavily-built, pot-bellied merchant in an embroidered fez and oriental clothes of fine quality. A servant had preceded him into the compartment, laid out his travelling bed—it is wise to travel everywhere in India and Pakistan with one's own roll-up bedding—and rudely obliged the student to move up into a narrow quarter of what was a wide seat. When the merchant himself came, the stationmaster saw him in, with unction. Seating himself cross-legged on his bedding, the merchant, without glancing at anyone, began reading a book in Arabic lettering, probably Urdu. His servant, who travelled in another part of the train, brought him small things to eat and drink at each stop. Though the rest of us were sharing what we had, he did not offer to share anything of his. When the Sindi business man spoke to him, he gave a monosyllabic answer and said nothing else for the rest of the time he was with us. If he did not eat everything his servant brought, he carefully placed the lid on the ornate pot in which it had come, and at the next stop the servant took it away.

When we were some hours out of Lahore he rose from his bedding, produced a mat from his possessions, unrolled it on the floor in the middle of the wide compartment, knelt down in our midst, and began addressing his ritual prayers, in a pious murmur and with many bowings to the ground, directly to where I sat cross-legged on my chaddar. For an anxious moment I thought he was possessed—I was once worshipped as an avatar by a Hindu who was possessed, and the memory dies ill—until from a calculation of the direction the train was going in I realized I was sitting in the West, the direction of Mecca, to which Islamic prayer should be addressed. I hastily buried my eyes in a book until, unable to concentrate and feeling ridiculous, I took refuge in the lavatory.

My fellow-travellers, who were of course also Muslims, stopped talking as the prayers began, but it was noticeable that none of them paid attention. One looked out of a window, the others read books or magazines.

'Does this sort of thing always happen?' I asked the airport official when we descended to stretch our legs at the next stop.

He pursed his lips with a look of resignation, but said nothing.

Some time in the afternoon more passengers got in, and for one of these the rich merchant moved up slightly, though without interrupting his reading, allowing the newcomer to sit on part of his outspread bedding, which the student had not been permitted to sit on. The newcomer was an old Muslim with thin old-fashioned spectacles and a white beard. He wore a long black surcoat, leather slippers with upturned pointed toes, and a strangely shaped and decorated fez. I took it that he was some kind of Islamic scholar or teacher. Without a word to anyone, he took out an illuminated edition of the Koran and began to read it under his breath, holding the book close to his tired eyes. His lips moved open and shut in a mesmerizing little movement, producing in gentle rhythm the sound ps-ps-ps-ps, broken from time to time when he drew the page to his lips and kissed the letters he was reading, though with the cold prudish sound of one who does not know what love is, the sound of one sipping tea.

This time the airport official, more forthcoming, gave me the smallest indication of a smile, while the Sindi business man, looking at me over the top of his newspaper, winked.

The other newcomers, without beds and therefore identifiable as travelling only a short distance, included two men who, from their physique and bearing, and from their sober but well-cut western suits, were clearly army officers. As the Muslim divine continued his reading, one of them took a cautious glance at me, trying to gauge my reactions. Both of them looked faintly embarrassed by the old man, and spent the time talking to each other in low tones.

From the impeccable good taste they showed in western clothes, I judged they had both been to Europe. Possibly they had done part of their training at Sandhurst. In any case, they belonged to that small circle of quiet, level-headed people, to be found in every country, for whom the words East and West imply no barrier.

But we had not yet been given the full treatment. At the next station a thin be-fezzed intellectual in a long robe got in. He had a satchel strung from his shoulder, and as soon as he had sat down he produced from this a sheaf of leaflets in Arabic which he handed round, one to each person in the compartment, with the exception of myself. They were religious tracts. When the train started he began to speak to everyone in Sindi, in a whining voice, like a Pharisee of the New Testament, his speech full of subtle interpretations and distinctions. He was a mean, narrow-minded man, with no milk of human kindness in him.

While he spoke, everyone stopped talking and read the leaflets—except the young airport official who, after a glance at his leaflet, spent the rest of the time looking out of the window. When the speech finished, the others all re-read the leaflets right through, turning them over to reach the end. I was surprised to see even the officers read theirs. I had expected them to pay no attention.

When this was over there was no more conversation, no sound except the rolling of the train and the ps-ps-ps of the old man, and his dry kisses on the leaves of his Koran. Not even the Pharisee could beat this.

It intrigued me to know what would have happened had another hour of prayer occurred while they were all in the compartment together. There would have been no room for all of them to spread out their mats. But fortunately this situation did not arise.

At the next stop, the officers, the rich merchant, the divine, the Pharisee and several others descended. The Pharisee, busy stowing away his leaflets in his satchel, was the last to descend to the platform. As he got down, the airport official crossed to the door, tapped him on the shoulder, and pushed a leaflet back in his hand. He did this with a remark in Sindi which I could not understand.

The Pharisee looked up at him with the devil's anger in his eyes, clutched his satchel to him, and strode fiercely away like an actor in a Hollywood religious film.

Looking back at the others in the compartment, I saw they were all quietly laughing.

'What was it?' I asked the airport official. 'What did you say to him when you gave him back the leaflet?'

He smirked.

'I said "You have greater need of this than I." '

This time everybody laughed openly. The compartment was now ours again, and our conversation became more relaxed. When night fell and we had dinner, it was like a party at which each was partly host and partly guest. It was an enjoyable evening, despite the ever-increasing grime of our clothes, the irritation of the dust between vest and skin, and the steady filtering of more and more dust between the slightest crevice in closed window and door.

'But why do you all pay attention to people like that?' I asked. 'Why did those officers read the stuff? You're not telling me that they were orthodox believers.'

'True,' replied the business man. 'But that is how Pakistan is. And we dare not offend them. They can make a lot of trouble.'

'You didn't mind offending that fellow with the tracts,' I said to the airport official.

He sniffed.

'Him! Well, once in a while doesn't matter. That one deserved it.'

(v) *Karachi*

Karachi, which as capital of the former Indian province of Sind was once a remote and stagnant place, had grown enormously and come to life as capital of Pakistan. It was pleasant to see camel caravans passing in the main streets. It was impressive to see the large new housing scheme of which government and people were justly proud. It was amusing to ask people where they were born, and hear the speed with which they proudly named Indian cities —Delhi, Amritsar, Khanpur, Allahabad. They were not—pah— Sindis. It was disappointing to find, having expected to hear some good classical Indian music, that many of the best-known Muslim musicians had stayed behind in India. It was arresting to see the way in which Karachi desperately tried to keep its head up in surroundings of more serious inexperience and inefficiency than at Lahore. It was disquieting to be approached by quite as many young men as those who discussed the matter with me during my few days there with requests for advice about migrating to other countries. This was something I had encountered nowhere else, and what impressed me about it was that most of the men who spoke to me of migration were young, intelligent and reasonably well educated—men who perhaps, could they have been persuaded to admit it, might have regretted that they left India, but whom nothing would persuade to return there.

Inviting a Muslim friend out to dinner, I found another harkback to united India. What restaurant did I intend to go to, and what sort of food would I order? Did I propose to drink alcohol? The taboos of religion, which used to poison social life in India, but which on this visit since independence I had not noticed at all, still lingered on, it seemed, in Karachi. Having satisfied my friend on all his doubts, he accepted my invitation—on terms, as it were.

When the evening came, however, it was a convivial one. With another European friend to urge him on, our guest relaxed to the extent of drinking a small glass of beer, having first drawn the curtain of our private room in the restaurant, and, for once out of the deep freeze of Islam Triumphant, which in prudishness is only rivalled by Chinese communism, openly and honestly discussed the tribulations of the new state.

At last he asked me the question which is invariably the lot of travellers who have only been in a country a few days, no matter what country it is.

'What do you think of Pakistan?'

Usually I try to avoid answering when this question comes. But this evening the company and the hour seemed right, and, having been trying for several days to find an answer to this particular question, I decided to test out my findings on my guest. Fearing that I might be wide of the mark, I spoke slowly and with diffidence.

'The greatest social issue in Pakistan, it seems to me, has not yet come to the surface. That issue lies between people of western education and ideas, like yourself, who would like to make Pakistan into a modern state, similar and equal to those of Europe, and the old orthodox Muslims who fear such a development, because they know it will bring a wider knowledge that will end by destroying their power and influence over the masses.'

Before I had finished I saw in the gravity of my friend's expression that we were not at variance.

'In fact,' he said at last, 'you speak as I think. If it had not been for the threat of war with India, over Kashmir, which has held the country together, this deeper problem would already have been right on the surface, bringing—well—far worse troubles than we have at present. When the Kashmir problem is settled, then we shall have to face it.'

(vi) *Ship-cities*

From Karachi I flew to Basra, in Iraq, and after a few days there went up by train to Baghdad.

In these cities of the desert, the curious realization that cities can be like ships, surrounded by a contrary element from which they must give protection and in which they must somehow survive, came back with greater force than when I had first vaguely noticed it in Lahore. Never having been in a desert before, I found it disturbing. Though it looked so neutral, flat and unchanging, I could not help regarding it warily, as if in reality it were as restless as the sea. Its emptiness, and the fact that the city was not, like a ship, moving towards some friendly port, but was fixed motionless for ever within the emptiness, gave me a sense of insecurity and helplessness. If the ship-city could not move, then I must move. I could not live, like the men of that city, with no prospect of reaching a port. Confined within the city, I would begin to feel like a prisoner, with a frustration that would ultimately become suicidal. Or else, in more practical vein, I would be unable to rest contented until I had made green the country round about the city, dividing it into privately-owned plots and public roads, with boundary stones and milestones—altering it, in other words, into the element I was accustomed to from birth.

An Arab of the desert would laugh at me. He would, I suppose, despise me too. But I like my garden, with its modest fence marking the area that is mine, and I like my city that is the outcome of a prosperous countryside, the point on which roads converge. I prefer cities to be, like ours, restless and instable central points in a landscape of stability, rather than, like desert cities, relatively stable points in an expanse of instability.

Even in the heart of Baghdad, one was constantly reminded of the contrary element surrounding it. In some of the Arab homes I saw there were so few possessions—though the families were well enough off—that the whole contents of a house could without trouble have been loaded on three camels and borne away. The more prosperous-looking men wore fine town clothes, designed somewhat on the lines of a European suit, but they still wore their traditional head-dress above, while certain adaptations in design made the suit convenient to wear when riding a horse or camel. The desert dust wafted in among the streets, and when the wind blew even the sky was filled with it, as if to remind the city that it only existed on sufferance, that its lanes and walls and laws belonged to an artificial way of life which might try, if it wished, to subsist in the desert, but which the desert could not acknowledge as its own.

It went deeper too. The city, because it provided satisfaction for certain low pleasures, might be desirable for men to visit, but to live in it implied a surrender to the baser side of nature. It was a place of moral escape, fit only for weaklings, men softened by easy living, Jews, Christians and other degenerates. If a man was forced by circumstance to settle in the city, and his descendants to become shopkeepers or clerks, he could only do so, if he had any moral fibre, with the mental conflict of a deserter, with a sense of guilt. Though with one side of his mind he might know that such sentiments were unreasonable, the daily sight of men coming in from the desert, and their faintly superior attitude towards him, kept alive the uncomfortable sensation that he had allied himself to what was ignoble. It produced what one might call the malaise of desert cities.

As in Pakistan, not a day passed without some unknown young man introducing himself, usually in the morning when I was alone in some public place drinking coffee and reading a newspaper, and asking for advice about migration abroad. And again as in Pakistan, it was not the wretched or the throw-outs who enquired. On each occasion the questioner was smart and intelligent, with a good education and a fair knowledge of English. Could I say whether he would be able to make a living in Singapore, or West Africa, or

London, or the United States? There was pathos in it, and, as the scene kept on repeating itself, a touch of comedy.

In such men the conflicts of the malaise were more pronounced because their education had brought them more potently in touch with the world of boundary-stones and milestones, the world whose principal concern with deserts is how to irrigate and sow them, how to divide them up into plots with roads passing through. In each case the conflict presented itself in an intense Iraqi patriotism, opposed by a profound desire to get away, to earn a living in some country where, as they thought, the education they had received would be of more value.

In others the malaise produced less balanced results. A chance word with a talkative and friendly shopkeeper, while buying cheroots or stationery, and coffee would be ordered, neighbours invited in from across the street, and I would have to listen to such torrents of anti-British abuse as I have seldom heard—all in the friendliest spirit, of course. . . . 'This is not necessarily what we personally think, but people in Iraq say . . .' after which came what they personally thought, delivered with impassioned gusto.

Even by going out into the desert they could not be entirely free of the conflict lying at the root of the malaise. Here and there in the vast emptiness beyond the city were the remains of great irrigation works built by kings of powerful dynasties that once ruled this land, long before the Arabs possessed it, and who used its fine clear rivers to make fertile much that has for centuries now been dust and waste. Parts of Iraq were once a green land, and the narrow strip of luxuriant vegetation that today fringed the great rivers showed what a remarkable country it must have been in those ancient times.

In the days of Islam's greatness, days of slow travel and small populations, the desert was life and strength. But the sowers had altered the world, encircling the desert, bent on preventing its further spread, while within the desert zone, as elsewhere in the world, loomed the problem of too many children and not enough food.

Circumstance—the movement of history—was forcing this race of tent-dwellers to settle down to traditionally less worthy ways of life as merchants and cultivators. The process made them feel stifled and hemmed in, surrounded by inexorable forces which, over small glasses of sweet black coffee, they personalized as the foreign nations representing boundary-stone civilization. It was these nations that were the cause of their frustration. Showering invective on them, they felt mentally more comfortable. The deeper reality was unbearable.

(vii) *Coming in from the desert*

On the next phase of my journey I decided to take the train from Baghdad to Istanbul, the Taurus Express. This would take four nights and three days, the train being affectionately described by English people as the Tortoise Express. When I purchased my ticket the agent said he hoped I would remember to take enough food, because for the first two nights and two days there would be no restaurant car. The Syrian customs officials, he explained (the route ran through Syria), had formed the habit of inviting themselves to free meals on the train, bringing their friends with them, and causing the company such a loss that the restaurant car service had had to be partially suspended. It would be joined to the train in Turkey, once we were clear of the Syrians.

This was a decided nuisance. I had no cook to prepare palatable provisions, and the prospect of eating canned food for two days did not appeal to me. Accordingly, when I went with some Iraqi friends to a provision store to buy my requirements, I settled on a loaf of bread, half-a-pound of butter, and twelve large bottles of beer. My friends were astonished.

'But you can't live on that for two days!' they protested.

'No,' I admitted, 'it may be difficult.'

'What will you eat, then?' they asked. 'Can you live on beer?'

'No, I can't,' I replied, 'but somehow—well, I've got a hunch, that's all.'

'What sort of hunch?'

'Well, it may not come off, of course, so I don't think I'd better say.'

Mystified, they were confirmed in their view that all Englishmen are a bit odd, and, with misgivings, said no more, while I arranged for the beer to be sent to the railway station.

I dined in Baghdad before starting, and when the train reached

Mosul the next morning we breakfasted well at the station restaurant. By this time I had made friends with people in other compartments—I was alone in mine,—an elderly English couple on one side and a young Turkish business man on the other. When lunchtime came, everyone started opening their provisions, well prepared by servants and relatives, and containing, as I had hoped, more than any of them could eat.

I was hungry, and the time had now come to test my design.

'Would you like a bottle of beer with your lunch?' I asked the Englishman, looking into his compartment.

The reaction was instantaneous.

'Beer!' he said in astonishment. 'Have you got some beer?'

'Yes,' I said nonchalantly. 'Plenty. I'll fetch a bottle.'

By the time I returned to his compartment with the beer his wife was ready for me.

'Won't you try some of this,' she said, offering some cold chicken and salad.

'Thank you very much,' I said. 'It looks delicious.'

It was, too.

So having taken some of their lunch, I went and offered beer to my other neighbour, the Turk, who was equally astonished and delighted. He had just been mentally blaming his servant, he said, for forgetting to put any in his hamper.

However, if his servant had forgotten beer—as something had told me all the servants and relatives would—he had forgotten nothing else. Being a Baghdad resident, with his own household there, his food was rather superior to that of the kindly English couple, and there was enough of it to feed a platoon. He had so much, and he liked beer so much, that I ate with him for the rest of the journey, until the restaurant car was coupled on. Apart from anything else, the beer won me an engaging and informative companion, with whom the journey was admirably passed.

Some people get along in this world by trying to remember everything. Others, less hopeful of success in this, have to get along by remembering those things that others are liable to forget.

.   .   .   .   .

By nightfall at the end of the first day we were nearing the frontier of Iraq, and the following day, descending into Syria, I watched with relief the desert recede and give place to a land of low hills and bright tumbling streams, olive orchards and vineyards, orange groves, and flocks with their dogs and cloaked herdsmen. The weather had changed. Here it was a warm late November day, but a softer climate, its warmth less torrid than that of Iraq.

With the passing of the desert I experienced feelings of relief and reassurance similar to those felt when leaving Burma and entering India. But my Turkish companion had no such sentiments. For him we were still beyond the pale of civilization, in a dark backward age where Muslim and Jew squabbled over their beliefs and rights, and petty nationalism inflated its chest with hot air. Not till evening, when we crossed the Turkish frontier and headed into a still more orderly and settled land, did he relax.

There was now a restaurant car, and the train unaccountably began to move much faster. Here was another tempo of life, and another temper. In the restaurant car we had pleasant exchanges with the Turkish merchants, farmers and others who joined us temporarily from station to station. Life was more convivial and mellow. We were coming in from the desert.

All the next day was spent passing through the noble wildness of Anatolia, reaching Ankara some time after dark. The following morning, the fourth in the life of the now cantering tortoise, revealed an entirely new landscape, with populous towns and villages, houses owing something to French provincial architecture, and, after a short time, the Bosphorus with its many islands and tree-lined shores. Not long after breakfast we came to a halt at Haidar Pasha, the railway terminus in Asia.

(viii) *Entering Europe*

It was over. We had arrived. Readjustments had to be made, and a small stretch of water crossed that would bring me to a place which as a child I had considered impossibly far away and strange, but which now seemed like the gate of my own home, its people already my people, by contrast with the way I had come.

My Turkish companion was met by a large group of relatives, so I bid him a momentary goodbye and took the ferry alone to cross into Istanbul and Europe. It was a cool fresh morning, blue and misty, with a trembling sea, and sitting in the ferry I thought how pleasant it would be if one could everywhere pass from one continent to another as easily as this. Ahead, only the shore houses were visible. Above them the city was veiled in thin mist, from the higher levels of which soaring minarets and low Greek domes issued tentatively.

As the view showed, it is not with continents and cultures that the difficulties lie. Trouble starts at a lower level, with nations. Where a single nation bestrides two continents, as Turkey does, movement from one to the other is effortless. The continental division is reduced to what it properly should be, a line on a map, an idea, not a physical obstruction. Nations are, after all, ideas. But whereas, crossing from Asia to Europe at Istanbul, we are pleased to contemplate the immateriality of continental boundaries, we disconcertingly add that of course national frontiers are something entirely different.

Entering Europe through this Islamic gate, where every landmark was a mosque, it occurred to me that my sensations of arrival corresponded closely to those of a Bengali re-entering India at Bombay. Yes, this was home so far as other races were concerned, but in another sense there was still a long way to go. People in the streets spoke an incomprehensible language, and their customs were unknown and interesting. Similarly, a Chinese of Suiyuan or Yunnan, arriving at Canton, would feel happy and say to himself that he was home, when in fact he still had to travel hundreds of miles before reaching people speaking his own language. There are times when the provinces of China and India look as large and clearly differentiated as nations. There are times when the nations of Europe look like provinces.

(ix) *The incomparable city*

Of all the cities that exist, Istanbul is surely the fullest expression of what Yo meant when he spoke of a world place. It is like a man playing host to many guests who, though they may quarrel outside, must within his walls keep peace. I spent hours in a street in Beyoglu, the more modern residential part of the city, where within fifty yards one could find bookshops selling the literature of nine major languages. The waiter in the hotel I stayed at spoke seven languages

—Turkish, Greek, Hebrew, German, Italian, French and English—
and sitting in the hotel lounge in the evening one might expect to
hear them all being spoken. Parts of the city reminded me strongly
of Paris, with shuttered windows, cobbles, tree-lined streets, and
Turkish women attired with Parisian taste and elegance. But down
a flight of steps, out of the bustle of the main streets, and here was a
quiet lane overhung with vines, beneath which old men sat as in a
pale green tunnel drinking coffee or wine at the doors of modest
shops. Or passing beyond the vines, the hill dropped abruptly,
giving an oriental view of minarets and domes. On one side of the
street was an old fountain decorated in stylized Arabic calligraphy,
on the other an ancient Christian church with mosaics that were
probably portraits of people who lived here in the age of Justinian.
Or calling on Turkish friends with a garden, one might be shown a
vase, belonging to several hundred years before Christ, which they
dug up accidentally last year while planting roses.

History has no beginning or end in Istanbul. One moment I
was talking to a Jewish shopkeeper whose ancestors escaped from
Spain during the persecutions of Ferdinand and Isabella and whose
family still used expressions belonging to an archaic form of Spanish.
Another moment I was buying decorative modern pottery in the
great covered bazaar, under a vault built in the ninth century or so,
or else standing in dazed admiration before the unique collection of
Chinese porcelain in the Sarai, the gifts of Chinese emperors to
Turkish sultans of the past.

This city has a personality, a genius of its own, which makes it
culturally impregnable to change or conquest. Greeks, Romans and
Turks have ruled it, countless nationalities have lived in it, but it
must be hard to find any who did not adapt themselves to its ways,
identify themselves with it, pride themselves on being part of it. One
feels certain that, however ruthless the assault of a conqueror, however destructive his victory, a month later he would be making
sentences beginning 'In Istanbul, we . . .' Like Peking, its culture is
gently adamant. Things must be done in the proper way. There is
no other that is so entirely suitable.

In my early enthusiasm for the Aya Sofya and other Christian
buildings of the Constantinople that was, and with the sense of
grievance which I think many Europeans feel about great Christian
works of art having been plastered over with Islamic designs or in

other ways despoiled, I found I had underrated the contribution which the Turks themselves have made to Istanbul, along lines of tradition that follow effortlessly from the earlier Christian epoch. It was a surprise to me to find that the mosque and tomb of Suleiman the Lawgiver, for example, designed by the great Turkish architect, Sinan, is as much inspired by the architecture of Justinian's time as any work of a Christian emperor, while in their use of decorated tiles to beautify the interiors of mosques, Turkish artists have with striking originality added to the artistic richness of the city whose religion and writing they changed.

In Istanbul I sat down for ten days to reoccidentate myself. I wasted innumerable hours in the houses of Turkish friends, talking, drinking coffee, and eating the world's most exultantly sticky cakes. The Turkish homes I visited again reminded me of Paris. Without words they told of a people who love fine things, and who show unusual discernment in matters of material quality, down to details which we in England would not worry about, but which people in France or Japan would.

But when I attempted to praise these or any other qualities, I was hastily assured that I had come too late. Istanbul was of course a splendid place—it always would be—but how could anyone judge today what it was really capable of? An elderly Turkish lady shook her head wistfully: '*Ah, Monsieur! Dans le Temps! Vous n'avez rien vu. Il y avait des merveils, des splendeurs!*'

Dans le Temps! How often, and with what fervour, that expression occurred in the speech of older people! It is, of course, a special Istanbul phrase, meaning 'Time was' or 'In the old days', and referring to the time of the Sultans.

One evening this same lady gave a dinner at her home for some members of her family and myself. She lived in a small flat on her own, graciously furnished with the last of the family's antiques and carpets. Over the doors and windows were framed specimens of Islamic calligraphy, for in Turkey, as in China and Japan, good calligraphy is collected by connoisseurs. As in China, too, we dined at a round table, eating slowly, with much conversation, and with many toasts drunk in small goblets of strong Turkish wine.

During dinner stray items from the past—*dans le Temps*—slipped in amongst us. The old lady spoke of a time when her father used to receive gifts of Nubian slaves—as many as fifty on one occasion—from a friend of his who was a provincial governor. In those days, in the private mosque in their house, at the noon prayers seldom less than three hundred people knelt down.

'*Ah, Monsieur! Dans le Temps!*'

And here she was, silver-haired and alone, entertaining us with the aid of a single woman servant, in one room, with the gracious, unaffected manners of her day, speaking in her slow melodious French, humbled, some would say, by circumstances—I would prefer to say shriven,—yet unscathed, having sacrificed wealth and power, but not one whit of the nobility and distinction to which she was heiress.

Since that visit, whenever Muslim friends of mine are going to Europe, I always beg them to go to Istanbul. In the West, it is so long since we engaged in our struggle to free our thinking from the fetters of orthodox religion that we no longer reckon the true value of what this struggle did for us. In Turkey today, now that public Islamic worship is no longer prohibited by law, an interesting comparison has been created between those Muslim countries which have not passed through their period of liberating struggle, and Turkey itself, which has. We see in Islam what once could be seen long ago in Christendom, a form of religion that impedes understanding, and a form that fructifies and enriches it. From being a renegade from Islam, Turkey has unexpectedly reappeared in the Islamic orbit, but in a new guise, as an exponent of the balance that can be achieved between pragmatic openmindedness and doctrinaire religion, a balance which other Muslim countries, from the Near East to Indonesia, have also to reach if they are ever to fulfil their political ambitions and rid themselves of the sense of guilt, grievance and dissatisfaction which the unresolved problem engenders. To orthodox Muslims, Istanbul is a despised place of free-thinkers, an outcast from the fold. But the evolution of a little more time may show that in reality it is the foremost Islamic city—as it already is indisputably in terms of art and culture. It is here that the true riches of Islam can be seen at their best, in the calm atmosphere of a mind that has found its balance in a new age.

For all its antiquity, it is a place where a fresh wind blows. It has done its spring cleaning, and is pleased with the effect, even though, for those who are old, it is comforting to talk with mystic reverence of the glory and splendour that once was—*dans le Temps.*

VII

Three weeks later, in Paris, I found myself one morning trudging through the snow beside a group of children going to school. Listening to their chatter, I was impressed by something relatively unfamiliar, the cultural unity of their lives. They were talking in French, their schoolbooks were in French, they were going to be given lessons in French, their lives were being moulded into a form achieved by hundreds of years of study and experiment in a definite direction—a French direction.

I found myself thinking back to the heavy warmth of tropical Manila, to Trining and her children. Applying their situation to these Parisian boys and girls, I began to conjure up an imaginary picture of Trining's children, with some of their friends, trudging through the Paris snow with their books.

Although, in this image, they were all of them French, the books they carried were not in French. In village schools the mother tongue might be taught, but not in Paris. Here they had their higher education either in English or Spanish. On the way to school, most of them chattered in French interspersed with English and Spanish phrases, some of the elder boys speaking entirely in English. They were furthermore divided into two groups, for some of them went to a school where the medium of instruction was Spanish, while others went to an English-language school. Once inside the school gates, of course, no more French would be spoken, because they must at all times practise the language of higher education. Though most of the teachers were French, they too spoke all the time in English or Spanish, while some of the best teachers were foreigners.

It had been difficult for the parents to decide which school to send their children to. The education in the Spanish school was academically superior, but an English education was more useful. Grandfather had the revolutionary idea that it would be better if they were taught privately, entirely in French, but that was of course unpractical. None of them would ever succeed in making a living if that was all they could speak.

.   .   .   .   .

This, in a single image, is the difference between Asia and the West. It never occurs to us to wonder, for example, what language our children should learn. Naturally they will learn our language, which is the medium of instruction in all the schools we know of. There is no choice in the matter.

In the East today an important element of choice enters into almost everything in life, from the moment a child is born. If he has a nurse from the country, he will grow up talking the provincial language. Would it not be wiser to engage a nurse from the city, so that right from the start he will learn the national language? If we can afford it, shall we send him later on to a foreign-language school, and if so which foreign language do we prefer? The choice is fundamental. On it depends the entire development of his thinking and the type of career he will be eligible for. If he is going to be a doctor, this language would be preferable to that, but if he is to be a lawyer this would not be satisfactory—another language would be more appropriate.

Leaving the personal level, and moving into that of the school itself, and of the government that partly finances it, the situation is equally fraught with choice. Which of the provincial languages is to be made into the national language? How much will it cost, and how many years will it take, to translate into this language all the textbooks required, particularly scientific books, or to write new textbooks? And is this, in any case, a sensible move? Since students will benefit by higher technical studies abroad, would it not be an advantage to them to have their grounding at home in a foreign language? If so, which language should it be?

Added to these are a variety of internal problems. The written versions of many of the leading oriental languages are not the same as the common speech. If these languages are to be reformed, again comes the difficulty of having to rewrite all existing textbooks. Would it not be simpler to do away with old scripts and romanize the spoken language? But there again, is it worth doing this for political and sentimental reasons, when the cheapest, quickest and most effective decision will be to set aside these vexations of an old continent and decide that there is nothing to be ashamed of in thinking and being educated in a foreign language?

.   .   .   .   .

The withdrawal of direct western control in the East has done far more than cause new governments to come into existence and new flags to fly. For about a hundred years the forms which eastern endeavour has taken have been prescribed by the patterns of colonial or semi-colonial association with the West. These patterns having been removed, in their place is a void which the East is now free to fill with whatever it likes.

Asia's reaction to this situation, which was not fully foreseen during the struggles for independence, has been unexpectedly shrewd. Far from trying to fill the void, it has paid hardly any attention to it. Instead, by deep instinct, it has seen this as the moment in which to conduct a complete overhaul of oriental life. Before any thought is given to filling the void, all that the East at present possesses is being revalued. Religion, customs, family conduct, morality, social obligations, political values, theories of government, all are being subjected to examination. Nor is it only the East that is familiar to us which is involved in the process. The withdrawal of western control has caused various aspects of the Asia that existed prior to the colonial period to re-emerge, and these too are being included in the revaluation.

Not the least interesting feature of it is that it is being conducted along lines of reasoning which are very largely western. The East is judging itself today according to standards derived from us. It is criticizing itself as we, in similar circumstances, would try to criticize ourselves.

Two distinct systems are being used in conducting the overhaul. In one—the communist system—all important decisions are taken by governments and committees, the people thereafter being told what to do. In the other, governments may, by popular consent, make such decisions as concern them, but the real burden of decision rests with families and individuals.

On the journey described in this book, we have been concerned with countries following the latter of these two systems, and from our western point of view what chiefly preoccupies us is whether, as a result of this phase of choice and revaluation, these countries

259

and other parts of the East are going to pursue a course that will bring them nearer to us in understanding, or draw them further away.

On a short visit to Burma some time ago, my arrival in Rangoon happened to coincide with one of the country's periodic outbursts against the use of the English language. The newspapers were full of it, well-known people were making impassioned speeches on the subject, and international agencies were sending news of it all over the world. I felt depressed.

Around sundown, being alone in the house—my Burmese host and hostess were attending a social function—and wanting a drink of sweet lime, I called for a servant. There was no reply. When a second time I called and there was no answer, I went down to the kitchen to find out what was happening. It was empty. Passing through it out into the servants' quarters, I found these too were deserted.

Fearing that something untoward might have happened, I continued my search as far as the cowshed, where I found the herdsman, a dark-skinned country boy clad only in shorts and a singlet.

'Where is everybody?' I asked. 'I want a drink.'

He laughed with caustic Burmese frankness.

'No use looking for them at this hour,' he said; 'they're all at night school,' and added, with a humorous slant of the eyes at the colour of my skin, 'You shouldn't complain—they're learning English.'

In Asia, as indeed in other parts of the world, what is shouted from the rooftops is generally of less importance than what is being quietly done in the rooms below.

Hongkong